CRUSADES

THE ILLUSTRATED HISTORY

CRUSADES

THE ILLUSTRATED HISTORY

General Editor: Thomas F. Madden

DUNCAN BAIRD PUBLISHERS
LONDON

Crusades: The Illustrated History

First published in the United Kingdom
and Ireland in 2004
by Duncan Baird Publishers Ltd
Sixth Floor
Castle House
75–76 Wells Street
London W1T 3QH

Editor: Peter Bently
Designer: Allan Sommerville
Picture researcher: Julia Ruxton
Managing designer: Manisha Patel
Managing editor: Christopher Westhorp
Commissioned illustrations, decorative borders and
maps: Peter Visscher and Allan Sommerville

A CIP record for this book is available from the
British Library

10 9 8 7 6 5 4 3 2

ISBN: 1-84483-040-3

Typeset in Bembo and Trajan
Colour reproduction by Colourscan, Singapore
Printed in China by Imago

NOTES
The abbreviations CE and BCE are used throughout
this book:
CE Common Era (the equivalent of AD)
BCE Before the Common Era (the equivalent of BC)

Captions to illustrations on pages 1 and 2:
Page 1: *A 13th–14th-century Islamic stucco "tile,"
probably from Toledo, Spain. Mudejar craftsmen inserted
the arms of their Christian lords in the shield shapes
which formed at the intersections, the central stars carried
emblems of their own. This example has letters in Kufic
script intertwined to produce a lobed arch, which is the
main feature of the tile.*
Page 2: *A 13th-century mosaic of a soldier with a sword
in Veneto-Byzantine style, from the interior of the basilica
of San Marco, Venice.*

**Captions to the chapter opener illustrations
are on page 223.**

CONTENTS

INTRODUCTION

Religious warfare, once thought to be an artifact of a distant past, has reemerged in recent years. A spate of Islamist terrorist attacks have reminded the western world that for many people religion is still a reason to kill and to be killed. That is a hard lesson for the West, which long ago relegated religious belief to personal preference and celebrates religious diversity; it requires westerners to look beyond modern sensibilities to a medieval world view that, for them, has largely passed away—for it has not passed away everywhere.

Out of a desire to understand today's events, many commentators turned to Christianity's holy wars: the crusades. It was their legacy, some contended, that had led directly to the attacks. When President George W. Bush spoke of the new war on terrorism as a "crusade" he was roundly criticized for the perceived suggestion that it was a war of Christianity against Islam. His aides apologized, saying that the president had only used the term in its sense of a campaign, but in the Middle East the remark was thought to confirm a popular assessment of Americans and Europeans as "crusaders."

The taking of Jerusalem in 1099 during the First Crusade, from a mid-14th century edition of History of Jerusalem *by William of Tyre. In 2001, just weeks after the terrorist attacks against New York and Washington, D.C., former U.S. president Bill Clinton claimed that the capture and sack of Jerusalem was still remembered by Muslims in the region, implying that the descendants of crusaders ought to shoulder their burden of the blame. Many other observers likewise began to see the root causes of Islamist attacks as lying in the crusades of the Middle Ages.*

So what were the crusades and who were the crusaders? After many decades of rigorous investigation by historians of the Middle Ages we are now much better able to answer. However, much of this research lies in academic publications aimed at specialists rather than lay readers, while many books aimed at a mass market perpetuate errors and misunderstandings that were corrected decades ago. As a result, outside the academic world the crusades remain badly understood.

The purpose of *Crusades: The Illustrated History* is to satisfy the popular desire for answers about the crusades with the fruits of years of exacting historical research. The professional historians assembled here have each made significant contributions to our understanding of the crusades—and here they have written fascinating narratives that reflect the latest conclusions of modern scholarship.

During the Middle Ages virtually all western Christians believed that the crusades to the East were divinely sanctioned wars against the enemies of Christ and his church. Even after the fall of the crusader states in 1291 the recapture of the Holy Land remained an important matter for western Christians. Then the expansion of the Islamic Ottoman empire (see Chapter Eight) forced Europeans to put aside any ideas of reclaiming Jerusalem and instead defend Europe. In the sixteenth century, when western Europe was in the gravest danger of Muslim conquest, the crusades as an institution began to collapse utterly. As secular authority in Europe increased, religious unity crumbled. The Protestant Reformation severely undercut the crusades because doctrines were rejected that were central to crusading—in particular the secular authority of the pope and the doctrine of indulgence. Martin Luther insisted that the crusades were the tool of a corrupt papacy. However, even Luther was aware of the threat that the power of the Islamic Turks posed to Christian Europe, and the old ideal of Christian unity in the face of the Muslim threat never died entirely—in 1571 the victory of a Catholic admiral over the Turks at Lepanto was celebrated in Protestant lands no less than in Catholic ones (see pages 194–195), and more than a century later Protestants joined the ranks of the pope's Holy League which, in the last crusades of all, began to roll back the frontier of the Ottoman empire (see pages 198–199).

Writing the History of the Crusades

By this time, histories of the earlier crusades had begun to appear. In his very popular *Historie of the Holy Warre* (1639), the English divine Thomas Fuller questioned the wisdom of the medieval crusades, which, in his view, had spent European lives and wealth for nothing more than a faraway plot of land and a few relics. His view was not untypical of Protestant writers. However, the French Jesuit historian Louis Maimbourg praised the movement and its participants in his own *Histoire des croisades* (*History of the Crusades*, 1675).

The eighteenth century saw a dramatic shift in western thinking. Not only had the Ottoman threat been averted, but European states were now expanding on a global scale. With the Muslim danger passed, many Europeans belittled it and cast doubt on its former gravity. It was the age of the Enlightenment, with its emphasis on rational thought, religious toleration, and anticlericalism—in such an intellectual atmosphere the medieval crusades did not fare well, and they were denounced by Voltaire, Hume, and others as a bloody manifestation of medieval barbarism, ignorance, superstition, and fanaticism in which thousands of the foolish had set out in a pitiful attempt to save their souls. In *Über Völkerwanderung, Kreuzzüge und Mittelalter* (*On the Migration of Peoples, Crusades, and the Middle Ages*, 1791), Friedrich Schiller even suggested that the crusades could be better understood as a continuation of the barbarian migrations and invasions that had destroyed ancient Rome.

However, the Romantic movement of the late eighteenth and nineteenth century embraced the chivalric piety of the medieval knight. In *History of the Crusades* (1820), the British historian Charles Mills criticized Enlightenment scholars such as Edward Gibbon for projecting modern values on medieval men. He judged that the crusaders were heroic, selfless, and courageous. Nationalism also changed historians' views, particularly in France, where the crusades began to be seen as an important part of the national heritage. The six-volume *Histoire des croisades* (1817–22) by Joseph-François Michaud extolled the achievements of the French crusaders.

Colonialism and racism were also interwoven into the fabric of crusade history in this period. By the nineteenth century the Muslim Near East had not only ceased to be a threat, but to most Europeans it appeared backward, quaint, exotic, or just barbarous. The crusades, therefore, were frequently celebrated as Europe's first colonial expansion. During the wars of the late nineteenth and early twentieth centuries—including the First World War (see page 204)—the romantic image of the chivalric crusader marching off to fight a foreign nemesis was pressed into service. Even after the carnage of the First World War, Europeans and Americans continued to characterize it as a noble "crusade" and the dead as fallen martyrs.

The Crusades in the Twentieth Century

In the twentieth century new methodologies and sources gave a new generation of historians the tools to unlock many of the mysteries

Opposite, top: *Remains of the citadel of Antioch, one of the most ancient of all cities in Christendom and a patriarchal see, conquered by the Seljuk Turks in 1085. It was restored to Christendom by the First Crusade in 1098, until Sultan Baibars destroyed it and massacred the inhabitants in 1268.*

Opposite, bottom: *An illustration from the 12th-century* Chirurgia *by Roger of Salerno, showing a doctor extracting an arrow from a man's back. Developments in surgery in Europe were assisted by the practical experience derived from treating battle wounds, but more fundamentally the debt was owed to the Muslim world—firstly, for the brilliance of reference works written by men such as Albucasis, a scholar and surgeon from Córdoba, and secondly because of the availability of translations of ancient Greek works on surgery.*

of the crusades. The starting point for modern investigations into the basic questions of definition and motivation is Carl Erdmann's groundbreaking book, *Die Entstehung des Kreuzzugsgedankens* (*The Origin of the Idea of Crusade*, 1935). He argued that the crusades were not so much the result of events in the East, but born of the eleventh-century reform movement in Europe, which had abandoned Christianity's ideal of withdrawal from the world and embraced instead the secular militaristic culture in order both to purify that culture and to use it as a tool of purification. The crusades, therefore, were neither an ad hoc reaction nor an aberration, but an organic element of the medieval world.

It is unsurprising that the rise of Nazi Germany and the ensuing world war changed the way historians approached the crusades. Western scholars reflected the popular aversion to wars of conquest and campaigns of fanatical ideology; racism joined colonialism in the West's collection of discarded doctrines. Western intellectuals began to view the crusades much as their Enlightenment predecessors had done two centuries earlier. Many historians who had observed how totalitarian leaders had covered their wars of aggression in the mantle

of glorious moral crusades expressed cynicism for the professed motives and purposes of medieval kings, popes, and crusaders. Rather than heroes, crusaders were described as opportunistic conquerors cloaking their true motives behind a veil of pious platitudes.

The most influential proponent of this view was Sir Steven Runciman. In his three-volume work, *A History of the Crusades* (1951–54), Runciman downplayed the role of piety, stressing what he saw as the base motives of rapacious men. Runciman's history, which had the benefit of being beautifully written, quickly gained a wide readership outside the academic world and remains a best-selling history of the crusading movement. It is no exaggeration to say that he almost singlehandedly crafted the modern popular view of the crusades. When one reads or hears media coverage about the crusades today it is invariably Runciman's judgment that reigns supreme.

Yet Runciman was by no means the last word on the crusades. Since the 1960s there has been a boom in crusade studies. The Society for the Study of the Crusades and the Latin East, a professional organization of crusade scholars, has at present nearly 500 members in thirty countries and hundreds of scholarly studies are published each year. As a result of all of this research, modern scholars have

The land walls of Constantinople, mammoth fortifications that defended the capital of the Byzantine empire for many centuries. Steven Runciman, a historian of Byzantium, had a natural sympathy for the subject of his studies and he accused the western crusades of weakening the empire that they had sought to sustain. More than the Turks, who would ultimately conquer Constantinople and its territories, Runciman blamed the crusaders for the fall of Byzantium.

largely rejected Runciman's conclusions, returning instead to the idea that medieval people should be understood on their own terms rather than ours.

The Crusades Today

One of the most exciting areas of recent crusade research is the investigation into the identity, methods, and motivations of those who took the cross. In the past, scholars have had to generalize about crusaders who were not in the ranks of the highest élite based on incomplete or impressionistic information. It is still not possible to learn very much about the poorest crusaders. However, through the use of the thousands of medieval charters held in European archives one can uncover the preparations and conduct of many thousands of otherwise unknown knightly crusaders. Charter studies have been around for a long time, but it is only relatively recently that historians have been able to employ new computer technologies in order to organize and evaluate these documents.

Using these methods, scholars such as Jonathan Riley-Smith have exploded the old myth that crusaders were Europe's second sons, landless men leaving home to seek profit and wealth wherever it could be found or plundered. On the contrary, we now know that the costs of crusading were staggering. This has led many historians to the conclusion that the overriding motivation for crusaders to the East was not greed but pious idealism. Crusaders truly believed that in endeavoring to expel Muslim conquerors from formerly Christian lands, they were doing God's will. Crusading was, for them, an act of charity and love through which they sought to do penance for their sins and thereby merit eternal life. These beliefs may not seem very modern, but neither were the people who held them.

Did the crusades to the East lay the foundation for modern anti-western terrorism? It is hard to see how, since Muslim conquerors not only destroyed the European crusader kingdom but went on to occupy much of Europe itself. Attempts to view the crusades through the lens of modern ideologies, though, do play a role in present-day rhetoric (see Chapter Nine). However, to seek to force the medieval crusades into nationalist, colonialist, or racist molds is to distort their fundamental character, and as a result the crusades are today among the most misunderstood phenomena in history. *Crusades: The Illustrated History* seeks to dispel that misunderstanding.

Thomas F. Madden
Professor of History
Saint Louis University.

Crusaders from a 13th-century mosaic from the basilica of St. John the Evangelist in Ravenna. Medieval warriors often joined the crusades in groups—members of the same family, same place of origin, or same feudal arrangement would travel together, assisting each other along the way. Crusades were dangerous endeavors: almost half those who left Europe never returned.

HiEROSOLiMA

Ierosolma

TEPLVM·SALOMÕIS·

1

CHRISTENDOM AND THE UMMA

ALFRED J. ANDREA

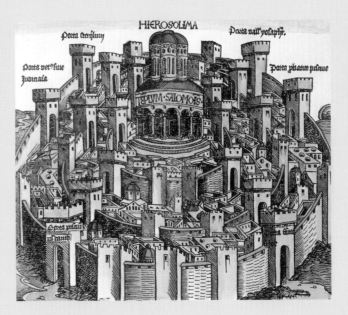

CHRISTIAN UNITY AND DIVERGENCE

Unity of faith and worship has been a Christian ideal from the beginning, but never a reality. In the early 50s St. Paul upbraided the Christians of Corinth for their factionalism, and their divisions were not unique. In the fourth century church unity was threatened when many North Africans, refusing to accept the authority of priests who had submitted to a recent Roman persecution, created the Donatist church, named for their leader Donatus (died 355).

In the midst of this crisis, the emperor Constantine I ("the Great," ruled 306–37) adopted Christianity as his favored religion. In 325 he called a council of church leaders at Nicaea (present-day Iznik) in Asia Minor to resolve the even more divisive Arian controversy. Arius, a priest of Alexandria in Egypt, claimed that Jesus was God only by adoption and "not of the same substance as the Father." The council promulgated the Nicene Creed, which affirmed Jesus' full godhood and condemned the Arians as heretics, or false-believing Christians.

In 330 Constantine shifted the focus of the Roman empire eastward by dedicating a new imperial capital on the Bosporus: Constantinople (present-day Istanbul). But despite Constantine's belief that he had breathed new life into the empire, deep divisions persisted within the imperial church. The council of Nicaea had not extirpated Arianism, and in the following centuries new theological controversies arose. To settle such disputes, the church held six further ecumenical councils between 381 and 787, which articulated

OTHER EASTERN CHRISTIANS

According to tradition, the first state to accept Christianity as its official religion was not Rome but Armenia, a kingdom south of the Caucasus mountains, which adopted the faith ca. 314. Sometime thereafter (traditionally in 333), the king of Ethiopia, in northeast Africa, accepted Christianity as the official state religion. The Georgians of the southern Caucasus also accepted the faith sometime in the fourth century, probably owing to Armenian and eastern Roman influences.

Some eastern Christian churches deviated from the orthodox faith as defined by the seven ecumenical councils (see main text). For example, the council of Chalcedon in 451 declared that two perfect and complete natures, divine and human, are joined in Jesus' single, indivisible person. The Coptic church of Egypt, as well as the churches of Ethiopia and Nubia (Sudan), rejected this idea in favor of Monophysitism, the doctrine that Jesus had a single, divine nature.

Monophysites were frequently persecuted by the imperial church of Constantinople and in the seventh century they tended to welcome conquering Muslim armies as liberators.

the core of the orthodox ("correctly taught") faith, defining what was to be believed and proscribing as heresy all contrary beliefs. However, these councils also divided Christians, because no doctrinal decision was accepted by every disputant.

During the same centuries, two competing centers of church authority emerged: Constantinople, whose emperor claimed to be *isapostolos*, the peer of the apostles; and Rome, whose bishop claimed the title of pope (Latin *papa*, father) by virtue of the powers of St. Peter, the putative prince of the apostles and first bishop of Rome.

Pope Leo I ("the Great," 440–61) was emblematic of the Roman papacy's self-image and emerging status in the West. Leo, self-styled "primate of the bishops," managed to suppress an attempt to accord Constantinople ecclesiastical parity with Rome. Moreover, as imperial authority became weaker in the West in the face of invasions by Germans and other "barbarians," popes and other western church leaders found it necessary to provide security for their people. In 452 Leo apparently persuaded Attila, leader of the Huns, not to attack Rome. Three years later he negotiated a mitigation of the sack of Rome by the Vandals. In 494 Pope Gelasius I was confident enough to upbraid the emperor for interfering in church affairs; in doing so he articulated the papacy's classic expression of the responsibility and authority of pope and emperor (see sidebar on page 16).

The situation was quite different in the eastern Roman empire, where emperors were able to control church leaders effectively, and

This detail from a Russian icon depicts the first ecumenical council of Nicaea (325), and the fifth (553) and sixth (680) ecumenical councils, both of which were held in Constantinople. The ecumenical councils (formal assemblies of church leaders that in theory represented the entire church) and other convened assemblies of experts were instrumental in defining the "correct," or orthodox, faith. Novgorod School, 18th century.

POPE AND EMPEROR:
A QUESTION OF AUTHORITY

In 494 Pope Gelasius I wrote to the emperor Anastasius I to affirm the supremacy of the church over the secular authorities. This is an extract:

"Although you take precedence over all mankind in dignity, nevertheless you piously bow the neck to those who have charge of divine affairs and seek from them the means of your salvation, and hence you realize that, in the order of religion you ought to submit yourself rather than rule. ... No one can ever raise himself by purely human means to the privilege and place of him whom the voice of Christ has set before all."

Charlemagne expressed the opposing view in a letter to Pope Leo III in 795:

"It is our royal duty to defend the church of Christ from the attacks of pagans and infidels...and to enforce within the church acceptance of the catholic faith. It is your duty, Most Holy Father, to aid us in the good fight by raising your hands to God...so that, by your intercession, the Christian people might always and everywhere be victorious. ... Abide by the strictures of church law in all matters and always obey the teachings of the holy fathers, so that your life can serve as an example of holiness to everyone, and your holy admonitions might be observed by the entire world."

The self-image of the eastern Roman (Byzantine) emperors as universal rulers is strongly conveyed in the Barberini Ivory, an ivory panel from the early 6th century. The emperor, probably Anastasius I (491–518) or Justinian (527–565), rides in triumph as Christ (top) gives his blessing and a general (left) offers a winged figure of victory; in the lower register easterners (Scythians and Indians) bring tribute, including an elephant tusk.

the chief prelate of the eastern church, the patriarch of Constantinople, was generally an imperial appointee. Emperor Justinian I ("the Great," 527–565), for example, was convinced that as God's viceroy on Earth he was uniquely responsible for the well-being of Christendom and of the faith, and closely controlled the patriarchate. He even bent Pope Vigilius to his will in a doctrinal dispute.

The sixth century was pivotal for Roman imperial Christendom. In the East a new Christian culture and civilization arose that is called "Byzantine." Centered on Constantinople (site of the ancient Greek city of Byzantium) and its imperial court, the Byzantine empire was an amalgam of late-Roman autocracy, Eastern Christianity, and the Hellenistic culture of the Levant. Byzantines saw and referred to themselves as Romans, but they belonged to an essentially Greek-speaking empire that persisted until 1453.

In the West, another new culture and civilization was taking shape. Variously termed "Latin Christendom" and the "First Europe," this new western culture was an amalgam of the vestiges of Latin Roman civilization, the cultures of the West's new barbarian inhabitants, and a Christianity increasingly centered on Rome and the popes. Pope Gregory I ("the Great," 590–604) personified this transformation. Although a loyal subject of the emperor in Constantinople, he found himself guiding a western church that was drifting away from imperial control. Through his actions, personal example, and writings, Gregory was a key agent in the evolution of the Roman papacy as the moral and spiritual leader of the West.

In the meantime, the secular rulers of the West continued to look to the rulers in Constantinople as models of imperial majesty and legitimacy. The most successful early imitator of Byzantine imperial greatness was Charlemagne (Charles the Great), king of the Franks (768–814), who carved out western Europe's first medieval empire. But his claims to unrivaled power never went unchallenged. At his coronation as "emperor of the Romans" in Rome on Christmas Day 800, Charlemagne probably expected to be acclaimed emperor by the people and venerated by the pope, in the style of the Byzantine rulers. He also probably expected to place the crown on his own head. But Pope Leo III upstaged Charlemagne by crowning him, spotlighting a basic tension running throughout medieval European history—the struggle between popes and western emperors for supremacy over Christendom.

The Byzantines were outraged that a German barbarian should usurp the imperial title, but in 812, after much wrangling, their emperor Michael I agreed to accord Charlemagne the title "emperor" (but not "emperor of the Romans").

By 843 Charlemagne's empire had split into three kingdoms and it was dead before the ninth century ended. In 962 the western empire and title were revived when Pope John XII found it expedient to crown King Otto I of Germany as Roman emperor, laying the foundations for the later Holy Roman empire. John was to regret this coronation. When he realized that Otto intended to rule Italy with full imperial authority, he turned against him; Otto then engineered John's deposition.

Otto and his successors saw themselves as the true heirs of the Caesars and Charlemagne, but they were also aware that to their east lay a larger, richer, and grander "Roman" empire. And they knew that these "Romans" were in fact Greeks—Christians with suspiciously different rites. They viewed Byzantium, one might say, with a mixture of envy, mistrust, and even a degree of contempt.

At the turn of the millennium, popes and western emperors were not the only authorities in Latin Europe. Most of the Christian West, which by then extended from Greenland to Poland, Bohemia, and Croatia, was divided into a dizzying array of kingdoms and feudal lordships. This political pluralism, which stood in stark contrast to Byzantium's centralized autocracy, would prove to be a dynamic factor in the history of western Europe.

A reliquary of gold, silver, and precious stones in the form of a bust of Charlemagne, presented to the treasury of Aachen cathedral by the Holy Roman emperor Charles IV in 1349. The Holy Roman emperors saw themselves as the successors of Charlemagne, who, as the protector of the church and its people, a patron of learning and the arts, and a warrior of God against pagans, became the West's archetypal Christian king and emperor.

THE RISE OF ISLAM

The angel Gabriel recites the word of God to Muhammad. The face of Muhammad is veiled, in accordance with Islamic strictures against depicting the features of the Prophet. A 16th-century Turkish painting.

Islam, which means "submission [to God]" in Arabic, is a faith, culture, and community whose members are known as Muslims ("they who are submissive"). Muslims are theoretically united in belief and practice because the will of Allah (Arabic *al-Ilah*, which means "*the* God") is unchanging, undivided, and unambiguous. That is the theory; historical reality presents a different picture.

Islam traces its lineage back to Adam, Abraham, and a line of other prophets (including Jesus) but claims to have received the fullness of divine revelation through Muhammad (ca. 570–632), the "Seal of the Prophets," the last and greatest of God's messengers. Around 610, Muhammad ibn Abdullah, a prosperous merchant of Mecca (Makkah) in Arabia, received revelations that impelled him to preach the oneness and uniqueness of God; the imminence of the resurrection of the dead, the coming of a Day of Judgment; an after-death hell fire for unbelievers and the unjust; and a paradise of bliss for all who believed and lived righteous lives according to a strict code of conduct.

Most Meccans initially rejected Muhammad's message, and in 622 the Prophet, preceded by most of his small band of converts, journeyed to Yathrib (later Medina), an oasis town that invited him to serve as an arbiter among rival factions and as its *de facto* ruler. This migration, known as the *hijra* ("breaking of ties"), meant that these first Muslims abandoned their tribal bonds and became members of a new community, or *umma*, that was defined by a shared Islamic faith and not by blood kinship. In the eyes of Muslims, this pivotal act, which led to the creation of a theocratic community at Medina, inaugurated Year 1 of the Islamic Era.

At Medina, Muhammad added the duties of statesman and warrior to that of prophet. After more than seven years of *jihad*, or holy war (see pages 26–27), against the Meccans and others who rejected his message, Muhammad and a reputed 10,000 followers were able to enter Mecca in triumph in 630. Mecca now became Islam's premier holy city, while Medina remained the political capital of the Umma. Because of his triumph, many of the tribes of Arabia united under the leadership of the "Messenger of God."

When Muhammad died in 632, many Arabs severed their ties with the Umma, believing that their loyalty had lain personally with Muhammad. One of Muhammad's closest companions, Abu Bakr, emerged to assume the office of "commander of the faithful," a title later changed to *khalifah* (caliph), or "successor" (of the Prophet). As commander or caliph from 632 to 634, Abu Bakr claimed not to be a prophet (since prophecy had ended with Muhammad) but simply the head of the indivisible community of Islam. He prosecuted war against all who would cut these ties, as well as against the remaining pagan Arab tribes. By his death, just two years after Muhammad's, Abu Bakr had welded together a vigorous community of believers that encompassed the entire Arabian peninsula. What is more, he had forged an Islamic army that was ready to advance against Arabia's two neighbors, the Byzantine and Sassanian (Persian) empires.

Islam's second caliph, Umar (634–644), launched raids against unbelievers outside the peninsula that soon turned into wars of conquest. Byzantium and Sassanian Persia, exhausted after more than a century of wars and suffering bitter internal divisions, were unprepared for the onslaught. Before Umar's death in 644, the Byzantines had lost Syria-Palestine and Egypt—Christianity's most ancient and sacred lands—to Islam, and the Arab conquest of the Sassanian empire (essentially present-day Iraq and Iran) was almost complete.

THE FIVE PILLARS OF ISLAM

The *Hadith of Gabriel* originates from the Prophet's friend Umar, Islam's second caliph, and contains the Prophet's enunciation of the "Five Pillars," core practices enjoined on every Muslim:

1. **Shahadah (Bearing Witness).** Proclaiming publicly: "There is no god but Allah, and Muhammad is the Messenger of Allah."
2. **Salat (Prayer).** Praying five times daily facing Mecca: before dawn, at noon, mid-afternoon, after sunset, and in the evening.
3. **Zakah (Purification).** An annual tax of 2.5 percent of one's income to support the poor and for other worthy purposes—including *jihad* (see pages 26–27).
4. **Siyam Ramadan (Ramadan Fast).** Abstaining from food, drink, and sex from dawn to sunset in the month of Ramadan.
5. **Hajj (Pilgrimage).** Making a pilgrimage, at least once during one's life, if possible, to Mecca during the first ten days of Dhul-Hijah, the twelfth Islamic month (see pages 22–23).

THE QURAN AND HADITH

The *Quran* (Recitations), Islam's holy book, consists of the revelations given by Allah to Muhammad at Mecca and Medina between 610 and 632. Delivered to the Prophet by the angel Gabriel, and spoken by Muhammad to the Umma, they are the fullness of divine revelation and coeternal with God. Its verses, each a perfect, poetic gift from God, are both doctrine and sacred law (Sharia).

Supplementing the *Quran* is Hadith (Tradition), collections of stories and sayings attributed to the Prophet and his Companions (the first Muslims) that provide models for behavior in every aspect of life. The individual *hadiths* (stories) are associated with the Prophet and so have the authority of divine inspiration, but unlike the *Quran* they are not God's literal word. Sunnis and Shias revere the same *Quran* but honor different collections of *hadiths*. Shias have a third source of divine inspiration: the pronouncements of their *imams*.

An early manuscript of the Quran. *Abbasid period, 8th–9th century.*

PEOPLES OF THE BOOK

Because Arab Muslims initially looked upon Islam as a uniquely Arabic faith, and because Christians and Jews were "People of the Book" (that is, God had given them their own books of divine revelation), conquered monotheists were normally offered *dhimmi* status. This meant that they accepted a contract, or *dhimma*, that obliged them to serve and to pay tribute (*jizya*) to their Muslim overlords in return for limited but real toleration. Even many Persian Zoroastrians were offered *dhimmi* status. However, despite this tolerance, many non-Arabs chose to convert to Islam.

Further territories were conquered with astonishing speed over the following century. By 751, when Islamic forces defeated a Chinese army at the Talas river (in present-day Kazakhstan), lands under Islamic domination stretched from Spain in the west (see page 120) to present-day Pakistan and Central Asia. The Byzantine empire was a truncated version of its former self, having lost Syria-Palestine, Egypt, and North Africa to Islam.

In the mid-eighth century, the community of Islam was a vast multi-ethnic empire. Despite the influx of non-Arab converts, many subject Christians and Jews (and to a lesser extent Zoroastrians) remained faithful to their ancestral religions. On the eve of the crusades, ca. 1095, Christian and Muslim populations were probably of equal size in Syria-Palestine. In many Muslim-dominated regions, such as southern and eastern Anatolia (modern Asiatic Turkey) and northern Syria, Christians still greatly outnumbered Muslims.

As Muslim armies were establishing an empire in the seventh century, a schism arose. Many Muslims, especially members of the Prophet's clan, the Hashim, accused the third caliph, Uthman (644–656), of favoring his own clan, the Umayya (Umayyads). The result was rebellion, Uthman's assassination, and civil war. One faction, the Party of Ali (Shiat Ali), favored the claim to the caliphate of Ali ibn Abi Talib, the Prophet's cousin and son-in-law. The other, led by Muawiyah, a kinsman of Uthman, represented the Umayyads.

The war ended with Ali's assassination in 661. Most Muslims acknowledged Muawiyah as caliph, ushering in the Umayyad caliphate (661–750). The political capital of the Umma was moved from Medina to Damascus, in part in recognition of Islam's expanding horizons but also because Medina had been Shiat Ali's center of support.

THE IMAMS OF THE SHIAS

Shias traced the rightful succession of leadership of the community of Islam from Muhammad and Ali through a number of subsequent *imams* (religious leaders of the Umma) who claimed descent from Ali. They also developed the notion of a messianic Hidden Imam, or Mahdi ("Guided One"). According to this theological vision, the *imams* of the family of Muhammad were infallible teachers, divinely appointed at birth, who spoke with the same authority as the Prophet. However, because of enemies who martyred each *imam* in turn,

this line of earthly *imams* came to an end. (Here various Shia groups disagree as to who was the last *imam*.)

But the imamate was not destroyed. Rather, the last visible *imam* had, through the power and mercy of God, withdrawn from human sight into a state of spiritual concealment, as protection against his enemies, especially false Muslims. There he would remain until some future time when he would reappear as the Mahdi to gather his faithful, persecuted followers, usher in an Islamic holy age, and herald the Last Judgment.

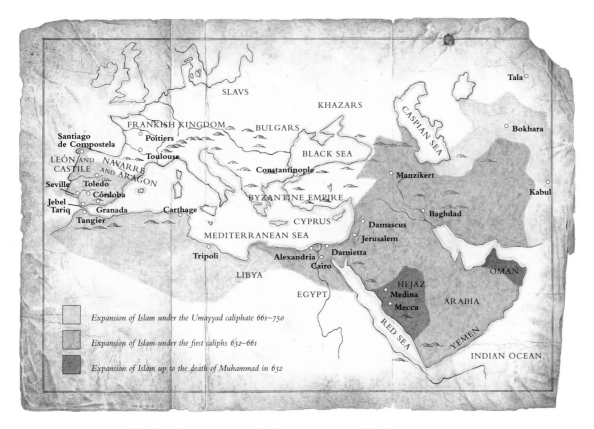

Expansion of Islam under the Umayyad caliphate 661–750

Expansion of Islam under the first caliphs 632–661

Expansion of Islam up to the death of Muhammad in 632

Upon Muawiyah's death in 680, war broke out again with the supporters of Ali's family, more commonly known as Shias or Shiites ("Partisans"). The Shias held that the caliph must be a blood relation of the Prophet, which meant al-Husayn, Ali's son and grandson of Muhammad. But on 10th October 680, al-Husayn and most of his family were massacred at Karbala in Iraq, an event still commemorated by Shias. By 692 the Umayyads had crushed their rivals, but it was a shortlived victory. In 750, supported by many Shias, non-Arab converts, and other disaffected Muslims, the Abbasids, a family tracing its lineage to the Prophet's uncle, overthrew the Umayyads in a bloodbath and established the Abbasid caliphate (750–1258).

Most Shias, who believed that only a descendant of Ali could be the rightful *imam,* or religious leader of the Umma (see box), were as hostile to the Abbasid caliphs as they had been to their predecessors. Mainstream Muslims, who accepted Umayyad and Abbasid authority, styled themselves Sunnis—followers of the path of tradition (*sunna*) as it evolved from the days of the Prophet. Underlying the Sunni self-image is the belief that God's community is infallible. Consequently, the practices and institutions of mainstream Islam are always correct.

The Abbasids moved their capital from Damascus to Baghdad in 762, in recognition of Iraq's geographic, economic, and cultural centrality. Muslim Spain (al-Andalus), remained outside the sphere of Abbasid authority. An Umayyad prince, Abd al-Rahman, who had escaped the bloody coup of 750, defeated the resident governor of Córdoba and in 756 established an independent Umayyad state that ruled Muslim Spain until 1031 (see pages 120–123).

Above: *The dramatic three-phase expansion of Islam saw its armies conquer territory that in little over a century extended Islam's influence into western Europe and Central Asia.*

Below: *The courtyard of the Great Mosque of Damascus, constructed in the early 8th century by the Umayyad caliph al-Walid I as part of his dynasty's program to underscore the legitimacy of its claim to the caliphate.*

PILGRIMAGE

Pilgrimage, the ritual of traveling to and worshipping at a sacred place, is an almost universal religious practice. Its goals include the sanctification of the worshipper, the affirmation of their place within a community of believers, and the expiation of sins through the rigors of the journey. Since the earliest days of Christianity, the primary pilgrimage destination for Christians has been the Holy Land—the region in which Jesus, the first Christians, and the biblical prophets were active. Of its many holy places, the most sacred is Jerusalem, and the most venerated place within the city is a small area—said to be where Jesus was crucified and buried—encompassed by the church of the Holy Sepulcher. A pilgrimage church has stood on the site since the emperor Constantine I dedicated a basilica there in 335. Other important pilgrimage destinations for Latin (western) Christians include Rome, which claims the tombs of saints Peter and Paul and other early martyrs, and Santiago de Compostela in Spain.

After the Arabs captured Jerusalem from the Byzantines in 638, Christian pilgrims continued to travel in substantial numbers to the city and nearby sites. They were usually unmolested by the region's Muslim occupiers, who allowed the Holy Sepulcher and many other churches and shrines to remain in Christian hands. However, in 1009 the Fatimid caliph of Egypt ordered the destruction of the Holy

THE ORIGINS OF THE HAJJ

Part of the genius of Muhammad was marrying the Kaaba and its pre-Islamic rituals of pilgrimage with the monotheistic religion of Abraham, thereby transforming Mecca into Islam's premier holy city. The transformation of the pagan *hajj* to Mecca into an Islamic pilgrimage with roots that go back to Ibrahim (Abraham) can be seen in the twenty-second *surah* (chapter) of the *Quran*, verses 27–30, where Allah speaks to Ibrahim:

"Announce to the people the Pilgrimage [Hajj]. They will come to you on foot and on every lean camel, coming from every deep and distant highway that they may witness the benefits and recollect the name of God in the well-known days over the sacrificial animals he has provided for them. Eat thereof and feed the poor in

want. Then let them complete their rituals and perform their vows and circumambulate the Ancient House [the Kaaba]. Such is it. Whoever honors the sacred rites of God, for him it is good in the sight of his Lord."

Three months before his death on 8th June 632, Muhammad made his Farewell Pilgrimage to Mecca. On Mount Arafat, outside the city, he delivered his Farewell Sermon, reminding the pilgrims that "every Muslim is a Muslim's brother." This dictum is underscored in the many rituals of the Hajj, all of which emphasize that Muslims, regardless of status or ethnicity, are equal members of Allah's family. All Muslims are enjoined to perform the Hajj at least once, if they are able (see sidebar on page 19).

Sepulcher. It was reconstructed under his more tolerant successors and completed ca. 1040, with Byzantium funding much of the work.

In the eleventh century, western Europe experienced a dramatic economic upswing and significant population growth, and one manifestation of this was a growing number of large-scale pilgrimages to Jerusalem. Many spurious legends also arose linking Europe's heroes, such as Charlemagne (see page 17), with the Jerusalem pilgrimage. Charlemagne never left Europe, but the fact that this great warrior of God became associated with the Jerusalem pilgrimage suggests a growing psychological readiness among eleventh-century Europeans for the idea of crusade, which combined the pilgrimage to the Holy Land with holy war.

Holy war and pilgrimage (Arabic *hajj*) are linked in the origins of Islam's most sacred site, Mecca. In 629 Muhammad negotiated a truce in his *jihad* with the unbelieving leaders of Mecca that allowed him and about 2,600 followers to enter the city, where they worshipped at the pilgrimage shrine known as the Kaaba (the Cube), an ancient cultic center of pagan Arabia, which at that time contained 360 idols. The Kaaba also housed a black stone altar that Muslims believe was set there by the prophet Ibrahim (Abraham) and his son Ismail (Ishmael), the ancestors of all Arabs. After his victory over the Meccans in the following year, Muhammad cleansed the Kaaba, known also as the House of God, of its idols, and the shrine became Islam's holiest site and the focus of the Hajj (see box).

THE SHARED HOLY LAND

"Glory be to Him who carried His servant by night from the Sacred Sanctuary to the Distant Sanctuary, whose surroundings we have blessed, that We might show him some of Our signs" (*Quran, surah* 17.1). According to tradition, this passage refers to a mystical Night Journey in which Muhammad was transported from the Kaaba (the Sacred Sanctuary) in Mecca to Jerusalem's Temple Mount (the Distant Sanctuary), the massive raised platform on which Judaism's First and Second Temples had stood and which Muslims know as al-Haram es-Sharif (the Noble Sanctuary). From there the Prophet was taken up to Heaven, where he encountered the prophets Abraham, Moses, and Jesus and received revelations. In 621, shortly after this mystical experience, Muhammad instructed his followers to pray daily facing Jerusalem. Another revelation in 624 changed the direction of prayer to Mecca, but for Muslims Jerusalem has always remained al-Quds (the Holy Place), Islam's third most sacred city and a place to be defended against profanation by unbelievers, even Christian and Jewish "People of the Book."

Above: *A Roman ivory plaque of ca. 400CE depicting the tomb of Jesus and the rotunda built over the Holy Sepulcher in the 4th century.*
Opposite, above: *Jerusalem, from a 6th-century Byzantine mosaic found in Madaba, Jordan showing the sacred sites of the Holy Land.*
Opposite, below: *The interior of the Dome of the Rock. The rock (center) marks the spot where in the Jewish tradition Abraham was to sacrifice Isaac, and in Islam it is from where Muhammad rose to Heaven (see main text).*

When the armies of Caliph Umar captured Jerusalem in 638 they discovered heaps of refuse on the Temple Mount. The caliph ordered it to be cleared and a small mosque was erected on the site. Between 688 and 691 the Umayyad caliphs constructed on the Temple Mount what many regard as Islam's most beautiful place of worship—the Dome of the Rock. This domed octagonal structure is not a mosque, or place of public prayer; rather, it is a place of pilgrimage and private prayer dedicated to the memory of the Prophet. Built over the tip of Mount Moriah, the traditional site of the Temple of Solomon's Holy of Holies, the Dome of the Rock affirms Islam's Abrahamic roots but also its superiority over Judaism and Christianity. Arching over the spot that Muslims consider to be the center of the world, its dome exactly matches the dimensions of the rotunda that then covered the Holy Sepulcher—but its magnificence far surpassed that of the Christian shrine. Early in the eighth century the Umayyads erected a second place of worship on the Temple Mount, al-Aqsa mosque. Built perhaps on the site occupied by Umar's original mosque, al-Aqsa was constructed in imitation of the Church of the Holy Sepulcher but on a much grander scale.

Jews, Christians, and Muslims also equally claimed other holy sites outside Jerusalem as their own. A case in point is Hebron's Cave of Machpela (the Tomb of the Patriarchs), the supposed burial site of Abraham, Isaac, Jacob, and their wives. A stone enclosure constructed in 65BCE by King Herod the Great suggests that Jews in the pre-Christian era probably venerated the tombs as a site of holy pilgrimage. It later became a place of Christian pilgrimage and in the fourth century a church was constructed at the site. Evidence shows that by the sixth century Jews were also offering prayers at the site.

The Muslim conquerors who swept through the region early in the seventh century allowed Jews and Christians to continue worshipping there. More significantly, sometime before the mid-tenth century, Muslims erected their own mosque at the cave, the Haram al-Khalil (Sanctuary of the Friend), dedicated to Ibrahim (Abraham), the Friend of Allah. Writing in the mid-eleventh century, a Persian Muslim reports that up to 500 pilgrims—probably representing all three faiths—arrived daily at the sanctuary.

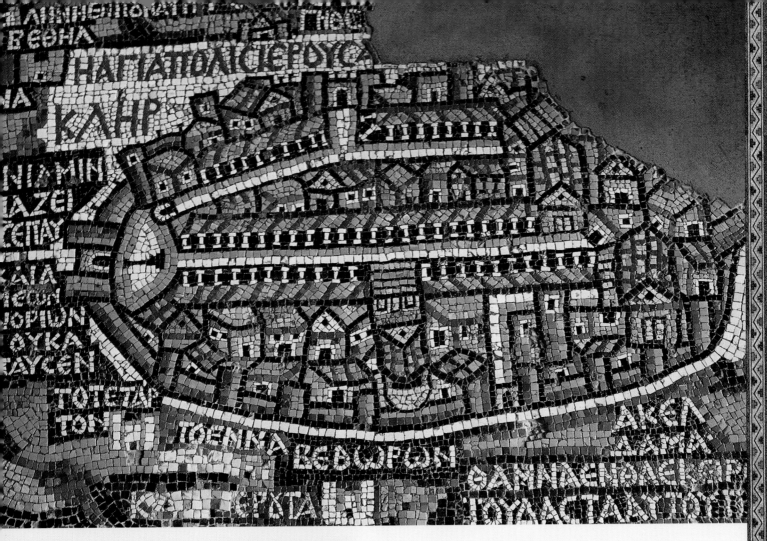

A place sacred to both Christians and Muslims is the Shrine of the Ascension, which stands on the Mount of Olives outside the old city of Jerusalem on the presumed spot whence Jesus ascended to Heaven. This octagonal shrine dates to the twelfth-century Latin kingdom of Jerusalem and marks the site of an earlier fourth-century church. Muslims also believe (although it is not mentioned in the *Quran*) that Jesus, the Islamic prophet Isa, ascended into Heaven, and following Saladin's conquest of Jerusalem in 1187 the Shrine of the Ascension became a Muslim place of pilgrimage. Today both Christians and Muslims worship at the Shrine, which remains in Muslim hands.

Muslims and Christians also venerated places in the Holy Land unique to their respective faiths. The church of the Holy Sepulcher is one such Christian shrine; another was the Cenacle, or Upper Room, on Jerusalem's Mount Zion, where twelfth-century pilgrims viewed the supposed table of the Last Supper. The principal mosque of Acre housed the tomb of Salih, an Islamic prophet (*Quran, surah* 7.73 ff.). During the Christian occupation of the city (1104–87; 1191–1291) the mosque became a church, but Muslims were allowed to worship at the small portion that contained the tomb.

CHRISTIAN HOLY WAR AND JIHAD

All the monotheistic religions that arose in the Near East—Judaism, Christianity, and Islam—have articulated some form of holy war, in which God calls believers to be agents in a cosmic struggle against evil. Holy war may be understood metaphorically, as when Christian ascetics are called Soldiers of Christ, but also as physical combat. The Hebrew Bible (Old Testament) has many examples of God commanding the Israelites to fight heathens.

St. Augustine (354–430), the early western church's foremost theologian, developed the idea of Christian Just War by defining it as warfare against sin. For him, war was both a consequence of sin and its cure. If waged by a proper authority for moral reasons and with due restraint, war is not simply an acceptable defensive action but a positive moral act benefiting both the just warrior and the sinful enemy. Augustine and later western church leaders faced barbarian invaders who were either Arian heretics (see page 14) or pagans. Pope Gregory I (590–604) instructed his officials to act as "warriors of the Lord" against the Arian Lombards, assuring Italy's civil authorities of divine aid for their act of armed resistance.

The distinction between a defensive just war fought on Christian principles and a "holy war" directed by God and sanctifying those engaged in it had become blurred by the time of Charlemagne. His defense and extension of Christendom (notably his conquest of the

THE FOUR JIHADS

Islamic jurists interpreting Sharia have historically named four forms of *jihad* demanded by God: *jihad* of the hand, which means doing good deeds, especially acts of charity; *jihad* of the mouth, which means proclaiming the faith; *jihad* of the heart, which means self-transformation to the point of becoming God-centered; and *jihad* of the sword, which means defending Islam as a *mujahid*, or warrior of God. Sufis, Islam's mystics, add a fifth: *jihad* of the soul, or the struggle to reach God through mystical experience.

In his *Treatise on Law*, Ibn Abi Zayd al-Kayrawani, a distinguished tenth-century Islamic jurist of northwestern Africa, defines *jihad* of the sword as "a precept ordained by God" and went on to maintain that

"it is preferable not to begin hostilities with the enemy before they have been invited to embrace the religion of God, unless the enemy attacks first. They have the choice of either converting to Islam or paying the poll tax. Failing either, war will be declared against them....

"There is no prohibition against killing white non-Arabs who have been taken prisoner. But no one may be executed who has been granted the *aman* [promise of protection]....Women and children must not be executed, and the killing of monks and rabbis must be avoided unless they have taken part in the fighting. Women who have participated in the fighting may also be executed."

pagan Saxons) was the main reason that the pope crowned him emperor and, therefore, defender of the Roman church (see page 17).

While accepting the necessity to defend Christendom and to uphold civil peace, most western church leaders continued to see war as inherently sinful, and requiring penance. This changed in the eleventh century, when the papacy began to justify military action as a righteous act when used to reestablish right order in the world. From there it was a short step to the idea of crusade, a Christian holy war seen as a penitential act that cleansed the souls of its participants.

Islam has also prosecuted holy wars, or *jihads*, a term often misunderstood simply as a bloody war against non-believers. But in fact *jihad* means "striving" and there are various forms of spiritual *jihad* as well as "*jihad* of the sword" (see box). One *hadith* (story) relates that after a victorious military campaign Muhammad told his followers: "We have returned from the lesser *jihad* to the greater *jihad*." That "greater *jihad*" is a moral struggle against evil. In this sense, all true Muslims are *mujahidin*, holy warriors, in a lifelong struggle to follow the way of God by practicing the Five Pillars (see sidebar on page 19) and fighting their lower selves. This in no way negates the fact that the Prophet and his followers were warriors who engaged in pitched battles with their enemies. Almost from the beginning, Islam has accepted that holy war in defense of the true faith is an obligation on all able-bodied men. What is more, those who die in defense of Islam are martyrs and assured of Paradise.

The first Muslims generally tried to convert by force only Arabia's pagans. When the Muslims exploded out of Arabia in the 630s, they were driven more by their warrior traditions and a simple desire for conquest than by a mission to convert unbelievers through the sword. Conversion to Islam in lands outside of Arabia was a long process rarely accompanied by armed threats.

THE HOUSE OF PEACE AND THE HOUSE OF WAR

According to traditional Islamic thought, people who embrace the Faith or who accept *dhimmi* status within a Muslim state reside in Dar al-Islam, the Abode of Islam, literally the House of Submission (or Peace). Conversely, unbelievers outside of these states reside in Dar al-Harb, the House of Chaos (or War). The two Houses are mutually hostile. By the late eighth century, most Islamic jurists agreed that while there might be brief strategic truces for reasons favorable to Muslims, the Houses could never be permanently at peace. Indeed, for the true believers of Dar al-Islam, holy war is inevitable, necessary, and an act of piety. Consequently, Islamic legal theorists crafted treatises on the law of *jihad*, in which they set out rules governing the calling and prosecution of a *jihad* of the sword (see box, opposite).

According to medieval tradition, this fine and elaborately wrought sword belonged to the emperor Charlemagne, the powerful Christian ruler of western Europe who reigned as the king of the Franks (768–814) and emperor of the Romans (800–814). However, it probably dates from no earlier than the 12th century.

THE WEST AWAKES:
THE ELEVENTH CENTURY

POPE GREGORY VII
CALLS FOR HOLY WAR

The age of the crusades might have begun two decades earlier—in 1074 rather than 1095. In 1073, two years after the disastrous Byzantine defeat at Manzikert (see page 34), the Byzantine emperor, Michael VII, appealed to Pope Gregory VII for aid against the Seljuk Turks. On 1st March 1074 Gregory dispatched a letter to the Christians of the West, appealing for them to go to the aid of their fellows in the East: "The example of our Redeemer and the duty of brotherly love demand that we set our hearts on delivering our siblings. Just as He offered His life for us, so we should offer our lives for our siblings. Let it be known that we, trusting in God's mercy and the might of His power, are preparing in every possible way to carry aid to the Christian empire as soon as possible, with God's help."

The Investiture Controversy broke out soon afterward (see main text) and nothing immediately came of Gregory's plan. But his successors did not forget the dream of armed intervention to aid eastern Christians against the Muslims.

For much of the tenth century western Europe was on the defensive, its lands attacked by Vikings from Scandinavia, Magyars (Hungarians) from the steppes of Central Asia, and various Muslim powers from North Africa. However, before the century ended the West's fortunes took a turn for the better. It managed to absorb the Scandinavians and Magyars into the mainstream of Latin Christian culture and began to beat back Muslim attacks in the Mediterranean. Additionally, by the year 1000, the West was experiencing a sharp population rise and an economic revitalization that enabled it to begin to confront Byzantium and Islam as an equal. In fact, during the eleventh century momentum shifted substantially to western Christendom, as it became an aggressive Mediterranean force that threatened Byzantium and Islam on several fronts.

In Spain, the caliphate of Córdoba fragmented in 1031 into a number of petty Islamic states, and Christian powers were quick to take advantage. In 1063 Pope Alexander II (1061–73) offered relief from all penance owed for sins to any knight planning an expedition to Spain. By this papal act, the Christian war against Islam in Spain became a holy war (see pages 121–122).

Farther east, Norman adventurers—French warriors whose Viking ancestors had settled in Normandy (Land of the Northmen)—were on the move to southern Italy, Sicily, and the Balkans. Under the leadership of the Hauteville brothers, especially Robert Guiscard, southern Italy was wrested from Byzantine control in a series of campaigns from ca. 1035 to 1071. Sicily, which North African Muslims had taken from the Byzantines in the ninth century, fell to Guiscard and his brother Roger of Hauteville in a campaign that lasted from 1061 to 1091. With eyes on other Byzantine lands, including probably Constantinople itself, Robert invaded the Balkans in 1081. His death in 1085 brought the invasion to an inglorious end, but he had set a precedent for two centuries of western designs and assaults on the lands of the Byzantine empire.

When Roger invaded Sicily he bore a papal banner granted by Pope Alexander II, and when Guiscard invaded the Balkans he did so with the approval of Alexander's successor, Gregory VII (1073–85), who mistakenly believed that Robert was trying to restore the rightful emperor of Constantinople. The papal blessing of these wars was a manifestation of a radical reorientation of the papacy and the western church that began ca. 1049 and continued well beyond 1100.

In essence, papal reformers attempted to free the church from control by lay rulers and in the process asserted that the Roman papacy was Christendom's ultimate, God-ordained authority. Claims to spiritual preeminence that had been articulated by earlier popes, such as Gelasius I (see page 16), were now transformed into the ideology that right order could only exist when the laity was subject to clerical authority in all moral and religious matters and the Roman papacy was recognized as the head of all churches. In 1075 Gregory VII went so far as to declare that the pope had the right to depose emperors and absolve subjects of their loyalty to unjust lords.

Such an attack on traditional notions of imperial and royal authority were ill received by the emperor at Constantinople and by western emperors and kings. The result in the West was a struggle between the papacy and some sovereigns that lasted from 1076 to 1122. Known as the Investiture Controversy (or Contest), this struggle ostensibly centered on the issue of whether or not lay rulers could install clerics in office and invest them with the symbols of

Above: *A gold and enamel panel depicting St. Procopius (left) and St. George as soldiers. Byzantine, 10th century.*

Opposite: *The interior of the cathedral of Monreale, the Norman royal citadel just south of Palermo. Under the rule of the Norman Hauteville dynasty from the late 11th century, Sicily was home to a rich culture that reflected the island's Byzantine, Arab, and Norman heritage. The cathedral, built by King William II in the 12th century, combines romanesque and early Gothic architecture with Arabic elements and an interior covered with magnificent Byzantine-style mosaics, presided over by a huge image of Christ Pantocrator in the apse.*

their ministry. But the real issue was: who is the God-anointed head of the Christian people, the pope or a monarch? In other words, did monarchs (especially the western emperor) rule by divine ordination and did they have certain sacral rights over the church and clergy?

Both sides finally agreed to negotiated truces, with the kings of England and France reaching an accommodation with the papacy in 1107, and the emperor in 1122. The settlements were compromises that recognized two realities: the new importance of the papacy in western European affairs and the severe weakening of the ideology of sacred kingship championed by Charlemagne and his successors. At the same time, rulers retained a good deal of real power in directing the affairs of the churches in their domains. Pope Urban II's call in 1095 for what became the First Crusade must be placed against the backdrop of an ongoing struggle that was already two decades old.

In the East, the result of this assertion of papal authority was a magnification of the differences between the Byzantine and Roman churches (see box). Pope Urban II's appeal for the First Crusade must, therefore, equally be seen within the context of a radically reformed and revitalized papacy that wished to rescue fellow Christians in the East and "return" them to what it perceived as right order: subservience to papal authority.

THE MYTH OF THE SCHISM OF 1054

It is a common, but mistaken, view that the Roman and Byzantine churches entered into a state of permanent and irreconcilable schism in 1054. What did happen was a row between two churchmen that was symptomatic of growing cultural and ecclesiastical differences between the churches. These differences became pronounced during the eleventh century when advocates of papal supremacy emphasized the need for all Christians to acknowledge the primacy of papal authority and to conform to the practices of the Roman church.

In 1054 Pope Leo IX dispatched Cardinal Humbert of Silva Candida as legate to Constantinople to establish an alliance with the emperor against the Normans in south Italy. An outspoken advocate of Roman supremacy, Humbert took the opportunity to publish a tract condemning "erroneous" Byzantine practices such as using leavened rather than unleavened bread in the Mass.

Unsurprisingly, Humbert alienated Michael Cerularius, the equally uncompromising patriarch of Constantinople. The ensuing row came to a head when Humbert and his colleague delivered a bull of excommunication against the patriarch and his supporters—not, as it has often been portrayed, a general excommunication of the Byzantine church. Byzantine church authorities countered by excommunicating the two legates—not the pope or the church of Rome—and declaring them impostors.

At the time these events were seen as little more than a personal matter between cardinal and patriarch. In any case, Pope Leo had died before Humbert issued his bull, so its legitimacy was doubtful at best. The incident was largely forgotten. Ironically, it would be the crusades, initiated by the pope to aid fellow Christians and draw all Christians together in friendship, that would dramatically drive apart the churches of Rome and Constantinople.

2

THE FIRST CRUSADE
"IMPELLED BY THE LOVE OF GOD"

JOHN FRANCE

CHAOS IN THE EAST

As the papacy was asserting its hegemony in the West (see pages 29–30), the unity of the Islamic Near East was in decline. From the early tenth century the Abbasid caliphate of Baghdad had begun to fragment, and a rival Shia caliphate was established at Cairo by the Fatimids, who claimed descent from Fatima, the Prophet's daughter. The Fatimids soon seized large parts of Syria-Palestine from the Abbasids. In 1009 the Fatimid caliph al-Hakim bin-Amar Allah (996–1021), moved by austere morality, destroyed the Holy Sepulcher at Jerusalem—an act that caused great indignation in the West.

At first it seemed as if the vacuum created by the Abbasid collapse would be filled by Byzantium, which reconquered Antioch in 969 and pushed into Syria. But after 1025 Byzantium was riven with savage factional struggles and could not follow up those conquests.

It was at this point that the Turks, a nomadic warrior people of the steppes (see box), rose to prominence. In 1055, Turks in the caliph's army helped a group of tribal Turks, recent converts to Islam led by the Seljuk family, to seize power in Baghdad, where they ruled as sultans in the caliph's name. The Grand Seljuks, as the sultans of Baghdad were called, championed Sunni orthodoxy and reconquered much territory from the Fatimids, including Jerusalem.

Not all the tribes of Turks wanted to obey the Seljuk sultans and some of them took to raiding the Byzantine empire. In 1071 the emperor Romanus IV Diogenes (1067–71) responded by invading Seljuk territory, where his armies suffered a crushing defeat at the hands of the Seljuk sultan Alp Arslan (1063–72) at Manzikert near

THE TURKS

The Turks were one of many nomadic peoples of the Eurasian steppe who, beginning with the Huns, emerged periodically into neighboring regions. Some time before the tenth century, the Oghuz Turks, led by descendants of a legendary figure called Seljuk, came to dominate the lands between the Black Sea and Central Asia. These shamanist tribes fought *ghazi*, zealous Islamic volunteers, on the northern fringes of Persia until the Turks were converted to Islam. In the tenth century Turkish Muslim

powers emerged. From the time of Caliph al-Mu'tasim (892–902), Turks had been enlisted in the armies of the Baghdad caliphate. Their life as steppe hunters trained them as mounted marksmen who were able to maneuver together. The scholar al-Jahiz (died ca. 868) wrote: "The Turk can shoot at beasts, birds, hoops, men, sitting quarry, dummies, and birds on the wing...at full gallop to fore or rear, to left or right, upward or downward." loosing ten arrows before anyone else can nock one."

Lake Van in Armenia (now Turkey). The discredited Romanus was deposed, and Byzantium descended into civil war. Both factions invited Turks in to assist and thus Byzantium virtually handed Asia Minor to them, including a branch of the Seljuks who established themselves at Nicaea (Iznik) and Iconium (Konya) as sultans of Rum ("Rome," that is, Byzantium). The mass of the people in these areas remained Greek-speaking Christians.

When Grand Seljuk Malik Shah (1072–92) died, the sultanate fragmented. By 1095 the sultan at Baghdad was preoccupied with eastern affairs, while Syria was divided between two Seljuk brothers, Duqaq of Damascus and Ridwan of Aleppo.

The Byzantine emperor, Alexius I Comnenus (1081–1118) had stabilized the empire and was keen to take military advantage of the chaos in the Islamic lands, but he lacked the troops to reconquer Asia Minor. In 1095, he sent an embassy to ask Pope Urban II (1088–99) to appeal for soldiers to aid the Christian empire of the East, which Alexius probably claimed was in grave peril. Urban's appeal was even more ambitious in scope: he called for a great expedition that would not only help Alexius but also liberate the holy city of Jerusalem.

THE COMING OF THE TURKS

In his *Chronicle*, the 12th-century writer Matthew of Edessa describes the arrival of raiding Turks among the Armenian Christians of Asia Minor:

"In the beginning of the year [1016–17] a calamity proclaiming the fulfillment of divine portents befell the Christian adorers of the Holy Cross. The death-breathing dragon appeared, accompanied by a destroying fire, and struck the believers in the Holy Trinity. The apostolic and prophetic books trembled, for there arrived winged serpents come to vomit fire upon Christ's faithful.... At this period there gathered the savage nation of infidels called Turks. Setting out, they entered [our] province...and put the Christians to the sword. Facing the enemy, the Armenians saw these strange men, who were armed with bows and had flowing hair like women."

The Armenian cathedral of the Holy Cross, built by the Armenian king in the early 10th century on the island of Aghtamar (Akdama) in Lake Van, which is today in eastern Turkey. A century later, in the face of the threat posed by the Turks, the Armenian ruler submitted to Byzantine authority and many Armenians fought in the imperial army at Manzikert in 1071. In the wake of this disaster the Seljuk Turks occupied Armenia, and many Armenians followed those who had already migrated to Cilicia in southeast Anatolia. The Armenians came to dominate much of Cilicia, which was to play a key role as a Christian buffer region between Byzantium, the Seljuks of Rum, and the crusader states. (See also page 40.)

THE ARMIES DEPART

URBAN'S APPEAL TO THE FRENCH

In his *History of Jerusalem*, the French chronicler Robert the Monk gives one of many reports of Pope Urban II's appeal for a crusade at the council of Clermont in 1095. This is an extract:

"Let the deeds of your ancestors move you and incite your minds to manly achievements; likewise the glory and greatness of King Charlemagne, and his son Louis, and of your other kings, who have destroyed the kingdoms of the pagans, and have extended in these lands the territory of the Holy Church. Let the Holy Sepulcher of the Lord, Our Savior, which is possessed by unclean nations, especially move you, and likewise the holy places, which are now treated with ignominy and irreverently polluted with filthiness. Oh, most valiant soldiers and descendants of invincible ancestors, do not be degenerate, but recall the valor of your forefathers."

The arrival (left) and preaching (right) of Pope Urban II at the council of Clermont in 1095, from a French manuscript of the early 14th century.

In February 1095 at Piacenza, on his way to France, Pope Urban II encountered the embassy sent by Emperor Alexius I Comnenus to appeal for help against the Turks. Alexius was in no danger, but he needed troops to exploit the divisions among the Seljuks. Perhaps Urban was already thinking of a great initiative: relations with Byzantium had improved and he was taking a very keen interest in the war against the Muslims in Spain. In France he almost certainly visited the powerful Count Raymond of Toulouse before he attended the council of Clermont in November.

At the end of the council Urban preached an inspirational sermon calling for a great expedition to the East. There survive many and differing accounts of this appeal (see sidebar), but the pope probably called for an army to aid the eastern Christians and to liberate Jerusalem. Those wishing to go had to take a pilgrim vow to persist in the way of God to the end, or until death. In return they were promised church protection of their lands and the remission of their sins. This appeal had obviously been carefully prepared: Adhemar, the bishop of Le Puy, was appointed papal legate to lead the crusade and was the first to take the cross, and the count of Toulouse's delegates came forward. A date for departure—15th August 1096—was announced immediately, and crusaders were asked to gather near Constantinople. A storm of enthusiasm greeted the appeal—the crowd roared "God wills it"—and the assembled bishops dispersed to spread the word. Urban traveled through France preaching, and wrote letters to those in other lands. In Italy, Bohemond of Otranto, the son of Robert Guiscard (see page 29), gathered an army in the south and Genoa sent a fleet.

But the great surprise was the support from northern Europe. Count Robert II of Flanders, Duke Robert of Normandy, Count Eustace of Boulogne, and Count Stephen of Blois all took the cross, as did Hugh of Vermandois, the brother of King Philip of France. Most striking of all was the adhesion of Eustace of Boulogne's brother, Godfrey of Bouillon, the duke of Lorraine, who was a vassal of Urban's political enemy, the emperor Henry IV.

There is no record of the numbers who went on the crusade—people from all over Europe joined and probably about 100,000 took the cross, but there were losses and desertions, so that around

60,000 eventually gathered at Nicaea near Constantinople in June 1097, including up to 7,000 knights.

This was an amazing achievement. Jerusalem was distant and the journey expensive—Godfrey sold many of his lands, but with the option of buying them back if he should return. Moving such masses of men and horses was difficult. A modern horse needs 24lbs (11kg) of feed per day and cannot continue indefinitely on less or its condition will deteriorate. A man needed a minimum of 2lbs (900g) of bread per day, which meant a pack-horse—carts could only be used where there were good roads—could only carry rations for 150 men per day. The main burden fell on the Byzantines, who were taken by surprise by the "People's Crusade" (see sidebar) when it entered their territory in the summer of 1096 long before the armies of the great nobles, but thereafter they coped well.

Not One Army But Many

The First Crusade was actually a gathering of armies, which took a variety of roads to Constantinople. Godfrey followed the People's Crusade, via Ratisbon (Regensburg) down the Danube valley, arriving by Christmas 1096. Hugh of Vermandois traveled to southern Italy and crossed the Adriatic from Bari, only to be shipwrecked near

THE "PEOPLE'S CRUSADE"

The "People's Crusade" is the name given to a series of expeditions that preceded that of the great leaders, and which ended in disaster in Asia Minor. The expeditions have been attributed (in some cases wrongly) to a charismatic French preacher, Peter the Hermit. Clerics who wrote after 1099 were happy to dismiss Peter and his followers as a rabble.

However, northern France produced many noted religious leaders of humble origins at this time. Among those Peter inspired was a knight, Walter Sans-Avoir, whom he sent with eight other knights and some footsoldiers as a vanguard. Their arrival in the Rhineland triggered a wave of persecution of the Jews—a chain of events that had already begun in France. Walter's force made its way down the Danube, arriving in Constantinople in July 1096 after some clashes. Peter's main force also encountered problems en route but was at Constantinople on 1st August. Instead of awaiting the main crusader armies, Walter led Peter's whole force against Seljuk Nicaea. On 21st October it was all but destroyed by the Turks.

In its final battle Peter's army had 500 knights, and like other crusader armies it seems to have consisted of nobles, knights, infantry, and non-combatants. Its main problem was the lack of an outstanding leader. Peter's charismatic authority could inspire, but he could not lead in the field.

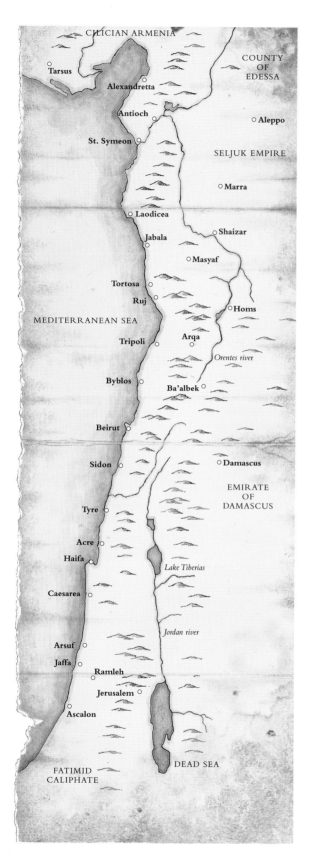

Dyrrachium (present-day Durrës, Albania), whence he made his way to Constantinople, arriving in November 1096. The count of Toulouse probably left Provence in December 1096, crossed Italy and passed down the Dalmatian coast, where his army was harassed by locals, arriving at Dyrrachium in February 1097. His large, undisciplined army then started to ravage, which led to skirmishes with its Byzantine escorts. Bohemond of Otranto set out with his small force on 1st November 1096 from Avlona, south of Dyrrachium, and did not reach Constantinople until early April 1097. He probably bypassed Dyrrachium, which had a Byzantine garrison, because he had earlier fought the Byzantines and wished to avoid hostilities until he was sure of a good reception.

Robert of Normandy, Robert of Flanders, and Stephen of Blois left in the fall of 1096. Robert of Normandy raised 10,000 silver marks for his journey by pawning the duchy to his brother, King William II of England (1087–99), but this huge sum took time to raise. Once in southern Italy only Robert of Flanders risked a winter crossing of the Adriatic, while the others delayed and did not reach Constantinople until May 1097. Many smaller, unchronicled groups also made their way east. It was a somewhat unwieldy structure for an army facing a long journey and many enemies. In the event, its first task was to deal with its ally, the emperor Alexius.

Why did so many people respond to Pope Urban's appeal for an expedition to the East? No part of Europe was untouched by it and such was the enthusiasm it generated that Urban forbade Spaniards from going lest they weaken the Reconquista. The crusaders' motives must have been primarily religious, but the suspicion that other factors were at work is suggested by the second canon of the council of Clermont, which declares: "If any man sets out from pure devotion, not for reputation or monetary gain, to liberate the Church of God at Jerusalem, his journey shall be reckoned in place of all penance." Urban proclaimed a fighting pilgrimage, giving a new dimension—that of salvation through slaughter—to an old and accepted idea. This pilgrimage was to the most prestigious of all goals, Jerusalem, which seems to have loomed large in the piety of western Christians.

By the end of the eleventh century, wars against Islam in Spain had begun to familiarize Europeans with the idea of holy war. Pope Urban II's determined campaigning, supported by other preachers, made an impact and occasional fragments of evidence bear witness to the pious motives of individuals: Achard of Montmerle, who died during the siege of Jerusalem in 1099, sold land to the monastery of Cluny "because I wish, fully armed, to join in the magnificent expedition of the Christian people seeking for God to fight their way to Jerusalem against the pagans and Saracens."

What we know of the major leaders suggests a mixture of motives. The counts of Toulouse, Blois, and Flanders were already immensely rich and it is difficult to see anything other than religious reasons for having taken the cross. Godfrey of Bouillon and Robert of Normandy were men in grave political difficulties. Bohemond of Otranto was an acquisitive lord who was trying to improve his fortune. Lesser men, such as Tancred and Baldwin of Boulogne, were obviously ambitious for land, and there may have been many others like them.

Perhaps the modern tendency in the secular West to be sceptical of spiritual and religious motives hinders understanding. The idea of holy war (see pages 26–27) was accepted at the time but it was popularly interpreted as attaining salvation by killing the enemy. Urban, who gave the concept a new dynamism by his indulgence of sins, did not outlaw rightful plunder and gain, he merely insisted that it should not be the prime motive. He probably recognized, too, that it would be necessary to establish states in the East and that these would have to belong to somebody. There were no contradictions for contemporaries, and worldly success could even be judged as a sign of heavenly approval. This was, after all, an age when the verdict in battle was seen as the judgment of God.

Above and left: *Knights and infantry heading for the First Crusade and (right) the "People's Crusade" led by Peter the Hermit (see page 37). Miniatures from the* Abreviamen de las Estorias, *a Provençal account of the crusades written at the beginning of the 14th century. The pope's appeal triggered a response by tens of thousands of individuals across western Europe. Urban's expectation was for an orderly force composed of knights and footsoldiers from among the ranks of the military-aristocratic gentry, but he stirred a reaction among the poor too, which resulted in ragtag bands of northern Europeans, such as that led by Peter the Hermit, heading for the Holy Land. Medieval writers were dismissive of the enthusiasm of the poor and feared that it might lead to heresy. According to the chronicler Albert of Aachen: "There was also another abominable wickedness in this gathering of people on foot, who were stupid and insanely irresponsible, which, it cannot be doubted, is hateful to God and unbelievable to all the faithful. They claimed that a certain goose was inspired by the Holy Ghost, and a she-goat filled no less with the same, and they had made these their leaders for this holy journey to Jerusalem; they even worshipped them excessively, and as the beasts directed their courses for them in their animal way many of the troops believed they were confirming it to be true according to the entire purpose of the spirit."*

THE CAMPAIGN IN ANATOLIA

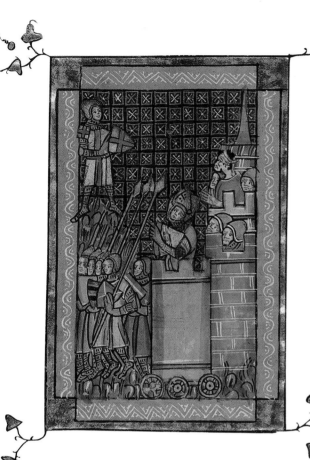

At Constantinople the emperor Alexius insisted that the crusade leaders swear an oath to become "his" men and promise to restore any former lands of the empire that they conquered. Raymond of Toulouse refused to accept the vassalage this oath implied but eventually swore a simpler oath to respect the emperor's life, honor, and interests. In return, Alexius promised the crusaders military and logistical support. As the chronicler Fulcher of Chartres remarked: "It was essential that all establish friendship with the emperor, since without his aid and counsel we could not easily make the journey, nor could those who were to follow us."

The ensuing Anatolian campaign opened the way for Alexius to reconquer much of western Anatolia in early 1098—the alliance worked because it also relieved the crusader army from the need to garrison captured cities. By 6th May Godfrey of Bouillon, Bohemond of Otranto, Robert of Flanders, and Hugh of Vermandois had begun the siege of Nicaea (Iznik), the capital of the Seljuk sultans of Rum. The Seljuk forces were skilled but small in number, and Sultan Kilij I Arslan (1092–1107) was away fighting the Danishmend Turks to the east. On 16th May he tried to relieve Nicaea but failed, and the crusaders were free to pursue the siege.

Nicaea was ringed by a 33-ft (10-meter) high Roman wall nearly 3 miles (5km) in circumference and studded with 114 towers. The ancient city was D-shaped: the western part of the

EDESSA: THE FIRST CRUSADER STATE

In the period of Byzantine expansion, many Armenians had settled in Cilicia and in cities stretching via Melitene to Edessa, while others had populated Antioch and north Syria. Their Christianity differed from that of Rome and of the Greek majority among whom they settled, but while many of their leaders resented Byzantine imperial control, they had nothing against the western church.

When Byzantium collapsed following the battle of Manzikert in 1071, the Armenians in Edessa and other places achieved a precarious autonomy. Some Armenians sought Byzantine support, and it was very likely at the court of Constantinople that they first encountered the

crusaders. This would help explain why the western armies were welcomed in Armenian Cilicia. Baldwin of Boulogne, the brother of Eustace of Boulogne and Godfrey of Bouillon, cultivated the Armenian leaders and came to the notice of Thoros, prince of Edessa, whose land was threatened by the Turks. Thoros probably just wanted to employ Baldwin as a mercenary, but reluctantly agreed to recognize Baldwin as his heir. Baldwin succeeded sooner than he expected. There were divisions among the people of Edessa and on 9th March 1098 they overthrew Thoros and accepted Baldwin as their prince. Edessa thus became the first crusader state in the East.

wall, the straight side of the D, abuts Ascanian Lake, so unless the attack was made in boats the defenders only had to man about half the length of the wall. The crusaders, reinforced by 2,000 Byzantine infantry under Tatikios, arranged themselves around the land wall and attacked it using penthouses—wooden structures on wheels with sloping armored roofs that were rolled up to the wall so that men within could undermine it—supported by catapults and archers.

In fierce assaults the crusaders suffered, but the garrison was weakening. On 17th June the emperor, who was at Pelekanum nearby, launched a fleet on the lake. This prompted the Turks to negotiate a surrender on 19th June, but to Alexius rather than the crusaders. The Byzantines concealed these negotiations, but the crusaders were not concerned because the alliance was working. Alexius gave them compensation for missing out on the city's loot and he asked Tatikios to lead a force on the crusade; he also advised the crusade leaders to send envoys to Egypt, whose Fatimid rulers hated the Seljuks.

On 26th June the army began to leave Nicaea, heading toward Dorylaeum (Eskisehir), the gateway to the Anatolian plateau. The army split, probably by accident, into a vanguard led by Bohemond, Robert of Normandy, and Stephen of Blois, followed at a distance of several miles by the main army. Kilij Arslan, who had returned with an army of about 10,000 Turkish horse, ambushed the vanguard as it turned south down the valley leading to Dorylaeum, above present-day Bozüyük. As Fulcher of Chartres recalled, "the Turks crept up, howling loudly and shooting a shower of arrows. Stunned, and almost dead and with many wounded, we immediately fled. And it was no wonder, for such warfare was new to us all." The sultan had achieved surprise, but he was then drawn into a close-quarter fight that gave the main crusader force time to arrive and defeat his army.

The victory at Dorylaeum opened Asia Minor to the crusade. The summer's heat took a heavy toll of people and horses even though the crusaders advanced via the well-watered city of Antioch-in-Pisidia (Yalvaç). The cities, still mainly Greek in population, opened their gates to them. After Heraclea (Eregli), the crusaders' objective was Antioch (Antakya), the greatest Syrian city after Damascus. The leaders sent a small force along the quickest route, over the mountains called the Cilician Gates into Cilicia and then over the Belen Pass into Syria. Most of the army went via Caesarea-in-Cappadocia, where they liberated the local Armenians from the Turks. In doing so they created a friendly zone to supply their attack on Antioch, where the main crusader army arrived on 20th October 1098.

Opposite: *Godfrey of Bouillon leads the siege of a city, from a 14th-century French manuscript. The crusaders are deploying a wheeled tower that could be rolled right up to the defensive walls—a similar structure was used during the siege of Nicaea (see main text).*

Below: *A 13th-century English bronze aquamanile (a ewer used for washing hands at table) in the form of a mounted knight, who originally held a lance and a shield, now lost. Horses played an important role on both sides during the crusades. The journey for the mounts of the western European knights for the First Crusade was mainly overland, but later many horses were transported directly to the Holy Land by sea. Among the Islamic forces in the Near East, a significant proportion consisted of Turk warriors steeped in traditions of nomadic horsemanship.*

THE SIEGES OF ANTIOCH

THE HOLY LANCE

In their desperation, besieged in Antioch by the enormous forces of Kerbogah (see main text), the basic religious motivation of the crusaders emerged to inspire them. On 10th June a poor pilgrim announced that St. Andrew had revealed to him that the Holy Lance, which had pierced the side of Christ, was buried in the ancient church of St. Peter at Antioch. The papal legate was skeptical, but the next day a respectable priest declared that Christ had confirmed to him in a vision that a token of victory would be revealed to the army.

Amid great religious fervor digging began in St Peter's church and on 14th June a lancehead was indeed discovered. This coincided with a startling event—a meteorite fell into Kerbogah's camp and he withdrew his forces from within the city. The clergy then fanned the fires of pious fervor with a series of celebrations. Thus incited, on 28th June the army marched out with the Holy Lance borne before them. Their victory owed much to Kerbogah's unwise dispersal of his army, and to Bohemond's tactical acumen. But without the inspiration of the lance and its "miracles" it seems unlikely that the starving army would have challenged Kerbogah. Little wonder that after the battle the relic enjoyed enormous prestige.

The crusaders arrived at Antioch to find that an English fleet had already seized its port, St. Symeon. The Roman walls of Antioch were strong, and half their circuit of 10 miles (16km) lay inaccessible in the mountains. The crusaders dared not attack because of the city's size; similarly, they could not surround it and so chose to strangle it by blockade. This strategy took time and involved constant fighting with the garrison and its supporters in outlying forts such as Harim.

By Christmas 1097 hunger within crusader ranks had forced them to send a foraging expedition led by Bohemond into Syria. On 31st January he fought a force under Duqaq of Damascus near al-Bara: a drawn affair, Duqaq retreated but the crusaders returned without food. With the army starving and its horses dying, Tatikios returned to Constantinople to seek more aid. Ridwan of Aleppo, freed from the threat of Duqaq, his brother and rival, now chose to strike. But Bohemond managed to gather a small mounted force with which he ambushed Ridwan's army, scattering it and seizing Harim. Relieved of Turkish pressure, the army could forage again.

On 4th March 1098 more English ships put into St. Symeon, and the crusaders used the equipment and skills of the new arrivals to build a fort outside Antioch's vital Bridge Gate. Despite savage resistance they succeeded and soon had closed off all the main gates. Spring meant more food became available and the crusaders were further encouraged by news of Baldwin's seizure of Edessa (see page 40).

At this time the crusaders made an alliance, against the Seljuks, with the Fatimid rulers of Egypt. Antioch's ruler, Yaghi-Siyan, appealed for help to Kerbogah of Mosul, who was subject to the Seljuk sultan at Baghdad. Kerbogah raised a huge army and from 4th to 25th May besieged Edessa, giving ample warning to the crusaders at Antioch. There, a tower-commander offered to betray the city to Bohemond, who demanded to be made ruler of the city. The other crusade leaders refused this as a breach of the oath to the emperor Alexius (see page 40), but the threat from Kerbogah was a very pressing one and in the end they agreed, but only on the condition that control of the city be ceded to Alexius if he came to claim it.

On the night of 2nd June an élite crusader force entered Antioch and the next day the city fell amid scenes of massacre. But the citadel on the walls held out. On 4th June Kerbogah laid siege to the heavily outnumbered crusaders in a city that was short of food. To make matters worse, his men could enter Antioch through the citadel and were only halted by desperate fighting. Stephen of Blois, who was absent when Antioch had fallen, fled when he saw the situation. He met Alexius at Philomelium on 20th June and told him that all was lost, whereupon the emperor returned to Constantinople.

In Antioch itself, sheer despair and pious zeal (see sidebar) had rallied the crusaders. Fired with enthusiasm, they appointed Bohemond as commander and on 28th June marched out of the city to defeat Kerbogah, who had unwisely let his army become dispersed.

The way south to Jerusalem now lay open, but the crusaders needed to rest and may even have hoped that the Egyptian alliance would deliver Jerusalem without a fight. Taking seriously the condition of their promise to Bohemond, the leaders sent a delegation to Alexius and postponed their advance to Jerusalem until 1st November—ample time for Alexius to claim Antioch. In the meantime, Bohemond behaved as a ruler and there was tension between him and Raymond of Toulouse, the champion of the imperial alliance.

By September, news of Alexius's "desertion" at Philomelium had hardened opinion against the Byzantines and at a council in early November the quarrel between Raymond and Bohemond paralyzed the army. Ultimately, Bohemond refused to go on to Jerusalem and when the other leaders had departed he ejected Raymond's men from Antioch, thus breaking up the unity of the crusade.

The crusader knights clash with Muslim troops during the First Crusade's second siege of Antioch, from a French manuscript of ca. 1200. The regional struggle for religious dominance had affected the fortunes of Antioch for centuries. As far back as 638 the Syrian city, which was where the new faith of Christianity was given its name, was captured from the Byzantines by the Arabs. In 969 the Byzantines recaptured the city by treachery after a long blockade. In 1097 the Byzantine general on the crusade urged a similar blockade, but the crusaders preferred to invest the city. However, they were unable to assault its strong fortifications and in the end it was betrayed to them by a discontented officer commanding three of its towers.

THE ROAD TO JERUSALEM

The sacred pools at the Halil Rahmna mosque in the city of Urfa, southeastern Turkey, and birthplace of Abraham. The mosque was built in 1211 on the site of the Mother Mary church erected in 504 by the Byzantines. At one time Urfa was known as Edessa, the seat of the first crusader state in the East when Baldwin of Boulogne engineered his succession to the city's Armenian prince. Baldwin's seizure of Edessa and Bohemond's effective takeover of Antioch showed that there were rich pickings for the ambitious and ruthless, and many crusaders seem to have stayed in north Syria rather than proceeding to Jerusalem. Edessa remained in crusader hands until 1144, when its loss to the armies of Zengi (see pages 54–55) prompted the Second Crusade.

The council of the army at Antioch in November 1098 had ended in what one participant called a "discordant peace" between Raymond of Toulouse and Bohemond, whereby each continued to hold sections of Antioch. Raymond then led some of the army south and attacked the Syrian city of Marra on 28th November. He was joined by Bohemond, but Godfrey of Bouillon and Robert of Flanders did not join in, so it is likely that this was a stop-gap activity pending a settlement over Antioch. Marra resisted strongly but fell on 11th December, and the bloodshed that followed was particularly brutal. Crusaders dismembered captives in the belief that they had swallowed money, and any citizens not killed were sold into slavery.

Delay in Marra resulted in the army starving—in their desperation some crusaders even dug up enemy corpses and ate them. The failure of supplies led some to abandon the crusade for cities such as Edessa. Raymond put an end to the food shortage by leading a raid into enemy territory which provided ample food.

Bohemond tried but failed to trade his section of Marra for Raymond's share of Antioch, causing further quarrels. In January 1099 Raymond called another council near Marra and offered money to those who would accept his leadership as far as Jerusalem (see sidebar). As a consequence, Bohemond refused to continue to Jerusalem and on 7th January ejected Raymond's men from Antioch. On 13th January elements of the now split crusader army left Marra under Raymond's command. Robert of Normandy and Bohemond's

nephew Tancred joined Raymond, while Godfrey and Robert of Flanders, apparently hostile to Raymond, remained near Antioch.

Sometimes dealing with the enemy proved more profitable than fighting them. Between the crusaders and Jerusalem lay many cities whose rulers had no wish to see a large enemy army ravaging their territory and were ready to pay to ensure a peaceful passage by such an army. This both enriched the crusaders and enabled them to pass on quickly to their goal. Thus the rulers of Shaizar and Homs paid tribute to the crusaders as they marched through Syria.

At the Homs Gap the crusaders decided not to take the inland route south via Damascus, but to make for the coast where friendly fleets could support them. As they neared the principality of Tripoli they faced a dilemma. Tripoli was nominally subject to the Fatimids, with whom the crusaders had made an alliance against the Seljuks. It was hoped that the Fatimids might hand over Jerusalem and the crusaders were awaiting the return of envoys they had sent to Egypt the previous spring. In order to occupy his men in the meantime, Raymond persuaded the army to attack the city of Arqa, which belonged to Tripoli, and he launched other raids against Tripolitan territory. He thus hoped to occupy and feed the troops, and to extort tribute from Tripoli, while refraining from outright hostilities.

Godfrey and Robert of Flanders had remained at Antioch, but, under intense pressure from their followers, who wanted to complete their journey, the pair departed at the end of February. However, they could not bear to join Raymond against Arqa and instead besieged Jabala. Only when mistaken news came of an enemy threat to Raymond's army did they march south, but even then the two forces remained aloof from one another. Earlier disputes now continued: Raymond wanted to seize Arqa and perhaps await help from the emperor Alexius, but Godfrey and his friends would have none of it. The army for its part was growing restless and anxious to move on to Jerusalem.

The deadlock was ended in May 1099, when an Egyptian embassy arrived. The Fatimids refused to concede Jerusalem. The crusaders reacted by immediately heading south into Fatimid territory, taking the Egyptians by surprise. They had no army in Palestine and had destroyed Jaffa, the port of Jerusalem, because they had no troops to defend it. In these circumstances the cities of the coast, such as Beirut, Acre, and Caesarea, paid tribute to the crusaders. Aware that the Egyptians would ultimately respond to their attack, the crusaders marched rapidly south and arrived outside Jerusalem on 7th June 1099.

THE PRICE OF LEADERSHIP

At the meeting at Ruj near Marra (see main text), according to Raymond of Aguilers, Raymond of Toulouse, who was the wealthiest of the crusade leaders, "wished to give the duke [Godfrey of Bouillon] ten thousand *solidi*, an equal amount to Robert of Normandy, six thousand to the count of Flanders and five thousand to Tancred and to the other princes accordingly" to accept his leadership. It seems likely that the offer to each leader depended on the size of his army. We know the terms, because the same source later reveals that "He [Tancred] had received five thousand *solidi* and two very fine horses on the agreement that he would remain in [Raymond's] service up to Jerusalem."

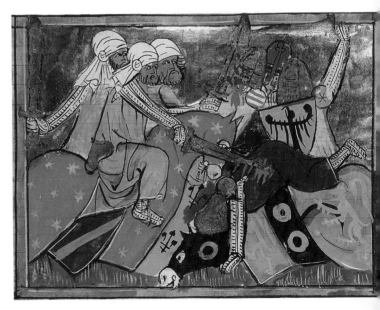

Saracens in combat against the crusaders, from the Roman de Godefroy de Bouillon et de Saladin, *a 14th-century French romance about the early crusades.*

THE FALL OF THE HOLY CITY

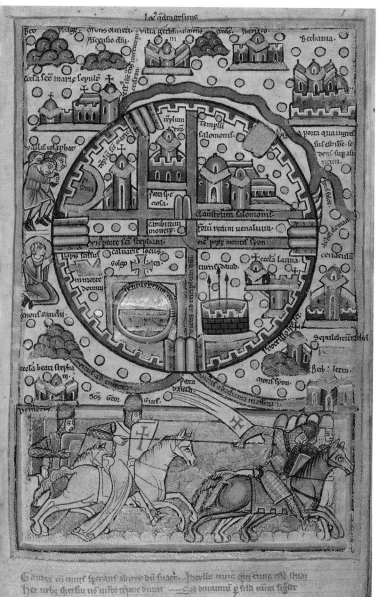

A 12th-century plan of Christian-held Jerusalem and its environs. In the bottom register, crusaders are shown driving off Muslims.

Jerusalem stands on a ridge with steep slopes to east and west. The city's north wall was much more vulnerable, but at that time it was reinforced with a ditch and an outer wall. Zion Gate, on the south wall, opens on to a small plateau but this too had a ditch. Before the crusaders arrived outside Jerusalem on 6th June 1099, the Egyptians had strengthened the garrison in the Tower of David on the west wall, and had devastated the area about the city, destroying all timber that could be used for siege machinery and blocking wells.

Knowing that the Egyptians would send a relief force, the crusaders launched an attack on 13th June, despite having only one assault ladder, built with wood found in a cave. This failed and they began to prepare a more systematic onslaught. Then, on 17th June a crusader fleet putting into Jaffa was surprised by Egyptian ships and forced to beach, but the crews salvaged the cargoes of food and ships' timbers which they took to Jerusalem.

It was decided to make a two-pronged assault. The northern French built a siege tower at the northwest corner of the city, and also a ram to break down the outer wall. Raymond hired a Genoese ship's captain, William Ricau, to build a tower outside Zion Gate and fill in the ditch. Both contingents constructed catapults. Foraging parties found light wood for ladders and mantlets (shields big enough to protect a man against arrows fired from the walls), and brought water, much of it foul, from a distance. Jerusalem's defenders strengthened the walls opposite the two crusader forces and brought up fourteen catapults, of which nine were directed against Raymond.

On 8th July the crusaders processed around Jerusalem like Joshua before Jericho, and the leaders were publicly reconciled. The decisive event came on the night of 9th–10th July, when the French dismantled their tower, ram, and catapults and moved them east to a weak point on the north wall. This was a huge task but to counter it the defenders had to start from scratch to reinforce the walls and build new catapults—and they were, in any case, divided by the need to keep a force on the south wall.

On 13th July the assault began. In the north the French ram breached the outer wall. By 14th July the tower was approaching the inner wall, where the knights in the tower would provide cover for an escalade (assault by ladder) and attempts to undermine the wall. But in the south, by the morning of 15th July, the defenders' catapults had wrecked Raymond's tower. This and the sustained Muslim assault demoralized the crusaders.

In the north, though, Godfrey of Bouillon had brought the siege tower up to the wall and the knights inside it were able to build a bridge onto the wall itself. Godfrey's men at once poured across the bridge and into the city, followed by Tancred's men, who occupied the Temple Mount while Godfrey opened the city gates. When news of this reached the south, the city's governor fled with his entourage into the Tower of David, but agreed to surrender the citadel to Raymond in return for safe passage out of the city. Most of the population fled and those who failed to do so were massacred (see box).

The crusaders celebrated their triumph, and completed their pilgrimage, in the church of the Holy Sepulcher. On 22nd July Godfrey was chosen as ruler of the city with the title advocate (protector) of the Holy Sepulcher. On 1st August Arnulf of Chocques, Robert of Normandy's chaplain, became the city's new Latin patriarch.

However, the leaders were aware of an Egyptian force building up at Ascalon on the coast. Emboldened by a sense that God was on their side, on 12th August the crusaders surprised and defeated the Egyptian army. For now, the crusader foothold in the Holy Land was secure, and most of the victorious army could return home.

"THE BLOOD OF PAGANS"

In his exultant account of the fall of Jerusalem, Raymond of Aguilers celebrates the slaughter visited upon the city's Muslims, seeing it as God's vengeance on those who had defiled the Holy City:

"It is sufficient to relate that in the Temple of Solomon [the Aqsa mosque] and the portico crusaders rode in blood to the knees and bridles of their horses. In my opinion this was poetic justice that the Temple of Solomon should receive the blood of pagans who blasphemed God there for many years. Jerusalem was now littered with bodies and stained with blood.... A new day, new gladness, new and everlasting happiness, and the fulfillment of our toil and love brought forth new words and songs for all."

THE MASSACRE OF 1099: MYTH AND REALITY

The slaughter that took place during and after the capture of Jerusalem in 1099 has become notorious, partly because later Muslim sources exaggerated the event in order to whip up the spirit of *jihad*. But the slaughter was not total. Many Muslims escaped, taking with them an important *Quran*, and created their own suburb of Damascus. The crusaders burned the synagogue over the heads of the hundreds of Jews who had fled there for safety, but surviving letters from the Jewish community in Cairo show that some Jews were captured and held for ransom.

The worst single atrocity took place on the morning after the fall. Tancred had given a group of Muslims protection on the roof of the Aqsa mosque ("Solomon's Temple"), but before he could ransom them they were

killed by other crusaders. Apart from this massacre, most of the killing took place when the crusaders broke into the city, and this must be seen in the context of the age. The earlier a city or castle surrendered, the better the terms for its population. The people in a stronghold that held out to the bitter end were "at mercy," and in the heat of battle there was likely to be little of that as the victors rushed through the streets in search of enemy troops and plunder.

By the same token, however, the chaos of battle could allow many to escape, and the east and west walls of Jerusalem were virtually unguarded by the crusaders. The fall of Jerusalem was certainly accompanied by terrible bloodshed, but not by all the imagined horrors of later generations.

THE GROWTH OF THE LATIN EAST

THE FATE OF THE PRISONERS TAKEN AT THE "FIELD OF BLOOD"

Walter, chancellor of the principality of Antioch, who was himself captured, gives a grim account of the execution of crusader prisoners after the disastrous defeat at the "Field of Blood" near Aleppo in 1119:

"Some…were hanged by ropes from a post, with their heads downwards, their feet upwards, and exposed to constant blows of arrows as the stuff of dreadful slaughter. Some were buried up to the groin, some up to the navel and some up to the chin in a pit in the ground, as the hands of the wicked ones brandished spears, and they underwent for Christ the end of a life full of sorrow. Several…were thrown with every limb cut off into [Aleppo's] squares and districts."

Bohemond's seizure of Antioch had caused hostility between Byzantium and the crusaders and wrecked the prospect of establishing a land route from Europe to the tiny crusader footholds in the East. Without easy access, these bridgeheads were starved of settlers, and a shortage of manpower from the West would always be a problem.

Another consequence was dependence upon the Italian maritime city-states. Although religiously inspired, they also sought trading bases in the East and to this end they helped Jerusalem to take coastal cities in return for trade privileges. In 1100 Godfrey of Bouillon died and his brother became King Baldwin I of Jerusalem (1100–18). Genoese ships enabled him to seize Arsuf and Caesarea in 1101 and Acre, with Pisan support, in 1104. In 1110 Genoese and Pisan ships assisted in the capture of Beirut and the Venetians helped to take Sidon. Tyre resisted in 1112 but was taken, with Venetian aid, in 1124.

The crusaders did not always call on the Italians. In 1102 Raymond of Toulouse sacked Tortosa without Italian ships, and attacked Tripoli in 1104, establishing Chastel Pelerin (Pilgrim Castle) as a base. In 1109, four years after Raymond's death, Tripoli fell to his son Bertram, who became count of Tripoli, a vassal of the crusader king.

A FORGOTTEN DISASTER: THE CRUSADE OF 1101

The fall of Jerusalem in 1099 was greeted with great enthusiasm across Europe, but there was great anxiety, shared by the new pope, Paschal II, that the conquests must be protected. Many who had taken the cross but not gone in 1095 were now pressured to fulfill their vows, and Stephen of Blois and Hugh of Vermandois, who had left the crusade, were obliged to return. An Italian force with very poor leadership arrived at Constantinople in March 1101. In May they were joined by the north French led by Stephen of Blois. The emperor Alexius appointed his ally, Raymond of Toulouse, as the overall leader of the crusader forces.

Before heading for Syria, the Italians insisted on a diversion to rescue Bohemond of Otranto, who had been taken prisoner by the Danishmend Turks, and Raymond led his force into dangerous country in northern Anatolia. A coalition of Islamic powers formed, and their forces surrounded the crusaders, whose army, already starving, gradually became weaker and was totally defeated at Mersivan in July 1101. Raymond, Stephen, and some of the other leaders escaped.

Count William of Nevers arrived in Constantinople with a small, well-disciplined army and set off after Raymond, but after failing to find his army he turned south and was destroyed by the victors of Mersivan near Heraclea (Eregli). Shortly after the count of Nevers had left, William of Aquitaine reached Constantinople with a force of Germans and French, but they were ambushed and defeated near Heraclea. The Turks had combined in the face of western attack, and learned to avoid the close-quarter battle until their enemy was weakened. This set the pattern for the clash of arms in the future.

Securing the coast was not Jerusalem's only priority. Egypt remained a real threat until the 1120s, when its internal problems came to the fore. Even then, Egypt retained Ascalon until 1153 as a base for attacks on the kingdom. Damascus was another threat; it was relatively isolated and close to the kingdom. In 1127–28 King Baldwin II (1118–31) appealed for a crusade to seize the city and envoys to the West arranged the marriage of his daughter Melissende to the powerful Count Fulk of Anjou, who thus became Baldwin's designated successor. Fulk raised men and money for a great expedition.

No crusade was proclaimed by the pope, but in the fall of 1129 a large Christian army menaced Damascus. However, ill fortune and an ill-advised raid into southern Syria that divided the Christians enabled the Muslims to force a retreat. Thereafter the isolation of Damascus and its anxiety to remain independent led to an intermittent alliance with Jerusalem.

The crusader state of Edessa effectively consisted only of the city itself and a series of fortresses, but it posed a threat to the Muslim city of Aleppo and offered the prospect of Christian expansion to the Euphrates river. Aleppo was also endangered by the proximity of the crusader city of Antioch, only 60 miles (100km) away. Prince Roger of Antioch (1112–19) had advanced on Aleppo in 1119 but died in the heaviest crusader defeat so far at the "Field of Blood," just west of the city (see sidebar). Antioch's fortunes revived, but its drive into Syria was halted after 1130 by succession disputes and the rise of Zengi, Aleppo's ruler from 1126 (see pages 54–55).

Above: *The crusader fort at Sidon, Lebanon. Baldwin I of Jerusalem besieged Sidon in 1110 with the aid of Norwegian ships under King Sigurd (1105–30). It surrendered after Venetian galleys drove off an Egyptian fleet. The aid that Venice and other Italian cities gave to the crusader kingdom helped them to establish a naval supremacy in the eastern Mediterranean that lasted until the 15th century.*

Below: *Crusader ships embarking for the East, from the 14th-century* Roman de Godefroy de Bouillon et de Saladin.

THE DIVERSITY OF CRUSADING

Opposite: *Pilgrim rock-cut graffiti crosses at the entrance to St. Helena's chapel in the church of the Holy Sepulcher, Jerusalem.*

Below: *A knight depicted as a Christian warrior confronting vices in the form of demons, from a fragment (ca. 1260) of the* Summa de Vitiis, *a treatise on the vices by the Dominican preacher William Peraldus (Peyraut) of Lyons. This popular work appeared at a time when the papacy saw the reform of Christian morals as crucial to the success of the wider crusade against the enemies of the church (see pages 146–147).*

The success of the First Crusade indelibly associated crusading with Jerusalem and even overshadowed the disasters of the "Crusade of 1101" (see page 48). Crusade was a form of sanctified warfare in which those participating were offered forgiveness of all their sins. The soldier in such a war increased his chances of entering heaven by the meritorious act of killing "the enemy."

This dynamic notion of salvation through slaughter drove the First Crusade. It was papal in origin and only the pope, as the keeper of keys to the "kingdom of Heaven," could offer such an "indulgence." Yet even before Urban II had launched his crusade he wrote to Count Robert of Flanders, probably in 1093–94, urging him, "for the remission of your sins," to help the bishop of Arras regain lands lost to the emperor Henry IV. This request embodied the essence of

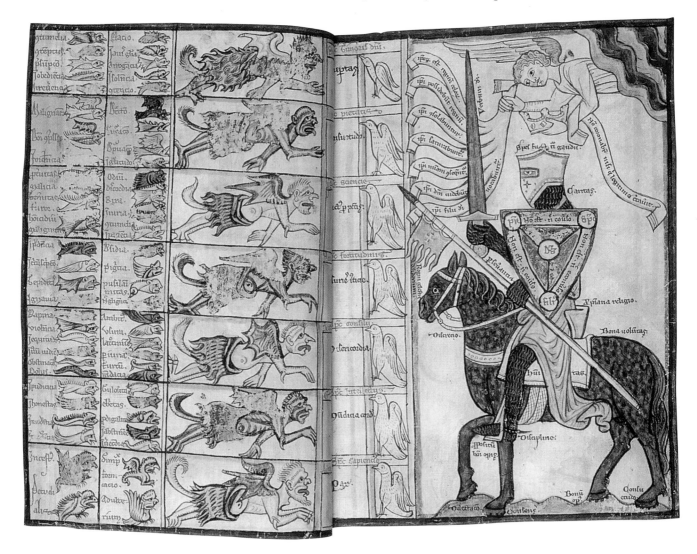

what he preached in 1095. Earlier still, in a letter of 1089 to Catalonia, Urban suggested that all who assisted the town of Tarragona, recently taken from the Muslims, should receive the same forgiveness of sin as those who went on pilgrimage to Jerusalem; this was repeated in 1091. Urban had, therefore, developed the essence of his ideas before 1095 and it is evident that he saw the expedition to regain Jerusalem as part of a universal struggle against Islam and the enemies of the church (see sidebar). Hence there was no necessary connection between Jerusalem and the crusade.

It took a long time for crusading to be absorbed into Christian thinking. The term crusade itself is derived from Latin *cruciatus* or *cruce signatus*—one signed with the cross—but crusading became sharply defined only in the reign of Pope Innocent III (1198–1216). It is difficult to understand how people a century earlier viewed the act of crusade and even whether they regarded it as distinct from pilgrimage to the Holy Land or from fighting the infidel in Spain. But it was clearly associated with the pope, since only he could offer the indulgence that went with it. When Pope Paschal II (1099–1118) wrote in 1103 to Robert of Flanders urging him to attack papal enemies at Liège, he virtually equated the merits of such an action with those gained from the First Crusade.

Further expeditions received papal sanction on similar terms. In 1105 Bohemond returned from Syria to Europe and persuaded the pope to proclaim a new crusade that raised many troops, especially from France. Bohemond, who may have misled Paschal as to his intentions, unsuccessfully attacked Byzantium in 1107. In 1114 Paschal proclaimed a crusade against the Muslims of the Balearic Islands and eastern Spain and in 1118 Pope Gelasius II (1118–19) promoted a crusading expedition which, with French help, captured Saragossa. In 1120, following the disaster at the "Field of Blood" (see pages 48–49), Pope Calixtus II (1119–24) proclaimed crusades to Spain and the Holy Land. This appeal produced the Venetian fleet that helped to take Tyre in 1124. A further crusade to Spain was proclaimed in 1125 and in 1127–28 one was requested, but apparently not granted, for an attack on Damascus (see page 49). In 1127 Pope Honorius II (1124–30) urged a crusade against the Normans of south Italy.

In 1132 two popes were elected, Innocent II (1130–43) and Anacletus II (1130–38). Both could claim legitimacy and both had some support. Anacletus called for a crusade against his rival and his appeal was confirmed by the council of Pisa in 1135, which offered the same remission of sins as had been decreed by Urban II in 1095. In the event, no crusade took place. Anacletus died in 1138 and his successor conceded to Innocent II.

URBAN II AND THE UNIVERSAL WAR AGAINST ISLAM

After the preaching of the First Crusade, Pope Urban II wrote to some Catalan lords who had taken the cross to suggest that rather than leave for Jerusalem they should stay to fight Islam in their own country:

"If the knights of other provinces have decided with one mind to go to the aid of the Asian church and to liberate their brothers from the tyranny of the Muslims, so ought you, with one mind and without encouragement, to work with greater endurance to help a church so near you resist the invasions of the Muslims. No one must doubt that if he dies on this expedition for the love of God and his brothers, his sins will surely be forgiven and he will gain a share of eternal life through the most compassionate mercy of our God. So if any of you has made up his mind to go to Asia, it is here instead that he should try to fulfill his vow, because it is no virtue to rescue Christians from Muslims in one place, only to expose them to the tyranny and oppression of the Muslims in another."

"WARRIOR MONKS": THE MILITARY ORDERS

Nowadays the idea of monks pledged to spend their life in warfare seems paradoxical, yet the creation of the Knights Templar and the Knights Hospitaller was a practical solution to some of the problems of the European settlements in the East. In its early years the crusader kingdom was a precarious place. The coastal cities fell only slowly (see pages 48–49), while Ascalon remained in Muslim hands until 1153 and served as a base for those harassing Christian pilgrims. Given this situation, ca. 1120 a French knight, Hugh of Payens, and some companions established a brotherhood sworn to protect pilgrims on the roads around Jerusalem.

By forming a fraternity Hugh and his fellows sought to emulate the long-lasting stability of a monastic community. Of course, the goal of monks was salvation, but that was also the objective of crusading, so contemporaries saw nothing at all paradoxical in the idea of an order dedicated to salvation through arms, while the adoption of religious oaths promised discipline for its fighting mission.

King Baldwin II (1118–31) gave the order the "Temple of Solomon" (as the Christians called the Aqsa mosque) as its headquarters, hence their name: the "Poor Knighthood of Christ and of the Temple of Solomon," or the Templars. The new order remained small until 1129 when Hugh of Payens solicited support in the West, culminating in the council of Troyes, where St. Bernard of Clairvaux threw his enormous spiritual authority behind it. As a result, a rule

TEMPLAR GREED AT THE SIEGE OF ASCALON

In January 1153 King Baldwin III (1143–62) laid siege to Ascalon, the last port of Palestine in Egyptian hands. The attackers then built a great siege tower that overtopped the city walls, but one night in late July the Ascalonites set it alight. A wind got up and blew the whole blazing mass against the city wall, whereupon the intense heat caused the stone to shatter and opened up a breach.

This happened in the Templar sector of the wall, and in the morning the Templars sent forty knights to seize the city. Members of the order then held off the rest of the crusader army, apparently to ensure that the Templars took the lion's share of the booty from the city. In the

event the Templars were trapped and slain, their bodies being hung over the wall by taunting defenders. The breach was repaired and the opportunity was lost.

Many of the crusaders were depressed by this display of selfishness and greed on the part of the Templars and wanted to abandon the siege, but the king pressed on and Ascalon eventually surrendered on terms on 19th August 1153. The citizens were allowed to depart with such of their property as they could carry.

It was not the last time that the Templars were to be accused of greed: this charge was to contribute to their spectacular fall a century and a half later (see page 175).

was devised and endorsed by the pope in 1129. Almost immediately the Templars received vast gifts of land from pious patrons.

The Hospital of St. John was founded in Jerusalem before 1099 to care for Christian pilgrims. Its enormous popularity brought early papal support and huge gifts to the monks who ran it. In 1139 the Order of the Hospital of St. John of Jerusalem (the Hospitallers) began its military career, taking over the castle of Bethgibelin near Ascalon at the request of King Fulk I (1131–43) and his barons.

The ascendancy of the military orders in Europe was sealed by the events of the Second Crusade (see Chapter Three). When Louis VII of France (1137–80) lost control of his troops in Anatolia he restored order by placing Templars in charge of each section of the army, which thereby fought its way through to Attalia. The orders' popularity brought enormous wealth that enabled them to recover from losses in the Holy Land. Alfonso I of Aragon (1104–34) left his whole kingdom to the orders, and although this bequest was annulled, they obtained huge lands in Spain. Later, as the nobles of the embattled crusader states became impoverished, the orders took over their lands and fortresses. Among the orders' strongholds were Crac des Chevaliers and Marqab, built by the Hospital, and Chastel Pelerin and Tortosa, which belonged to the Templars.

The orders were widely imitated. In the Holy Land, the Order of St. Lazarus, founded ca. 1130, consisted of leper knights, while the Germans founded the Teutonic Order (see page 85). In Spain there was a plethora of orders, and their remarkable discipline and continuity made them vital to the Reconquista (see pages 120–123).

In Jerusalem the Hospital and the Temple, with about 600 knights and a huge following of sergeants and footsoldiers, formed a powerful regular force—the indispensable core of the kingdom's army. The orders enjoyed great power and also remarkable autonomy, since they were subject only to the pope. They were inevitably involved in the politics of the crusader states.

After the battle of Hattin (see pages 74–75), in a testimony to their importance, Saladin ordered the execution of all his Templar and Hospitaller prisoners, declaring, according to his secretary Imad ad-Din al-Isfahani: "I shall purify the land of these two impure races." However, the orders' resources in the West enabled them to recover and become a power in the kingdom once more. By the time of the fall of Acre in 1291 they were its main land force, just as the Italian city-states were vital to command of the sea.

Opposite: A Templar knight in armor ready for battle, from a 14th-century French manuscript.

Below: A 13th-century ecclesiastical staff from Cuenca cathedral, Spain, traditionally said to have belonged to the legendary St. Julian the Hospitaller, who was revered as a patron of the Knights Hospitaller. According to tradition, Julian founded a hospital to care for lepers.

THE RISE OF ISLAMIC UNITY

ZENGI, CHAMPION OF ISLAM

In Imad ad-Din Zengi the crusader states faced a formidable enemy who portrayed himself as a champion of Islam. A *madrasa* (religious college) at Damascus bears an inscription of 1138 describing Zengi as "the fighter of *jihad*, the defender of the frontier, the tamer of the polytheists [Christians], and destroyer of the heretics." Zengi's devotion to *jihad* was matched only by his legendary cruelty. One Muslim chronicler remarked: "He was tyrannical and he would strike with indiscriminate recklessness. He was like a leopard..., like a lion in fury, not renouncing any severity, not knowing any kindness."

The crusaders had established themselves in the Holy Land because of the disunity of Islam. The Seljuks of Baghdad had been unable to destroy the Fatimids in Egypt, while Damascus and Aleppo had become alienated from Baghdad. After Roger of Antioch's victory at Tell Danith in 1115, the sultans of Baghdad left resistance in the north to local powers. The greatest threat to Jerusalem was Egypt, but by the early 1120s it was crippled by internal divisions.

If the Islamic powers united, the weak European settlements would be at risk. But the westerners, too, were disunited. Following the disaster of the "Field of Blood" in 1119 (see pages 48–49), Antioch recovered under Bohemond II (1119–30), but he quarreled with Joscelin I of Edessa (1119–31) and as a result they failed to take advantage of a period of political turmoil in Aleppo. This ended in 1128 when all the factions united behind Imad ad-Din Zengi, a tough Turkish captain who had served the Seljuk sultan and risen to be governor of Mosul, from where he asserted his power over Aleppo. Zengi spent much time and effort fighting fellow Muslims,

THE FALL OF EDESSA

When Zengi seized Edessa in 1144, hundreds died in the frenzy to seek safety in the citadel, and thousands more in the ensuing massacre. Zengi spared the native Syrian Christians, but massacred the Europeans. Archbishop William of Tyre, who was born in the East ca. 1130 and died at Rome in 1186, chronicled the history of the crusader states up to ca. 1184 in his monumental *History of Deeds done Beyond the Sea*. He gives this account of the city's fall and the ensuing panic and bloodshed:

"Zengi continued to attack the city [of Edessa] without intermission and ran through the whole gamut of injuries. No method was left untried which might tend to increase the woes of the citizens and help him to take the city. Through subterranean passages he sent in miners who dug tunnels under the wall. These were supported overhead by beams which were then set on fire. When the props burned away, a great part of the wall fell and left a breach. The enemy rushed together from all directions, entered the city, and put all to the sword whom they encountered. Neither age, condition, nor sex was spared.... Thus the city was captured and delivered over to the sword of the enemy.

"As soon as this happened, the more sensible and alert among the citizens fled with their wives and children to the citadel. Here they hoped their lives at least might be safe, if only for a short time. But the inrush of such a crowd of people caused a panic, and many perished miserably in the struggling mob."

notably in his many abortive efforts to seize Damascus, which as a result resorted to an alliance with the crusaders after 1140.

After the death of Bohemond II in 1130, Antioch lapsed into civil war, and Zengi was able to drive its frontier back to the Orontes river. Stability returned when Raymond of Poitiers acceded to Antioch in 1136. He disliked Joscelin II of Edessa (1131–59), but they both worked to resist a bid by the Byzantine emperor John II Comnenus (1118–43) to assert his overlordship of Edessa.

Then events turned to Zengi's advantage. John II died in April 1143 and in November King Fulk I of Jerusalem also died, leaving Queen Melissende as regent for a child king. The Europeans were thus deprived of military leadership in the field. In November 1144 Joscelin II marched to aid his Muslim ally, the ruler of Diyarbakir, against Zengi, and in his absence Zengi laid siege to Edessa. Raymond of Antioch refused to help, and on Christmas Eve 1144, before any troops could arrive from Jerusalem, Edessa fell (see box).

The county of Edessa had always been little more than a string of fortifications, including Edessa itself. Now Zengi set about picking off the outposts while the Europeans remained divided. Before he could complete the process, on 14th September 1146 Zengi was assassinated. Nevertheless, the capture of Edessa was the first great success of the *jihad*, establishing Zengi in the pantheon of Islamic warriors and providing his son, Nur ad-Din, with both prestige and a model for the future. It also brought about the Second Crusade.

Opposite: *This illustration to a 14th-century French manuscript depicts the overlord of the Mongol dominions, Kublai Khan, ordering the execution of two traitors. However, the khan and his executioners are depicted as stereotypical dark-skinned "Saracens" and the ill-fated traitors as fair-haired Europeans. The conflicts between Christians and Muslims during the period of the crusades influenced the western view of the Orient as a place ruled by arbitrary, violent, and cruel despots, exemplified by Zengi and others— notwithstanding the fact that the Europeans were also guilty of displaying savagery and brutality toward their enemies.*

CRUSADER CASTLES

Some crusader castles stand out as being among the most famous fortifications of the medieval period. But most of these date from the thirteenth century, and recent examination has shown that in the twelfth century most castles were quite simple, such as the Red Tower (al-Burj al-Ahmar) in the plain of Sharon. This was a square stone tower surrounded by an enclosure wall. Internally it had two floors. The lower floor was partly below ground-level and served for storage, while the upper floor was living space. Such relatively simple structures are found all over the crusader states and are clearly based on western models. They differed from most castles in the West in that they were of stone, not earth and timber, but timber was rare in the East and cut stone from ancient ruins plentiful.

These castles were very important as centers of lordly administration and agricultural exploitation, but while they could serve as refuges against raids, they could not hope to resist serious attack by an enemy army. There were some much stronger castles that were capable of real resistance to any enemy, such as Saone in the mountains of the principality of Antioch, a mighty fortress some 0.6 miles (1km) long. At Saone the crusaders took over and improved a Byzantine fortress.

Most castles simply grew out of the needs of individual lords or particular situations and were built only as elaborately as the situation demanded. In the twelfth century the defense of the crusader kingdom depended not on castles but on cities. These were extremely difficult to capture on account both of their size and their strong fortifications, which were all Roman, though modified over time. Once the crusaders had taken an important city it would be difficult for anyone to recapture it as long as the crusaders had a field army, and they were further hindered by the numerous crusader castles giving refuge to the Frankish population and serving as military supply centers.

By the mid-twelfth century, all over Europe, the Mediterranean world, and beyond, field armies were becoming better organized and more proficient at siege warfare, in part because of an improvement in the technology of catapults. Nur ad-Din strengthened the fortifications of Damascus and other places. The crusaders reinforced exposed Kerak, which defied Saladin until the kingdom's collapse. Belmont, near Jerusalem, a small square fortified enclosure on top of a hill, was reinforced

with a strong outer wall. At Belvoir, in 1168–70, the Hospitallers built a real concentric castle that held out from 1187–89 against Saladin (see illustration on page 91).

In the thirteenth century the city walls of Acre, Tyre, Tripoli, and Antioch continued to be the main strength of a shrunken kingdom, but complex fortresses such as Marqab, Athlit, and Arsuf were also necessary. From the great concentric castle of Crac des Chevaliers, close to Homs, the Hospitallers extracted tribute from nearby Muslim powers. But in the end each of these fortresses fell after a month of siege by the increasingly efficient Egyptian armies of the Mamluk sultans.

Nineteenth and early twentieth-century scholars were deeply impressed by crusader castles, especially Crac des Chevaliers, and it was presumed that the crusaders had copied Islamic and Byzantine models, whose features were then passed on to the West. Many writers dismissed this idea, notably the student T.E. Lawrence (Lawrence of Arabia), but it has persisted to this day.

In fact, most crusader castles were constructed along familiar western lines of a tower within an enclosure. It seems likely that fortification techniques in both the Islamic world and Europe were fundamentally learned from the Romans—Roman walls were a feature of some European and almost all

Near Eastern cities—with the addition of certain Byzantine techniques, such as enclosed and bent entrance-ways.

By the end of the twelfth century Islamic and European traditions were diverging. In Europe and the crusader states there was an emphasis on concentric design, as at Crac des Chevaliers, while in the Islamic world massive towers, some capable of supporting catapults, were constructed, as in the citadel of Damascus, built at the end of the twelfth century.

Above: *Saone (Sahyun, Syria), where the crusaders added massive square towers to the former Byzantine fortress as well as a deep stone ditch that isolated the end of the spur on which the castle stands.*
Opposite page and right: *Exterior and interior views of Crac des Chevaliers, a famous concentric castle between Tortosa and Homs.*

3

THE SECOND CRUSADE

WAR CRUEL AND UNREMITTING

JOHN FRANCE

DISASTER IN THE EAST

BERNARD AND THE JEWS

The church opposed violence toward Jews, because, as Pope Alexander II (1061–73) put it, they were "prepared to live in servitude." Kings and other powers taxed Jews to their profit and so disliked violence against them. But for zealous crusaders both Jews and Muslims were "enemies of Christ," and the launch of the First and Second Crusades saw savage persecutions in France and Germany. In the 1140s the authorities were better prepared to prevent such attacks, but there were still figures such as the monk Radulf, whose vitriolic preaching incited murders of Jews in northern France and the Rhineland. Responding to an appeal from Archbishop Henry of Mainz, Bernard of Clairvaux ordered Radulf back to his monastery and strove to end the violence. In 1146 he wrote to the archbishop:

"Is it not a far better triumph for the church to convince and convert the Jews than to put them all to the sword? Has that prayer which the church offers for the Jews, from the rising up of the sun to the going down thereof, that the veil may be taken from their hearts so that they may be led from the darkness of error into the light of truth, been instituted in vain? If she did not hope that they would believe and be converted, it would seem useless and vain for her to pray for them. But with the eye of mercy she considers how the Lord regards with favor him who renders good for evil and love for hatred."

In 1145, in response to the fall of Edessa, Pope Eugenius III (1145–53) addressed a bull to King Louis VII of France (1137–80) calling for a new crusade. Louis seems already to have resolved to go to the East, but his barons were unenthusiastic, so he called in Abbot Bernard of Clairvaux, the greatest spiritual authority of the age, to preach. On 31st March 1146, at Vézelay in Burgundy, thousands took the cross (see box), and enthusiasm soon spread across Europe. In the summer Bernard went to Germany to stop the anti-Jewish activities of Radulf, a fellow Cistercian (see sidebar), and he also persuaded the German emperor, Conrad III (1138–52), to join the crusade, which he did on 27th December. No ruling monarch had taken the cross before; now, momentously, two had done so.

Many German nobles proposed a campaign against the Wends (a pagan Slav people) rather than to the East, and in April 1147 Eugenius felt obliged to declare their expedition a crusade (see pages 126–127). In June, he also confirmed crusade status on an expedition by Barcelona and Genoa against Almería in Muslim Spain.

"HEAVEN'S INSTRUMENT": BERNARD OF CLAIRVAUX

It is a measure of Bernard of Clairvaux's eloquence that it was he who persuaded the French nobility to support the Second Crusade, rather than their own king, Louis VII. Odo of Deuil witnessed Bernard's preaching at Louis's court at Vézelay on 31st March 1146: "[Bernard] mounted the platform accompanied by the king, who was wearing the cross, and when heaven's instrument poured forth the dew of the divine word, as he was wont, with loud outcry people on every side began to demand crosses. And when he had sowed, rather than distributed, the parcel of crosses which had been prepared beforehand, he was forced to tear his own garments into crosses and sow them abroad."

Bernard's style of crusade preaching can be gleaned from a letter he wrote ca. 1150 to his uncle Andrew, a Templar knight fighting in the Holy Land: "Under the sun you fight as a soldier, but for the sake of Him who is above the sun. Let us who fight upon earth look to Him for largesse. Our reward for fighting comes not from the earth, not from below, but is a 'rare treasure from distant shores.' Under the sun we have no profit, our reward is on high above the sun."

In the event, Conrad III and his army left for the East in mid-May 1147. Eugenius, Louis VII and his queen, Eleanor of Aquitaine, left in mid-June, following Conrad down the Danube valley. As the armies entered Byzantine lands, Roger II (1130–54), Norman king of Sicily and south Italy, launched an attack on the Byzantines. The Byzantine emperor Manuel I Comnenus (1143–80) responded by making peace with the Seljuk Turks of Iconium, the greatest Muslim power in Asia Minor, to enable him to deal with Roger, whose rule both he and Conrad III refused to recognize. On 10th September Conrad reached Constantinople, followed on 4th October by Louis.

Relations between Manuel and the two monarchs were difficult; he had never been enthusiastic about the crusade, which served no Byzantine interest. He knew, too, that many in the French army were hostile to him and favored the claims of Roger, and he feared that Conrad might be lured into a Franco-Sicilian alliance against him. Moreover, both armies were poorly disciplined and had done great damage on their march through imperial territory.

Also in the force was a northern European fleet that assembled at Dartmouth in England on 19th May 1147 and en route helped to take the Muslim-held city of Lisbon in October (see page 122). By then it was winter and the fleet had to wait until the spring of 1148 to continue. Other smaller groups chose to travel independently.

Anxious to get the crusaders away from Constantinople, the emperor Manuel suggested that Conrad III should travel down the western coast of Asia Minor to the city of Attalia. But Conrad chose to follow the inland route of the First Crusade, across the Anatolian plateau via Dorylaeum. Despite raids by Turks on the plateau, the

Opposite: *St. Bernard of Clairvaux, from a 13th-century English manuscript. The outstanding churchman of the age, Bernard inspired great popular enthusiasm for the Second Crusade. When some of this zeal expressed itself in attacks on Jews, he intervened to prevent them; for this reason Jews came to regard him as a Righteous Gentile.*

DEFEAT SOWS DISTRUST

Bishop William of Tyre, writing in the 1180s, recorded the disillusionment toward the Franks of the East felt by those who had gone on the Second Crusade:

"Henceforward, as long as they remained in the Orient, and, indeed, ever after, the crusaders looked askance on all the ways of our leaders. They justly declined all their plans as treacherous and showed utter indifference to the affairs of the kingdom. Even when permitted to return to their own lands, the memory of the things they had suffered still rankled. … As a result, fewer people, and those less fervent in spirit, undertook the pilgrimage thereafter. From this time on the condition of the Latins in the East became visibly worse. Our enemies saw that the labors of our most powerful kings and leaders had been fruitless and all their effort vain."

larger cities were under Byzantine control and could offer support. Without waiting for Louis VII, Conrad left Constantinople. At Nicaea there were disagreements in his army and it was decided to send the infantry under Otto, bishop of Freising, along the coastal route recommended by Manuel. On 25th October 1147 the Turks destroyed Conrad's main force at Dorylaeum. The Germans blamed their Byzantine guides, but it is likely that their own indiscipline was the problem. Shortly afterward, the Turks also destroyed Otto's infantry.

Louis took Manuel's advice and took the more westerly route to Attalia, but in the mountains his troops suffered terrible winter conditions and the Turks inflicted heavy losses. Attalia gave the French shelter, but had limited food supplies. The barons argued that the army was no longer strong enough to force its way to Antioch, and Louis agreed to take them by sea. But there were so few ships that he had to abandon the infantry, most of whom perished.

When Louis arrived at Antioch in March 1148, Prince Raymond of Antioch urged him to attack Aleppo, which was ruled by Zengi's son and successor, Nur ad-Din. This might aid the recovery of Edessa—the loss of which had, after all, prompted the crusade—and secure the northern frontiers of the crusader states. But Louis

decided to head directly to Jerusalem. En route he refused to help Count Raymond of Tripoli with his own frontier problems, and as a result an offended Count Raymond refused to join the crusade.

The Failure of the Siege of Damascus

On 24th June 1148 Louis, along with Conrad III, who had landed at Acre with the remnants of his army, met the king of Jerusalem, Baldwin III (1143–63), and his barons to decide how to proceed. An attack on Egyptian-held Ascalon was rejected in favor of a move on Damascus. Although at times an ally of Jerusalem, Damascus was politically unstable and sometimes backed the kingdom's enemies; and in any case it was an obstacle to crusader expansion.

Internal squabbles among the Frankish barons, who were split between the parties of Baldwin and of his mother, Melissende, probably had an effect on the siege of Damascus, which was poorly conducted. On 24th July the crusaders arrived in the well-watered orchards on the city's southern side. It was a good place for a camp, but the trees also gave good cover for Damascene sallies, and on 27th July the barons persuaded Louis and Conrad to move into the open plain to the east. This move was so unwise—a shadeless, waterless plain in the height of summer, next to the strongest part of the city wall—that it prompted accusations of treachery. No army could exist for long in such inhospitable conditions and on 28th July, with Damascene raids continuing and a relief force under Nur ad-Din on its way, the crusaders withdrew. Thus the Second Crusade ended in a humiliating retreat.

From the Christian perspective the only positive results of the Second Crusade were in Iberia: Lisbon and Almería fell in 1147, and Barcelona took Tortosa in December 1148 with the aid of crusaders returning from the East. But this was a poor return for such a great effort and in Europe there were bitter recriminations, especially against Bernard of Clairvaux. The papacy had inspired the crusade, but had done little to organize or coordinate it; Eugenius III had not even replaced the papal legate to Conrad's army, who had joined the Wendish Crusade. Byzantium was much blamed for the losses in Asia Minor, but the pope had done little to prepare Manuel for the arrival of two enormous and at times ill-disciplined western armies.

However, the root cause of the failure was probably that Louis VII and Conrad III were poor and inexperienced commanders who failed to cooperate. Divisions among the Franks of the East further confused matters. The main results of the crusade were western suspicion of the settlers (see sidebar); an estrangement between Byzantium and the crusaders; and a rise in the prestige of Nur ad-Din.

Above: Jesus Drives the Moneylenders from the Temple, *a window (ca. 1400) in the church of Wiener Neustadt, Austria. One moneylender wears the conical hat that Jews in the West were obliged to wear in the later Middle Ages. The persecution of Jews at the time of the first two crusades (see page 60) was fueled in part by greed for Jewish wealth. In medieval Europe many Jews were moneylenders, since most other trades were forbidden to them, while usury (lending money at interest) was forbidden to Christians.*

Opposite: *The mountains of southwestern Anatolia (modern-day Turkey), through which the French crusaders passed on a gruelling winter march down to the coast at Attalia. Apart from the bitter weather, the French crusaders suffered when the indiscipline of their vanguard exposed them to attacks by the Turks.*

THE KINGDOM RECOVERS

Opposite: The strategically important Syrian fortress of Shaizar, one of Nur ad-Din's bases in the Orontes valley. It was besieged in 1157 by the Franks led by Baldwin III of Jerusalem, Count Thierry of Flanders (who had come to the East on crusade), and Reynald of Châtillon, the regent of Antioch, who had married the widow of Prince Raymond. The siege was abandoned, but shortly after the allies recovered another important fortress, Harenc between Antioch and Aleppo.

Nur ad-Din's rescue of Damascus had given him confidence and the city's ruler was obliged to ally with him. Emboldened by this, Nur ad-Din attacked Antioch, and on 29th June 1149 crushed its army and killed Prince Raymond at Inab. This victory convinced him that he was God's instrument and he began a systematic program of supporting mosques, schools, holy men, and scholars in the name of Sunni orthodoxy. He aimed to influence leaders of opinion in those cities, especially Damascus, whose leaders had made a truce with Jerusalem in May 1149. Nur ad-Din's propaganda made subsequent Damascene alliances with the Christians increasingly unpopular.

As well as backing Damascus against Nur ad-Din, Baldwin III of Jerusalem saved Antioch in the wake of Inab and forced the northern Frankish barons to agree to a Byzantine takeover of the remnants of Edessa. In January 1153, he exploited political instability in Egypt to besiege the city of Ascalon, which surrendered in August 1153 (see page 52). It was the last great crusader triumph.

Egypt reacted with a naval campaign against the crusaders. This distraction undoubtedly helped Nur ad-Din to take Damascus in

STRATEGIC DILEMMAS OF THE CRUSADER KINGDOM

The settlers in the Holy Land had been able to establish themselves because the Muslim world was divided, and the settlers were anxious that this state of affairs should continue. The crusader kingdom stood vulnerably between Syria and Egypt. Hence King Baldwin I established the castles of Shawbak and Petra, the nucleus of the later lordship of Oultrejourdain centered on Kerak, which dominated the Egypt–Damascus road.

The First Crusade leaders had briefly considered first attacking Egypt, in order to secure not only Jerusalem, which was in Fatimid hands, but the whole region. In the early years of the kingdom Egypt proved the greatest threat, mounting expeditions almost annually. In 1118 Baldwin I attacked Egypt, but died before anything was achieved. From the mid-1120s Egypt became distracted with internal affairs and ceased to be a threat, though it retained Ascalon as a thorn in the kingdom's

side. This enabled Baldwin II to plan an attack on Damascus but in 1129 his expedition miscarried and from this time there was usually an agreement to keep the frontier open, to the profit of both sides.

The crusader principalities of Antioch and Edessa looked toward Aleppo and the Euphrates for expansion, and were threatened by local powers and the Seljuk sultans of Iconium—as well as Byzantium, which regarded Antioch as a vassal state and had a foothold in neighboring Cilicia. The kings of Jerusalem wanted to prevent the emergence of a great Muslim power in north Syria, hence the first two Baldwins spent much time in the north. Baldwin III's acceptance of the Byzantine protectorate over the north (see main text) was a clear recognition of the weakness both of Antioch and the remnant of Edessa. However, this arrangement left Nur ad-Din free to concentrate his forces against Jerusalem.

April 1154, a victory that involved little fighting and was apparently welcomed by the Damascenes. He approached Egypt to propose a joint assault on Jerusalem, but this plan came to nothing. Nur ad-Din then launched a series of attacks on Jerusalem that ended in his defeat at al-Batihah, and in 1158 a truce was renewed for two years.

In 1158 Baldwin married Theodora, the niece of the Byzantine emperor Manuel, and the two rulers then joined forces to attack Nur ad-Din. However, Manuel and Nur ad-Din came to an agreement whereby Nur ad-Din would respect Byzantine frontiers in the north. Although some Franks considered the treaty a betrayal, Baldwin accepted it, because it established a Byzantine protectorate over north Syria, an area that Jerusalem could not defend alone.

In 1163 Baldwin III died, widely mourned as a just ruler. He had not prevented Nur ad-Din from uniting Syria, but he had retrieved the fortunes of the kingdom after the Second Crusade, and there is no doubt of the importance of the Byzantine protectorate of the north. He had rallied all the European settlers in the East and gained the respect even of his Muslim enemies. If he had less success in his active diplomacy to secure western aid, it was because Europe was preoccupied with its own affairs and still remembered bitterly the failures of the Second Crusade.

THE CHAMPION OF *JIHAD*

The chronicler Ibn al-Qalinisi, a senior official at Damascus when the city fell in 1154, describes how Nur ad-Din cleverly portrayed himself, in contrast to Mujir ad-Din, the ruler of Damascus, as the popular champion of *jihad*:

"Nur ad-Din sent a message to Mujir ad-Din in which he said: 'It is not my purpose...to seek to engage in warfare with you nor to besiege you. I have been prompted solely by the frequent appeals of the Muslims of the Hawran [south of Damascus] and the Arab cultivators whose possessions have been seized, whose women and children have been scattered by the hand of the Franks, and who have no one to assist them.... I am aware of your inability to guard and protect your dominions, and of the remissness which has led you to call upon the Franks for assistance in fighting against me.'"

EUROPEAN SETTLEMENT IN THE EAST

The dominant elements among the Europeans who settled in the Holy Land after the First Crusade were nobles and knights, but they could raise only 6,000–7,000 mounted men for battle, suggesting that their total number was relatively small. The rest of the European population could raise 5,000–7,000 troops, and probably more in an emergency, so the total settler population ca. 1187, with women, children, and other noncombatants, was perhaps about 120,000. This was not large, which is probably why the kings of Jerusalem encouraged settlement by native eastern Christians (Greeks and Syrians) and pursued a policy of toleration toward Muslims.

Knights and nobles continued to leave Europe for the Holy Land throughout the twelfth century, but in small

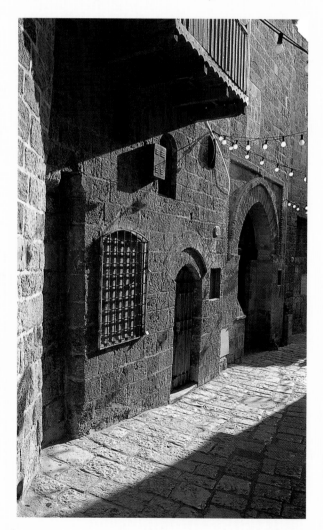

numbers. Jerusalem was a dangerous environment. Many adult males died in the almost constant fighting, but disease was an even greater killer, particularly of children. Young men who wanted to make their fortunes could do better fighting for Christ on the Spanish and German frontiers.

The key to European expansion in the East was the settlement not merely of knights and nobles but also of peasants—however, Jerusalem was distant; the risks that applied to the upper classes also applied to peasants; and the costs of sea travel were relatively high. It used to be thought that the Europeans in the East lived mainly in the cities, but the presence of 20,000 refugees in Jerusalem after the battle of Hattin in 1187 suggests strong rural settlement. Recent archaeology has also shown that in some areas, notably around Jerusalem, there were many villages of Europeans. Most settler villages were in areas occupied by native Christians, suggesting, when taken with other evidence, close ties between the groups. This may explain how King Guy of Jerusalem was able to raise nearly 20,000 troops in 1187. In areas such as Galilee, where native Christians were relatively few, there were also few westerners. By 1187 the Europeans had, after nearly a century of settlement, put down deep roots in some areas of the kingdom.

The crusaders inherited a system of confessional administration from the Muslims. The native peoples were grouped according to religion and lived by their own laws and customs, whether Greek Orthodox, Syrian Jacobite, or Muslim. The dominant group were the European settlers and the most subordinate the Muslims, who paid the poll-tax that their own rulers had formerly demanded from non-Muslims. Jews were banned from entry to Jerusalem and forced to wear special dress, while European clothes were prohibited to natives. The commercial courts that settled disputes over trade were the one place where locals and Europeans came together.

Left: *Crusader-period buildings in a street in old Jaffa, the port of Jerusalem in the 12th century.*
Opposite, above: *Olive oil production, using presses like this one, was an economic mainstay in the villages of the kingdom of Jerusalem.*
Opposite, below: *The church of St. Anne, Jerusalem. Constructed ca. 1140 during the reign of King Baldwin II, it is one of the few crusader churches of this period to have survived.*

Among the Europeans, nobles and knights enjoyed high privileges, and the leading families dominated the Haute Cour (High Court), the council that advised the king and decided, when necessary, among rival claimants to the throne. A Muslim prince, Usama ibn Mundiqh (1095–1189), wrote that "once the knights have given their judgment neither the king nor any other commander can alter or annul it." The leading families had a right to be tried in the High Court by their peers.

The European settlement in the Holy Land was polyglot, but their Muslim enemies lumped all the western Christians together as "Franks" (*franj*). As this term implies, most of the leading families were French in origin, and French was the dominant tongue in the kingdom of Jerusalem, with Latin used for legal and ecclesiastical purposes. The county of Tripoli used Provençal and the Norman dialect was important in the principality Antioch.

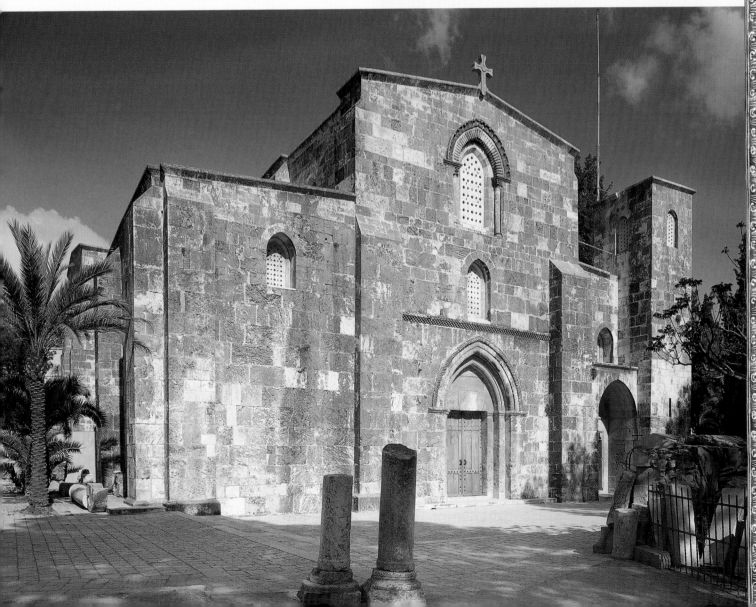

THE RACE FOR EGYPT

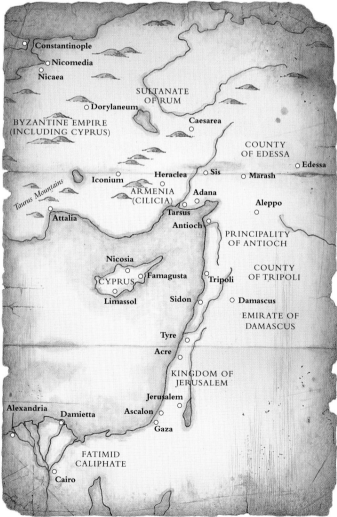

Below: The significant cities and distribution of power in the Near East at the time of the Second Crusade in the late 12th century.

In Egypt political and religious authority was in theory united in the person of the Fatimid caliph. However, in practice successive viziers (chief ministers) had increased their own authority and isolated the caliphs. The power of the viziers grew even further after the death of Caliph al-Hafiz in 1149, when there was a series of child caliphs of whom the last, al-Adid (1160–71), succeeded at the age of nine.

Amid this turmoil, in 1155 Egypt's rulers bought peace by the payment of tribute to King Baldwin III of Jerusalem. In 1163 the vizier Shawar was ousted by the court chamberlain, Dirgham, who refused to pay the tribute. This prompted the new crusader king, Amalric I (1163–74), to launch an invasion of Egypt, but his army was repelled by the annual Nile flood.

In the meantime, Shawar had sought help from Nur ad-Din to fight Dirgham. Nur ad-Din sent an army to Egypt to support Shawar under his Kurdish general, Shirkuh, and Shirkuh's nephew—Salah ad-Din, better known in the West as Saladin. They captured Cairo in 1164, but Shawar, seeking to play off his enemies and retain his independence, then called in Amalric.

In the event the fighting was indecisive and both the Syrian and Frankish armies withdrew. In 1167 Shirkuh and Saladin again invaded Egypt, and again Shawar called in Amalric. At the battle of al-Babyan the Franks were defeated, but not decisively. A truce was made and the crusaders agreed to evacuate Egypt, in return for an increased tribute to Amalric and the installation of a crusader garrison at Cairo.

In 1168 Gilbert d'Assailly, the grand master of the Hospital (see sidebar), persuaded Amalric to break the truce. In November Bilbais fell to the Franks and this time Shawar appealed to Nur ad-Din, who again dispatched Shirkuh. The crusaders had by this time suffered substantial losses and Amalric was forced to retreat.

In 1169 Shirkuh killed Shawar and became vizier himself, but died a few weeks later. Saladin now seized power. By August he had secured his position, in time to face a joint attack on Egypt by Amalric and the Byzantine emperor Manuel. The Byzantine fleet sailed in good time, but there were delays in gathering the

THE MILITARIZATION OF THE HOSPITALLERS

The order of the Knights Hospitaller was established to care for pilgrims (see page 52), but by the mid-twelfth century it was taking on an increasingly military role. The decisive period seems to have been the rule of Gilbert d'Assailly as grand master after 1163, when the order actively took over the defense of frontier zones and castles, and joined expeditions, including those to Egypt. Gilbert's policy seems to have strained the resources of the order, and it is possible that he pressed Amalric to attack Egypt in 1168 (see main text) because he hoped to restore the order's fortunes with booty and rich lands.

The failure of the expedition almost ruined the Hospital, and those among its leadership who were totally opposed to militarization forced Gilbert's resignation. During the crisis Pope Alexander III (1159–81) wrote to remind the knight-brothers that care of pilgrims was their primary concern (see box). In fact the order, with its vast resources in Europe, made a rapid economic recovery. However, it was now decisively launched on the military path.

crusader army because many men were reluctant to go to Egypt after the defeats of the previous year. In the event the allies besieged Damietta from October to December 1169, but then, amid mutual mistrust, the alliance broke up and the siege ended.

Saladin moved quickly to consolidate his regime. By 1174, however, he faced the possibility of invasion both by Nur ad-Din, who resented his independence, and by Amalric and the Byzantines, who had renewed their alliance. But Nur ad-Din died on 15th May 1174, and before he could exploit this situation Amalric also died, of dysentery, on 11th July. The advantage had now switched to Saladin.

DISEASE AND MEDICINE

The premature deaths of a number of prominent figures—such as King Amalric I who died in 1174 from dysentery—is evidence of the deadliness of disease in the medieval era and the need for effective medical care. Battle injuries were, of course, often severe and involved traumatic wounds. But in war, disease often killed many more than battle itself. The Knights Hospitaller had units that accompanied the crusaders to battle and evidence from skeletons suggests that there were some physicians who were good at setting broken bones. The order's main hospital at Jerusalem reputedly held 2,000 patients, who were prescribed sensible diets. Eastern physicians enjoyed a higher reputation than Europeans. A Christian Arab doctor put a poultice on an abscess on the leg of a knight, but a Frankish doctor insisted on amputation by axe—the patient died from the shock.

THE RISE OF SALADIN

When Nur ad-Din died in 1174, Saladin's priority was to annex his inheritance. Saladin was always at pains to portray himself as the champion of Islam against the European intruders, although in fact he spent much, if not more, of his career involved in war against members of Nur ad-Din's family, the Zengids (named from his father, Zengi), and other Muslims.

When he died Nur ad-Din was an *atabeg*, essentially a senior officer of the Baghdad caliph, commanding armies and governing territories. In practice his subservience to the caliph was nominal. He was the leader of a militarized, largely Turkish élite, and ruled a state embracing Aleppo, Damascus, and extensive lands toward the Euphrates. Other Zengids governed various parts of Nur ad-Din's domains on his behalf.

The strength of dynastic feeling among the Zengids created the presumption that Nur ad-Din's son, as-Salih Ismail, would succeed him. But there was no legal requirement that an officer such as an *atabeg* should be succeeded by his son, and on Nur ad-Din's death Saladin acknowledged as-Salih as his overlord but claimed to be the young boy's rightful regent. In consequence Saladin was invited into Damascus and in 1175 was acknowledged as ruler by the caliph.

THE TERRORS OF SIEGE

Siege warfare could be a protracted business and those inside a besieged city or fortress might suffer terrible hardships. In addition to the inevitable shortages of food and other privations there was the sheer terror of living under the bombardment of rocks hurled by siege catapults. Writing only months after the event, Bishop William of Tyre describes Saladin's siege of the great crusader fortress of Kerak (see illustration on page 72) in Oultrejourdain during his invasion of the kingdom in 1183, in which he subjected the castle to a constant assault from catapults arranged all around the fortress:

"Stones of such great size were hurled that no one inside the walls dared raise a hand or look out of the openings or try any method of resistance.... At one time those besieged in the fortress tried to set up a machine of their own. The enemy in charge of the engines outside, however, aimed the stone missiles with such skill that the Christians, appalled by the constant blows and fear of death which every stone seemed to threaten, abandoned the attempt. These dangers, which caused men to shake with terror, assailed not only those who crept forth from their hiding places to hurl weapons or stone missiles from the ramparts or to gaze down upon the besieging forces. Even those who had fled to the innermost apartments, the most retired seclusion, shrank with terror before the crash and roar of incoming missiles."

In the event, William reports, after a month of siege, Saladin learned that the army of King Baldwin IV of Jerusalem was close by and ordered his troops to retreat.

Saladin now had potentially vast resources in Egypt and Syria at his disposal, but a long series of wars to wrest Aleppo from Zengid control prevented him from devoting his full might to the cause of *jihad* against the crusader kingdom (see sidebar).

Jerusalem, however, was unable to take effective advantage of Saladin's conflict with Aleppo because it was in the grip of internal dissension. Amalric I had been succeeded by his son, Baldwin IV (1174–85), who was a leper. A regency was necessary because he was a child, and his illness, which prevented him from marrying, meant another regency was probable in the near future. Regencies inevitably unleashed tensions among the nobility, and this was immediately evident when Miles of Plancy was displaced as regent by Raymond III of Tripoli in 1174. When Miles was assassinated, his widow blamed Raymond III and married Reynald of Châtillon, the former regent of Antioch and now lord of Oultrejourdain. Reynald became an enemy of the regent. Gerald of Ridefort, the seneschal (administrator of the royal household) and later grand master of the Templars, was a personal enemy of Raymond III owing to an old dispute. Amalric I had left two ex-queens, Agnes of Courtenay (Baldwin IV's mother, supported by her brother Joscelin III of Courtenay), and Maria Comnena, who hated one another. Out of such personal enmities factions arose and competed for control of the kingdom.

Despite such tensions Raymond III assisted the Zengids against Saladin and arranged the marriage in 1176 of Sibylla, the king's sister and heiress, to William Longsword, the son of the marquis of Montferrat in Italy. As Sibylla's husband William would become king, but unfortunately for the kingdom (as events were to turn out) William died, leaving a child, later Baldwin V (1185–86). An effort was made to find another husband for Sibylla, but the existence of Baldwin V made her an unattractive prospect, because if a man accepted her hand and became king his own son could not succeed. An extended regency therefore seemed likely.

Moreover, in 1176 the Byzantine emperor Manuel was heavily defeated by the Seljuks of Iconium at Myriocephalum, reducing his ability to intervene in Syria. In 1177 Manuel sent his fleet to aid the Franks in another attack on Egypt, but Baldwin IV, who came of age that year, was ill and nobody could be found to lead an expedition.

After assuming full power, Baldwin IV generally favored his mother and Reynald (whose party was strengthened when they procured the election of Heraclius as Latin patriarch of Jerusalem in

Opposite and below: *Glazed tiles produced in Chertsey, England, ca. 1250–60 depict Saladin (below) being slain by Richard I of England. The popular medieval legend of Saladin's death in single combat with Richard was entirely fictitious but reflects his reputation for chivalric virtue.*

SALADIN, DEVOTEE OF HOLY WAR
Baha ad-Din ibn Shaddad was a member of Saladin's entourage and wrote his *Life of Saladin* toward the end of the 12th century. He describes his master's devotion to the cause of *jihad*:

"The sacred works are full of passages referring to the Holy War [*jihad*]. Saladin was more assiduous and zealous in this than in anything else. ... The Holy War and the suffering involved in it weighed heavily on his heart and his whole being in every limb.... For love of the Holy War and on God's path he left his family and his sons, his homeland, his house, and all his estates, and chose out of all the world to live in the shade of his tent, where the winds blew on him from every side."

1180). In November 1177 Saladin invaded the kingdom. Baldwin IV, now recovered, advanced to meet him, but so big was Saladin's army that Baldwin retreated into Ascalon. Saladin allowed his troops to disperse and plunder whereupon Baldwin fell upon them, gaining a great victory at Montgisard on 25th November 1177.

In 1178 Baldwin built a fortress at Jacob's Ford in Galilee to guard his vulnerable northeast frontier. Despite other preoccupations, Saladin could not ignore a fortress so close to Damascus and when Baldwin refused a large sum to dismantle it Saladin started to ravage the locality. On 24th August he began a savage assault on the castle itself, which fell five days later. The fortress (which was probably incomplete) was destroyed and its garrison massacred.

The immediate consequences of the loss of Jacob's Ford were not great because Saladin was intent on seizing Aleppo from the Zengids and he agreed to a truce with Baldwin in early 1180. But the raid into Galilee had demonstrated how vulnerable the north of the kingdom now was. The Seljuk defeat of Byzantium in 1176 and the death of the emperor Manuel in 1180 made matters worse, because it ended the Byzantine protectorate over the northern crusader states (see page 65) and left the crusader kingdom isolated. European

Remains of the crusader fortress of Kerak, the base of the lords of Oultrejourdain, the isolated crusader territories beyond the Dead Sea and Jordan river. It was built in the 1140s and dominated the southern end of the Dead Sea and the route between Egypt and Syria, withstanding a number of assaults by Saladin (see box on page 70) before finally surrendering to him after a year-long siege in 1188.

rulers, meanwhile, were too preoccupied with their own affairs to lend assistance.

In 1182 Reynald of Châtillon broke the new truce by raiding caravans traveling between Egypt and Syria, prompting another invasion by Saladin that was checked near Belvoir. In the same year, Reynald launched a fleet on the Red Sea, sacking the ports of Medina and threatening Mecca. The Umma was scandalized and Saladin was obliged to gather a great army, which invaded the kingdom in September 1183 (see box on page 70).

Baldwin was too ill to lead his army, which was commanded by Guy of Lusignan, a knight from Aquitaine. The head of the army was Guy's elder brother, Amalric, an associate of Agnes of Courtenay. Through Amalric's agency, Guy met and quickly married Sibylla, thereby becoming Baldwin IV's heir. In due course he was proclaimed regent for the incapacitated king, replacing Raymond III.

Guy refused battle, but shadowed Saladin's great army, which eventually melted away. Guy's enemies accused him of cowardice for not engaging Saladin, and Baldwin, rallying momentarily in his illness, deposed Guy as regent. Baldwin proclaimed his young nephew as his heir and, in an unprecedented move aimed at securing his succession, had him crowned as Baldwin V in November 1183, with Raymond III as his regent. Having arranged the succession, Baldwin IV finally succumbed to his illness in March 1185, aged twenty-nine.

In the meantime, in 1183 Saladin had defeated the Zengids and taken Aleppo. Despite continued Zengid defiance, he was now the clear master of Egypt and Syria.

Egyptian troops take part in a battle against European knights—note the helmeted figure at bottom right being unhorsed from his black charger—beneath the fortified walls of an unidentified city. A fragment of a 12th-century Egyptian drawing.

THE HORNS OF HATTIN

In 1186 the eight-year-old Baldwin V of Jerusalem died after barely a year as king. In such an event Baldwin IV had laid down a formula for choosing between the claims of Sibylla and Isabella, the daughters of King Amalric I by different wives. All the leading nobles had agreed to this, but in a palace coup Sibylla and her husband Guy of Lusignan were crowned. Most of the barons reluctantly accepted Guy as king, but Raymond III of Tripoli did not and retired to his lands in Galilee. When Guy threatened him Raymond concluded a treaty with Saladin, who promised to protect his lands.

In early 1187 Reynald of Châtillon breached a truce with Saladin by attacking a caravan passing from Cairo to Damascus. Saladin demanded compensation, but Reynald refused to pay, despite the insistence of Guy, his overlord. War with Saladin was now likely and Guy sent envoys to Tiberias to seek a reconciliation with Raymond III. Before they got there, Raymond had granted Saladin free passage across his lands to raid the kingdom. On 30th April, at the Springs of Cresson, the raiders annihilated a small force of Hospitallers and Templars who had unwisely challenged them.

This development brought Raymond III back to the fold. On 1st July 1187 Saladin, with a large army perhaps 30,000 strong, besieged

An illustration from Matthew Paris's account of the battle of Hattin. Paris dramatizes the loss of the sacred relic of the holy cross by showing Saladin himself seizing the cross from King Guy in the thick of battle. English, 13th century.

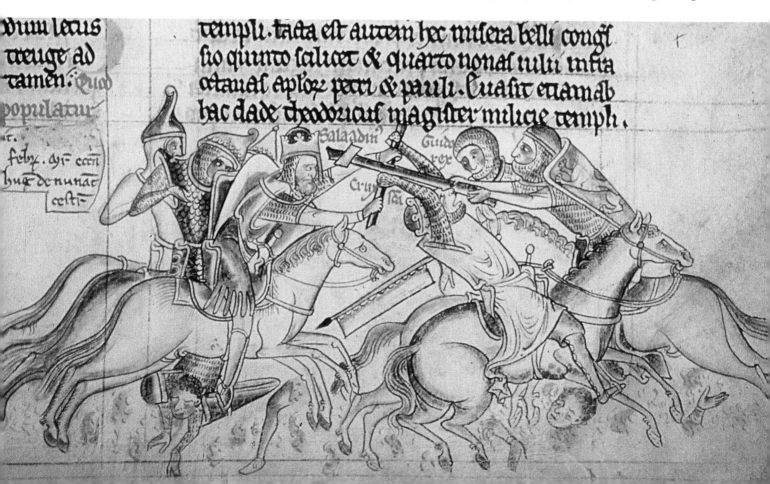

Tiberias, where Raymond's wife Eschiva was trapped. On 2nd July, Guy was at Saffuriyah (Sepphoris), 16 miles (26km) to the west, a strong well-watered position. Guy had stripped all city and castle garrisons to raise the biggest army the kingdom had ever fielded: 1,200 heavily-armed knights, numerous light cavalry, and nearly 12,000 footsoldiers.

Elements of Saladin's army approached Saffuriyah, but Guy refused battle. That night there was a dramatic and angry council: many sources suggest that Raymond III was in favor of declining battle while his enemies, including Reynald of Châtillon, took the opposite view. There was a good case either way. The tactic of shadowing the enemy, as in 1183, was attractive. If Saladin's army did not disperse it could be lured into battle on grounds of the crusaders' choosing. On the other hand Guy's huge army gave him a chance to defeat Saladin decisively, and the prestige of victory would help him to unite the kingdom.

Guy decided to lead the army eastward from Saffuriyah on 3rd July. He clearly intended to give battle, but it seems inconceivable that he expected to march to Tiberias in a day, exposing his army to terrible thirst in arid country. Whatever Guy's plan, it evidently went badly wrong. After the crusaders had left the springs at Turan, Saladin's cavalry encircled them, attacking the rearguard ferociously as it struggled uphill to Maskana. There, on Raymond III's advice, the army halted for the night, short of water and surrounded.

The next morning, 4th July 1187, Saladin held back until the heat of day began to take its toll. It seems that the crusader infantry, their will sapped by thirst, deserted the cavalry and took refuge on nearby hills known as the Horns of Hattin. The cavalry, now exposed to Saladin's mounted archers, were prevented from breaching the encirclement by Saladin's superior numbers. Only Raymond III, Balian of Ibelin, and a few others escaped. After a last desperate attempt to establish a camp on Hattin, Guy surrendered.

In the hour of his greatest triumph, and the crusaders' greatest disaster, Saladin displayed both his ruthlessness and his magnanimity. He was courteous to the defeated Guy and other nobles—but he beheaded the troublesome Reynald with his own sword. Two days after Hattin, all the Templar and Hospitaller prisoners were executed except the Templar grand master, Gerald of Ridefort. Guy and his brother Amalric were sent to Damascus, as were Gerald, Humphrey of Toron, and other noble prisoners. Eschiva, who had surrendered Tiberias the day after Hattin, was allowed to leave for Tripoli.

The twin hills known as the Horns of Hattin, the scene of Saladin's great victory over the crusader kingdom in 1187.

EUROPEAN MERCENARIES

At Hattin a knight called John, "having long served in Turkish armies," was asked by King Guy to give advice on how the army should fight. Western mercenaries took service with anybody who would pay during the Middle Ages, even Muslim rulers. As long as they did not abjure their religion this was regarded as perfectly respectable. When the Fatimids took over Cairo in 969 they had within their ranks European soldiers, and they were so numerous in North Africa that by 1147 they had their own priests and even a bishop. The Turkish sultans of Iconium regarded their corps of European soldiers as an élite and when one, an Italian, killed a local man, it was impossible to punish him because his 700 comrades threatened to revolt. More surprisingly, the *Livre au Roi*, the laws of the kingdom of Jerusalem, dating from the late twelfth century, permitted vassals of the king to serve Muslim princes providing they entrusted their fiefs to the king in their absence.

"SWEET VICTORY": SALADIN TRIUMPHANT

Saladin ravaging the Holy Land, from a manuscript of William of Tyre's history of the crusades. At the top a city is in flames, while beneath troops drive bound prisoners and livestock before them. French, 1250–59.

The disaster at Hattin left the large crusader settlements almost defenseless. Saladin generally preferred to offer mercy to cities and castles in the hope of a quick surrender, and was known for keeping his word. On 10th July, against the wishes of its citizens, Joscelin III of Courtenay surrendered Acre. Jaffa resisted and was stormed; its population was then sold into slavery. Tyre was prepared to surrender on terms until the end of July, when Conrad of Montferrat, brother of Queen Sibylla's first husband, arrived from Europe. Conrad organized Tyre and defied Saladin, who bypassed the city. But Sidon and Beirut surrendered, as did Ascalon and Gaza. By late September 1187 virtually all of the coast except Tyre was in Saladin's possession.

Saladin now moved on the greatest prize: Jerusalem. The population was defiant and swollen with refugees ready to fight, but they had no leader. However, the arrival of Balian of Ibelin (see box) provided strong and competent leadership. When Saladin arrived on 20th September the citizens made it clear they would fight. Saladin seems to have wanted a bloodbath to avenge the events of 1099 (see page 47), perhaps to satisfy the many religious zealots with his army. He refused a surrender on terms proposed by Balian and attacked, but his troops were repulsed. Balian now threatened to kill all Muslim prisoners and destroy the Dome of the Rock and the Aqsa mosque.

Saladin now suggested terms. He would allow all Christians to leave Jerusalem on payment of ten dinars for a man, five for a woman,

SALADIN'S GALLANTRY

One of the few survivors of Hattin was Balian of Ibelin (Balian the Old), the head of a family that had amassed vast lands in the kingdom. Together with Reynald of Sidon, Balian was able to break out of the Muslim encirclement in the later stages of the battle. He took refuge in Tyre, but his wife Maria Comnena (formerly the second wife of King Amalric I), remained in Jerusalem with their children. When Saladin threatened the holy city, Balian asked him for a safe conduct to the city to allow him to take his family back to Tyre. Saladin courteously agreed, as long as Balian traveled unarmed and did not spend more than one night in Jerusalem.

However, once Balian was in the city the population clamored for him to lead their defense and he reluctantly agreed. Balian wrote to Saladin to explain why he had to break his word, and for this courtesy Saladin sent his own troops to escort Maria and her family to safety. This was an extraordinary act of generosity on Saladin's part, and a reminder of the commonality between the non-native ruling elites who were contending to rule the Near East. It was also one of several episodes that contributed to the later European legends of Saladin as an outstanding figure of chivalry (see page 93).

and one for a child. Balian pointed out that many thousands of poor people would not be able to afford these sums, and Saladin granted a period of grace for money to be raised. In the end, perhaps 15,000 were left behind and taken into slavery, but the remainder were escorted to the coast.

"How sweet was it for him to be victorious," wrote Imad ad-Din of Saladin's capture of Jerusalem. The holy city's recovery for Islam was a great success, but it also allowed time for Tyre to organize its defense under Conrad. Saladin arrived at Tyre in November, but withdrew on 1st January 1188. It was his first defeat since his great victory at Hattin (see sidebar).

In May 1188 Saladin gathered an enormous army with which to attack the northern crusader cities. A Sicilian fleet prevented an assault on Tripoli. He seized Tortosa, but not its citadel. In the principality of Antioch he enjoyed much success. On 15th July Jabala fell, followed on 22nd July by Laodicea (Lattakiyeh). The fortress of Saone (Sahyun) surrendered on 29th July, as did Bourzey on 23rd August. When Baghras fell Saladin had virtually surrounded Antioch itself. However, his own considerable losses forced him to make a truce.

Elsewhere Saladin's lieutenants mopped up the remnants of the kingdom. Kerak in Oultrejourdain surrendered in November 1188 and Safad fell in December, while Belvoir held out until January 1189. Effectively, the kingdom of Jerusalem had ceased to exist, the county of Tripoli had been savaged, and Antioch was no more than a remnant. But the flow of reinforcements to Tyre was growing, and in Europe a new crusade was already underway.

CONRAD TRAPS SALADIN'S FLEET

Conrad of Montferrat's defense of Tyre rallied crusader morale in the aftermath of Hattin. The Old French *Estoire d'Eracles*, partly based on eyewitness accounts, tells how Conrad outwitted Saladin's fleet:

"The Saracens saw that the chain [across the harbor entrance] was down and decided to enter the port. In fact five galleys came in. When the marquis [Conrad] saw that the galleys had entered the port, he ordered the chain to be raised. As soon as the chain was up, the Christians [seized the galleys], together with two he had found at Tyre. He stationed plenty of well-armed knights and men on board. At dawn the following day they sailed out silently and attacked the [remaining] Saracen galleys. … When they could no longer endure the fighting, they ran five of their galleys onto the shore, and two others went off to Beirut."

Two ships engaged in battle, from a manuscript of ca. 1340. Conrad of Montferrat's defeat of Saladin's fleet was crucial to the revival of crusader fortunes after the losses of 1187.

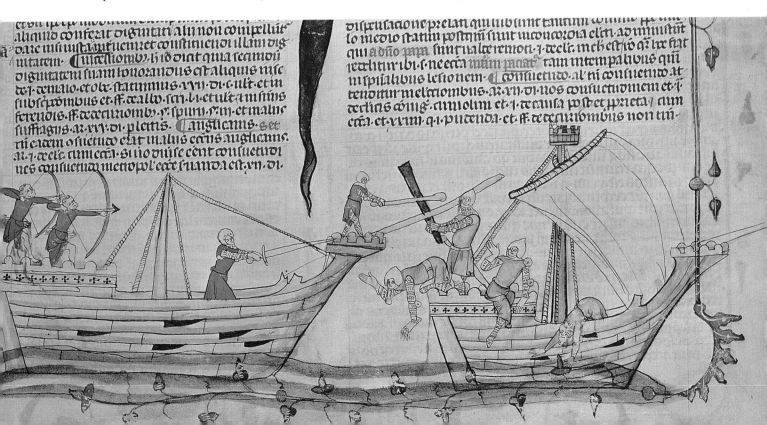

THE THIRD CRUSADE

A CAMPAIGN OF EUROPE'S ÉLITE

HELEN NICHOLSON

THE KINGS TAKE THE CROSS

THE *AUDITA TREMENDI*

Like all papal letters, Gregory VIII's appeal for Christians to aid the Holy Land is known by its opening Latin words, in this case *Audita tremendi* ("We have heard things that make us tremble"). This is an extract:

"We have heard things that make us tremble at the severity of the judgment that the Divine hand has executed over the land of Jerusalem.... We must be aware not only that the inhabitants [of Jerusalem] have sinned but also that we have sinned, as have all the Christian people.... Everyone must think about this and act on it, so that by voluntarily correcting our sins we may turn to Our Lord God. First we should put right the evil we do, and then we may turn our attention to the enemy's ferocity and malice.... We promise that those who take up this journey with contrite heart and humble spirit and depart in penance of their sins and in right faith will have full indulgence for their crimes and will receive eternal life."

The gisant (supine effigy) of King Richard I of England (1189–99), from his tomb in the abbey of Fontevrault in Anjou, northern France—one of eight English Plantagenet royal tombs there, including those of his parents, Henry II of England and Eleanor of Aquitaine. Owing to his involvement in the Third Crusade and his wars in France, Richard spent barely six months in his own kingdom.

In the fall of 1187 Archbishop Joscius of Tyre sailed from the East to Europe with the news of Saladin's victories (see Chapter Three) and to appeal for help. Christians in the West were horrified at what they heard. At the end of October, Pope Gregory VIII responded with *Audita tremendi*, an encyclical, or papal announcement, urging all Christians to go to the aid of their fellows in the East (see sidebar). One of the first to take the cross was Count Richard of Poitou, the rebellious eldest son of King Henry II of England. King William II of Sicily was the first western ruler to dispatch military aid, sending an armed fleet to harass the coasts conquered by Saladin.

The pope authorized Archbishop Joscius and Cardinal Legate Henry of Albano, a Cistercian monk, to travel north of the Alps raising recruits for the crusade. The kings of England and France (Henry II and Philip II Augustus) were at war, but in response to Joscius's preaching in January 1188 they agreed to make peace and go to the Holy Land. Henry planned to travel overland across Europe and sent letters to the rulers of the lands that he would need to pass through, asking for safe passage for his army.

In March 1188 the elderly emperor Frederick I Barbarossa, the ruler (1152–90) of Germany and northern Italy, took the cross in a great ceremony before the assembled German nobility at Metz in Lorraine. Frederick issued instructions that only experienced warriors who could equip and support themselves properly in a two-year campaign should join his crusade. Although the last leader in the West to declare his intention to join the crusade, in May 1189 Frederick was the first to set out (see pages 84–85).

In the meantime, war broke out again between the French and English kings. Then, in July 1189, Henry II died with his crusade vow unfulfilled, to the great disappointment of the Franks of the East, who had expected great things of him. In the past Henry had sent money to help the Holy Land, and he was closely related to the rulers of Jerusalem: he and Queen Sibylla were cousins, grand-children of Count Fulk V of Anjou, king of Jerusalem (1131–43).

However, Henry II's successor, Richard of Poitou (Richard I), immediately began preparations to fulfill his own crusade vow. On 4th July 1190, Richard and Philip II finally set out on crusade from Vézelay in Burgundy, where they made an alliance and agreed to evenly divide everything won on the crusade. The agreement was made as between equals, but Philip regarded Richard as his subordinate because he was overlord of Richard's vast French estates. Richard, however, saw himself as at least as great a monarch as Philip, with greater domains, resources, and military skills. Their relationship was not to be an easy one (see pages 87 and 95).

Although the two kings set out together from France, their large forces traveled separately. The armies were so big that if they had traveled together they would have placed an unbearable burden on the people whose lands they were transiting, who would not have been able to feed and supply so many. Richard assembled a fleet in England to transport his army to the East, while Philip hired ships at Genoa to carry his own troops.

The emperor Frederick I enthroned, flanked by his sons Henry (later the emperor Henry VI) and Duke Frederick of Swabia. The emperor is shown with his family's characteristic red hair and beard from which he derived the nickname "Barbarossa." (Redbeard). From a chronicle produced at the German monastery of Weingarten, 1179–81.

THE SALADIN TITHE

War was very expensive. Many crusaders paid their own way, but when they ran out of money they looked to the crusading leaders to support them. When they took the cross in 1188, King Henry II of England and King Philip II of France agreed to impose a new tax in order to finance the forthcoming crusade. Anyone in their kingdoms who did not take the vow to go on crusade would have to pay a tenth of the value of their revenues and moveable property. The tax, dubbed "the Saladin tithe" (tithe = "tenth"), was very unpopular, and in France it provoked so much resistance that Philip had to abandon its collection. In England, however, everyone eligible had to pay the tithe, and it raised a large sum.

Following Henry II's death, his son Richard I raised even more money by selling offices and rights to anyone who could afford them. He disposed of government posts, titles, castles, and land, and sold towns the right to govern their own affairs. One contemporary writer quoted the king as saying that he would even have sold London if he could have found a buyer.

THE CRUSADE HEADS EAST

RICHARD I CAPTURES CYPRUS

On their voyage to the East, some of King Richard I's contingent were shipwrecked on Cyprus, a Greek Christian island ruled by the usurping Byzantine "emperor" Isaac Comnenus. Isaac's mistreatment of the shipwrecked crusaders prompted Richard to attack the island, which he also wanted as a supply base for the crusade.

Richard's attack was successful, but to save the expense of defending the island himself, he sold it to the Templars. After a local revolt against their rule, the Templars returned the island to Richard, who subsequently sold it to Guy of Lusignan, the ex-king of Jerusalem. Guy successfully established himself as king and Cyprus was ruled by the Lusignans and other western Europeans until it was conquered by the Ottoman Turks in 1571 (see also pages 164–165, 176–177).

A fleet departs for the crusades, from the Cantigas de Santa Maria, *an illuminated manuscript in Galician commissioned by King Alfonso X of León and Castile (reigned 1252–84).*

Crusaders set out on the Third Crusade from all over Europe, especially from Italy, France, Germany, and England, but also from regions farther afield, such as Denmark, Frisia, and eastern Europe. People from all sectors of European society joined the crusade: men and women, young and old, peasants and merchants, as well as the nobility. Those who could not fight were expected to help the crusading armies by laboring, trading, carrying on a craft or simply by praying. Many clergy and monks went on the crusade, despite the fact that priests were not permitted to shed blood and monks were supposed to stay in their monasteries.

Some crusaders, especially the northern Europeans, completed the whole journey to the East by sea, while others went overland, such as the army of the emperor Frederick. Crusaders from France went by land as far as ports such as Marseilles or Genoa, then hired ships to the East. These were the routes taken by kings Philip II of France and Richard I of England when they set out in July 1190. In the Mediterranean the crusader fleets usually stopped to take on water and food at Sicily and Crete, as well as at Rhodes or Cyprus, or both. A winter crossing was risky because of the stormy conditions, so Richard and Philip overwintered in Sicily.

Philip reached the East in April 1191, followed at the start of June by Richard, who had captured Cyprus from the Byzantines en route (see sidebar). This was several months after the first of their followers, who had reached Acre by the end of September 1190.

The crusaders encountered many challenges on their way to the East. The Scandinavians, English, Frisians, and Flemish who sailed in summer 1189 stopped en route in Portugal, where they helped King Sancho to ravage Muslim territory and temporarily capture some fortresses and towns.

The English crusaders who arrived with Richard I in Sicily in early autumn 1190 were less well received by the local Greeks, Muslims, and Italians. The Sicilians resented a large body of foreigners who behaved with arrogance and could not speak the local language. The bad feelings were aggravated by a dispute between Richard and King Tancred of Sicily, who refused to hand over property belonging to Joanna, the dowager queen of Sicily, who was Richard's sister. Joanna's

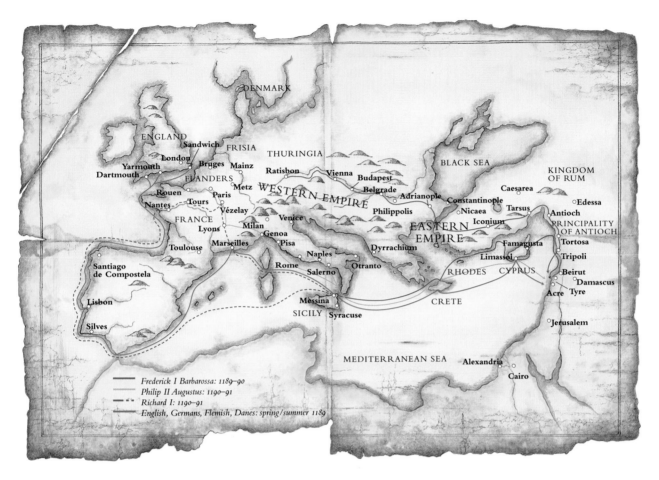

Frederick I Barbarossa: 1189–90
Philip II Augustus: 1190–91
Richard I: 1190–91
English, Germans, Flemish, Danes: spring/summer 1189

husband, King William II of Sicily, had planned to join the crusade, but died in November 1189 before he could set out. One of the reasons Richard went to Sicily was to collect both Joanna and her dowry, which he was hoping to use to help finance the crusade. The quarrel escalated into open battle, Richard besieged and captured the city of Messina, and careful diplomacy was needed to restore peace. The episode showed how the large crusader armies, with their huge need for food, water, and lodging, could pose a considerable threat to the stability of the areas through which they traveled.

The crusade faced other difficulties. Some crusaders never set out at all or else returned home early when they ran out of money or fell ill. But the most serious loss to the crusade was the great army that had left with Frederick I, which arrived in the East having lost its leader and most of its troops along the way (see pages 84–85).

All this did not bode well for the success of the crusade. Nevertheless, the English and French kings arrived in the East to find the vital port of Acre, captured by Saladin shortly after the battle of Hattin (see page 76), already under siege from the Franks of the East and their recently arrived western allies. The crusader counteroffensive against Saladin had begun.

To reach the Holy Land a variety of routes, both at sea and on land, were used by the major elements of the multinational force. Scandinavian and Flemish contingents sailed across the North Sea to England, where they linked up with the English and set sail from several south coast ports in spring and summer of 1189. Richard I set out from his ancestral possessions in western France, traveling up the Loire and then across land to Vézelay, while separately his fleet sailed from Nantes and headed for Sicily, where he planned to meet up with it for the onward journey. Philip's forces moved southward through France and either sailed direct for Sicily from Genoa or port-hopped along the coast of Italy, reuniting in Sicily for the journey east. Meanwhile Frederick I's army moved down the mighty Danube and various minor rivers then marched through Anatolia and the Kingdom of Armenia to converge on Acre.

BARBAROSSA'S CRUSADE

THE DEATH OF BARBAROSSA

An anonymous German cleric recorded Frederick I's death at first hand:

"The emperor, undaunted by every danger and wishing to cool himself and avoid the mountain peaks, tried to swim across the depths of the swift Selef river. Although everyone told him not to…, that man—who was so wise in other things—unwisely exercised his strength against the flow and current of the river, entered the water and was swallowed by a whirlpool…. All the nobles around him hurried to help him, although they were too late, and they carried him to the shore. Everyone was so distressed and struck with such terrible grief at his death that some, torn between fear and hope, died there with him; others despaired, as if they thought that God did not care about them, renounced the Christian faith, and joined the heathen."

Frederick I Barbarossa drowns in the Selef river, from a manuscript of the 13th-century Saxon World Chronicle, *a history of the world from the Creation written in Low German dialect.*

Setting out from Ratisbon (present-day Regensburg) in Bavaria early in May 1189, the emperor Frederick I and his army traveled down the Danube through southern Germany, into Hungary and beyond. The army marched on the south bank of the river while supplies were carried by boat. South of Belgrade, Frederick headed up the Morava, a tributary of the Danube, then crossed Bulgaria and headed for Constantinople, the Byzantine capital.

The Byzantine empire had assisted the first two crusades, but since the death of the emperor Manuel I Comnenus (1143–80) relations between it and the West had soured. Such was the mistrust that the emperor Isaac II Angelus (1185–95, 1203–04) had even made an alliance with Saladin, seeing in Frederick a serious military threat to his own position. When Frederick sent envoys to negotiate his passage through the Byzantine empire, Isaac had them imprisoned.

Frederick arrived in the Byzantine city of Adrianople (Edirne) in late November 1189 and established camp there for the winter. Over the following months his forces mounted raids in the surrounding countryside both to secure food for the army and to force Isaac to make peace. Isaac finally agreed to negotiate and in February 1190 the two emperors made a peace treaty that allowed Frederick and his army to continue toward the Holy Land.

The Turkish sultan of Iconium (Konya), in Asia Minor, had already promised Frederick free passage through his lands, but when

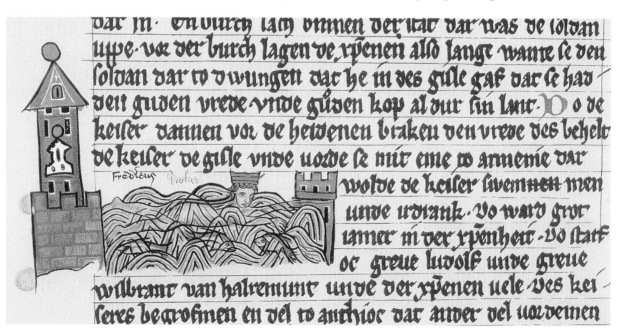

THE TEUTONIC ORDER

During the siege of Acre, German crusaders from the merchant cities of Bremen and Lübeck founded a hospital to care for their sick and wounded compatriots. As in western European hospitals at this time, the staff of religious men and women would have offered only limited medical care beyond alleviating their patients' physical sufferings and looking after their immortal souls.

Duke Frederick of Swabia (see main text) took the hospital under the protection of his family, the Hohenstaufen, and it went on to acquire extensive properties and rights in Germany. In March 1198 the institution was officially reestablished as a military religious order, its rule based on those of the Templars and the Hospitallers. The Order of the Hospital of St. Mary of the Teutons (Teutonic Order), never had great landholdings in the East. However, in the 1230s it became involved in the crusades against the pagans of northeast Europe and subsequently established an independent military-religious state in Prussia, which it ruled until the sixteenth century (see Chapter Six).

The Cappenburg Head, a gilded bronze reliquiary (container for holy relics) made ca. 1160. It takes the form of the head of Frederick I Barbarossa, German king and Holy Roman emperor 1152–90.

Frederick's forces came under Turkish attack in the sultan's territory, the emperor blamed him for breaking their agreement. In May 1190 Frederick captured and sacked Iconium before heading south into Cilician Armenia, a Christian land that was friendly to the crusaders.

Then, on 10th June 1190, disaster struck the expedition when the emperor was drowned in the Selef (Göksu) river. What exactly happened remains unclear, since the many contemporary accounts do not concur; some claim that he was fording or trying to swim across the river, and others that he was swimming for relaxation (see sidebar, opposite). Whatever its cause, the emperor's death was a heavy blow to his followers and the other crusader armies, and was greeted with great rejoicing by the armies of Saladin. The crusaders had hoped that Frederick and his huge army would lead them to a rapid victory. Instead, his crusade achieved little, although it led to the creation of a new military order, the Teutonic knights (see box, above).

Frederick's son, Duke Frederick of Swabia, took over command of the imperial army and led it to Antioch, where the emperor's body was buried. Some of the German crusaders died there of an epidemic, and many others simply decided to return home. It was with a much depleted army that the duke arrived in early September 1190 at the port of Tripoli (in present-day Lebanon) to take ship to Acre. The duke arrived at Acre in October 1190 to find the city already besieged by the crusaders.

THE SIEGE OF ACRE

King Guy of Jerusalem had been taken prisoner after the battle of Hattin (see page 75). Saladin freed him in July 1188 on condition that he cross the sea at once—that is, leave for Europe; but Guy simply sailed to Arwad off the Syrian coast before returning to the mainland. At Tripoli he was joined by the first crusaders from the West. He attempted to ally with Conrad of Montferrat, who took over the defense of Tyre in the late summer of 1188, but Conrad had ambitions to be king and refused to cooperate. So, late in August 1189, Guy marched to Acre, which Saladin had taken in July 1187, and despite his small forces began a siege. Saladin moved his troops inland, trapping the crusaders between the city and his army.

The crusaders' initial assaults failed, so they concentrated on blockading the city. By November 1189 the blockade was complete and Acre was running short of food. Saladin tried to send in supplies by sea, but after many naval clashes his fleet was defeated in March 1190 by Conrad of Montferrat, who had now been persuaded to help the crusaders. Yet still Acre did not fall, and on 25th July another

Philip II receives the surrender of Acre in 1191, from the Chroniques de France, *ca. 1325–50. An English cleric who went on the Third Crusade and gave an account of events in the* Itinerarium Peregrinorum et Gesta Regis Ricardi (The Journey of the Pilgrims and Deeds of King Richard), *describes the Muslim defenders of Acre as "outstanding and memorable warriors, who were men of admirable prowess, exceptional valor, very energetic in the practice of war, and renowned for their great deeds. No less, as they came out of the city almost empty-handed, the Christians were stunned at their fine bearing and appearance, which remained unaltered by adversity."*

attack on Saladin's camp was repulsed. But more crusaders were now arriving by sea from Europe and Saladin's army was growing demoralized. The duke of Swabia landed early in October 1190, but he died in January 1191 of a plague that swept the crusader camp, exacerbated by a food shortage. Conrad had promised food supplies if the crusade leaders allowed him to marry the heiress to the throne of Jerusalem (see pages 94–95). Once married, however, he had forgotten his promises and left for Tyre at the end of November 1190.

At last, on 20th April 1191, Philip II of France arrived to assume overall command, and Richard I of England landed on 8th June with more ships and siege equipment (see sidebar). As the siege engines took their toll the Muslims asked for peace, but Richard refused their terms. On 3rd July the wall was breached and within a few days Saladin agreed terms for the city's surrender. On 12th July Acre was given up to the crusaders, who kept around 3,000 hostages as a guarantee that Saladin would free his own prisoners and return the relic of the True Cross captured at Hattin. The kings divided the booty and negotiated a settlement between Guy and Conrad (see page 95). Philip then returned to France. He perhaps resented the prominence of Richard (see page 95), but he may simply have felt unable to continue: he had been very ill and his son was dangerously sick at home.

On 16th August Richard ordered the massacre of the hostages, an atrocity condemned by Muslim and Christian writers alike. He claimed that Saladin had not kept to the treaty; Saladin denied this, but each side gave a different version of the treaty and blamed the other for breaking it, so it is difficult to determine the truth. It is likely that Richard's motives were a desire to terrify the Muslims, and to avoid the expense of maintaining so many prisoners on the next stage of his campaign: the recapture of Jerusalem.

The port of Acre, (present-day Akko, Israel) stands on a promontory on Haifa Bay. Few remains of the crusader city are visible today above ground, but the breakwater built to create an outer harbor after the city's initial capture by the crusaders in 1104 can be seen. According to literary sources and maps, the crusader port also once included an inner harbor.

CRUSADER SIEGE ENGINES

When the crusaders blockaded Acre they filled in the ditch around the city to allow siege engines to be brought up to the walls, and dug defensive ditches around their camp. The Muslims were impressed by the elaborate siege equipment constructed by Duke Frederick of Swabia, Philip II, and Richard I to assail the city's defenses. Philip had a catapult for hurling stone missiles that his troops called the "Evil Neighbor," and the crusaders built a great siege tower that was probably like the one described by Saladin's secretary Imad al-Din al-Isfahani: "The Franks began to construct a terrifying tower on wheels, a machine heavy with menace that was topped with an object called a ram. This machine carried two long horns like lances, as fat as two thick pillars. The padlocks of closed walls opened before it without a key, for walls struck by its horns were reduced to dust!"

CONTROL OF THE SEA

Maritime power played a vital part in the Third Crusade because of the transportation of both men and supplies to the East. In addition, control of the sea was crucial in the fall of Acre in July 1191, and it enabled Richard I to recapture part of the Palestinian coast.

The Arabs only began to build warships after early Muslim rulers saw that they were needed to make conquests in the Mediterranean. They employed local experts to build and crew the fleets that defeated the Byzantines off Egypt in 654, and attacked islands such as Cyprus, Crete, Rhodes, and Sicily. In the late seventh century the Muslim governor of North Africa established shipyards at Tunis and built more than 100 ships. In the 840s a North African and Spanish Muslim fleet captured most of Sicily from Byzantium. In 904 an Arab fleet sacked Thessalonica, and throughout the tenth century Muslim ships dominated the Mediterranean. Although Muslim-owned warships were large, heavy, and slow, they were also stable and all-season vessels, unlike the Christian-owned types, which did not sail the Mediterranean in the winter. Most ships from Muslim territory operated as traders when they were not acting as warships and were hired by rulers on a freelance basis.

By the twelfth century improved western European ships, especially those of traders from the Italian cities of Venice, Genoa, and Pisa, were competing to control the Mediterranean. The most common warship was the long, narrow galley that sat low in the water and had the flexibility of oar- or sail-power, depending on the weather. The galley could be used for trade.

From 1177 Saladin began to improve the Egyptian fleet in order to defend his coasts from Christian ships and to attack

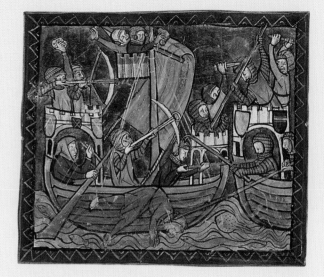

ports of the Christian East. He imported timber from Europe and tried to recruit suitable crews. (In 1179 the church banned Christians from serving as captains or pilots in Muslim vessels.) Saladin's improvements alarmed the Franks, who feared he would attack pilgrim ships and the crusader states—as he did in 1182, when at least thirty galleys unsuccessfully attacked Beirut.

After his victories of 1187 Saladin used his fleet to control the Syria-Palestine coastline. Only Admiral Margarit of Sicily resisted him in the north, while Conrad of Montferrat's fleet at Tyre defeated him in the south. In his attempt to evade the crusader blockade of Acre during the siege of 1189–91, Saladin even disguised vessels as Christian ships (by putting pigs on board). The crusaders used ships to transport troops and supplies and to attack Muslim fortresses, erecting siege towers on ships to create mobile fighting platforms. Conrad defeated the

Muslim fleet at Acre and Saladin's naval supremacy finally ended in June 1191 when King Richard I arrived with a large fleet of warships and transports. They carried supplies up and down the coast, protected the crusaders marching along it, kept Richard in contact with coastal bases even when Saladin blocked the road, and enabled him to relieve Jaffa quickly in August 1192.

After Saladin's death in 1193 Egypt's rulers paid less attention to naval power, but still needed a fleet both for defense and to attack Christian settlements. Later, the Mamluk sultan Baibars I built up a fleet and in 1271 attacked Cyprus. In 1302 Egypt captured the island of Arwad from the Templars. Further north, Turkish ships raided the Greek islands, and in the fifteenth century the Ottoman Turks emerged as the greatest naval power in the Mediterranean (see Chapter Eight).

Above: *An Islamic tin-glazed bowl of ca. 1425–50 from Málaga, Spain, decorated with what appears to be a type of vessel know as a carrack.*
Opposite, above: *A northern European cog with high sides, a straight prow, a flat keel, and a single square sail. From a manuscript of ca. 1270.*
Opposite, below: *Venice, a trading city whose networks and influence extended to the Black Sea. Galleys were suited to both trade and war.*

ADVANCE TO JERUSALEM

Opposite: *Belvoir ("Fair View"), standing high above the Jordan river valley, 12 miles (20km) south of the Sea of Galilee, was one of several fortresses that guarded the eastern frontier of the crusader kingdom. Rebuilt by the Hospitallers in 1168–70, it was a concentric castle, with a great deep moat, partly stone-lined, enclosing a mighty curtain-wall 425ft by 330ft (130m by 100m) long. The wall had projecting square towers on heavily splayed bases at each corner and in the middle of each wall. Within the wall was an almost identical enclosure. Belvoir held out against Saladin for a year and a half before capitulating in 1189.*

Almost immediately after executing the Muslim hostages, King Richard I began arrangements for the march south to Jerusalem. Determined to enforce discipline, he decided that the women of the army would be left in safety at Acre, except for those performing essential services that would not be performed by men, such as the laundry. He arranged for his supply ships to sail down the coast parallel to the army on the coast road. The army set out in late August.

Initially there were problems in keeping the crusader army together as it moved in such a long column, constantly harassed by Saladin's forces. Richard solved this to some degree by putting the military orders, the Templars and Hospitallers, in command of the vanguard and rearguard. Yet the march south, in the heat of late summer, was still very difficult. Many of the rivers had dried up and fresh water was hard to find. The infantry and ordinary pilgrims had to carry all their own possessions and some died on the road, unable to bear the harsh conditions. Food too was short: after one battle Richard arranged for the horses that had been killed to be sold for food. The road itself had become overgrown and was almost impassable. On 7th September 1191, on the road to the town of Arsuf,

LEGENDS OF THE LIONHEART

As a close relative of the queens Sibylla and Isabella of Jerusalem and arguably the closest heir to the throne of Jerusalem after them, Richard could claim to be a natural leader of the Third Crusade. His great skill as a military strategist and tactician was matched by his ability to inspire warriors to follow him, and the image of the king that comes through the contemporary sources—a figure of reckless courage and great military ability—was certainly one that the king encouraged. Even his notorious fits of rage—such as that which led to the execution of the Muslim hostages—were part of the "superhuman" image that the king created around himself. Richard's own subjects described exceptional deeds: he was the first in every attack and the last to withdraw; he was attacked by a huge wild boar that he killed singlehandedly; at Jaffa he leapt into the sea and

waded ashore to attack Saladin's forces, followed by his men. These stories were essentially true, and inspired his famous nickname, Lionheart. Later writers went so far as to claim that Richard had killed and eaten a lion, and even that he had devoured the flesh of dead Muslims.

Richard's Muslim contemporaries saw him as their greatest enemy. The historian Ibn al-Athir called him "the most remarkable man of his time for his bravery, cunning, activity, and prudence. Because of him the Muslims experienced an unparalleled calamity." Baha ad-Din ibn Shaddad called Richard "accursed," because he was such a great enemy of Islam, and emphasized his cunning and treachery as well as his judgment and military experience. Baha ad-Din's colleague, Imad ad-Din al-Isfahani, declared that Richard could never be trusted and that his troops were "demonic."

Saladin's forces attacked Richard's rearguard, but the crusaders drove off the Muslims and kept control of the field.

After this, Saladin withdrew and destroyed several key fortifications. The crusaders marched on to Jaffa, from where Richard organized repairs to fortifications controlling the road to Jerusalem. At the same time, he entered into negotiations with Saladin (see sidebar), but the talks failed because neither side trusted the other, and because Saladin was also negotiating with Conrad of Montferrat.

In late November 1191 the army continued its advance toward Jerusalem. The crusaders spent Christmas encamped in various castles on the road to the holy city, from which they launched raids across the countryside. The weather was very poor, with heavy rain.

Early in January 1192 a council of crusader leaders concluded that even if they captured Jerusalem they would not be able to hold it, since Saladin could easily bring an army up from Egypt to recapture the city. But the crusaders could cut his supply lines by refortifying Ascalon, on the coast road from Egypt to Jerusalem. Richard and the other leaders therefore decided to withdraw to Ascalon, a move that so distressed many of their followers that they left the crusade.

With the crusader threat to Jerusalem withdrawn, Saladin dismissed his army and abandoned his aggressive strategy to concentrate on improving the city's defenses. His Muslim enemies within his

DIPLOMACY AND NEGOTIATION

The conflict between the crusaders and Saladin was partly conducted through diplomatic channels. Christian sources are discreet about such negotiations, but Muslim writers record that Richard I was in contact with Saladin from his first arrival in the East in June 1191. Local nobles, notably Humphrey IV of Toron, often acted as his ambassadors, and Saladin sent his brother, al-Adil, as envoy to Richard. The leaders became fairly friendly, although—in spite of legends to the contrary—they never met.

However, the followers of Richard and Saladin feared that their leaders were betraying their principles by negotiating with the enemy. Each side also suspected the other of merely playing for time. Yet it cannot be denied that Richard's negotiations with Saladin over a long period helped him to gain a relatively favorable peace treaty in September 1192.

Scenes from the Maciejowski Bible of ca. 1250, illuminated in Paris and presented to Shah Abbas the Great of Persia by a papal mission. The upper register depicts a battle from the Old Testament, but the combatants are represented as mounted knights of the time the manuscript was produced. Their weapons would have been familiar to combatants of the Third Crusade and include a crossbow being aimed by the soldier in the tower at top right, which in 1139 at the Second Lateran council the Roman Catholic church had outlawed the use of against Christians, calling it "hateful to God"—but there was no objection to its use against non-Christians.

empire were close to revolt, but he could not fight them while the crusaders remained a danger. He could, however, encourage the quarrels between the crusaders, urging Conrad to attack Richard.

At Ascalon, meanwhile, Richard supervised the restoration of the city's defenses. But with their immediate goal of Jerusalem removed, the crusaders divided into quarreling factions. Then in April 1192 Richard received alarming news from England: his younger brother John, count of Mortain, was plotting to take over his kingdom. Urgently needing to reach a settlement in the East, Richard agreed to set aside Guy of Lusignan's claim to the kingdom of Jerusalem in favor of Conrad. He compensated Guy by selling him Cyprus, where Guy became the first of a long line of Lusignan rulers (see page 168).

In the event, however, the marquis was never to be crowned. At the end of April 1192 Conrad was returning alone to his quarters in Tyre one night after supper when he was murdered by two Assassins (see sidebar). The French blamed Richard, on the grounds that he wanted to remove a rival. Duke Leopold V of Austria, a cousin of both Conrad and Richard, also blamed the English king. The Muslim historian Ibn al-Athir claimed to have heard that Saladin had paid Rashid ad-Din Sinan, the leader of the Assassins' sect, to kill either Richard or Conrad; according to Ibn al-Athir, Sinan realized that if Richard died, Saladin would then be free to attack the Assassins, so he arranged the murder of Conrad. However, the true motivation for the assassination remains a mystery.

After the marquis's death, Count Henry of Champagne was elected king by the French with the approval of Richard, his uncle. Conrad's widow Isabella, the heiress to the kingdom (see page 94), accepted Henry as her husband and they were married, thereby resolving the succession problem.

The Crusade Runs Out of Momentum

In the meantime, Richard continued to campaign, capturing important fortresses, and in June 1192 the crusaders began a second advance on Jerusalem. However, Richard was reluctant to lay siege to the city because there was little water in the area for the besiegers,

Saladin would be able to cut off their supply lines easily, and the crusader army was too small to be sure of defeating him. Instead Richard advised an attack on Egypt, the heart of Saladin's power, but the French did not agree. The matter was still undecided when the crusaders heard that some of Saladin's supply caravans were approaching from Egypt. Richard captured one and distributed the booty, but he then withdrew from the advance on Jerusalem.

In the city, Saladin and his advisers rejoiced at this reprieve, but the crusaders were despondent at this second disappointment. Many set off for home, and the remaining French crusaders refused any further cooperation with Richard as leader.

Richard withdrew to Acre to plan an attack on Beirut. Meanwhile Saladin attacked and captured Jaffa, but Richard arrived by ship just in time to prevent Saladin's troops from capturing the citadel. In the ensuing battle, on 5th August 1192, Richard had only a small force, but deployed his archers and cavalry so skillfully that Saladin was unable to dislodge the crusaders and was forced to withdraw.

The battle of Jaffa turned out to be the final engagement of the crusade. After it Richard fell ill, offering his enemy a perfect opportunity to attack. But Saladin could not rely on his own hungry and demoralized army to fight, and instead he agreed to make a truce.

THE ASSASSINS

Members of an extremist Ismaili Shi'ite sect, the Assassins broke away from the domination of Fatimid Egypt in the late eleventh century, under the leadership of al-Hasan ibn al-Sabbah (died 1124). In 1091 they captured the fortress of Alamut in Iran, which became their power base, and early in the twelfth century some settled in the mountains of north Syria. They believed that if they served their leader without question they would be rewarded in paradise, and to this end members of the sect would seek out and murder anyone that their leader commanded. Outsiders called them Assassins after hashish, which they were rumored (falsely) to use in their religious practices. The Assassins of northern Iran were destroyed in 1256 by the Mongols, and in 1272–73 Sultan Baibars of Egypt visited a similar fate on the Assassins in Syria.

LEGENDS OF SALADIN

As a non-Arab (he was a Kurd, from Tikrit in Iraq) and an upstart, Saladin was not well respected by later Muslim historians until the twentieth century (see page 209), but his reputation in the Christian West was great. He was honored as a just and merciful ruler, kind to the weak, trustworthy, pious, and an excellent warrior. In his own lifetime it was reported that he had been knighted by one of the Frankish nobles of the East, just as if he were a Christian warrior. The next generation of Western writers claimed that Saladin was descended from a French noblewoman, and that he had become a Christian on his deathbed. Later writers added a love affair between Saladin and the queen of France on the Second or Third Crusade.

Although these stories were inventions they show the respect in which medieval western writers held the Muslim leader, who came to be regarded as the epitome of the chivalrous, cultured, and pious ruler—in implied contrast to the Christian rulers of the West.

Saladin, Sultan of Egypt. *A detail of a miniature from an Egyptian manuscript of ca. 1180.*

DISCORD AND RIVALRY

On his return to France, King Philip II invaded Richard I's extensive lands there, and the two former allies remained at war for the rest of Richard's reign. This scene from a French manuscript of ca. 1325–50, Chronique de St. Denis, *depicts Richard attacking Philip's army at Gisors in 1198.*

The effectiveness of the Third Crusade was seriously undermined by the personal rivalries between Philip II of France and Richard I of England (see sidebar) and between the local leaders, Guy of Lusignan and Conrad of Montferrat. But these rivalries simply provided a focus for deep rifts that existed within the entire crusading army. To begin with, the crusaders were never united under a single leader. Individual nobles made their own way to the East with their own warriors, and once there they tended to ally with crusaders from their own area, simply because they shared a common language.

When Philip II returned to France in August 1191, Richard I became the commander-in-chief of the crusade. However, he could only really rely on his own subjects—the English, Normans, Angevins, and Poitevins—to support him. The other groups acknowledged Richard's command only for as long as he could pay them, and when his funds ran low they deserted him.

The Italian cities of Genoa and Pisa were fierce competitors in maritime trade and they brought their rivalry to the crusade, supporting opposite sides in any dispute. Chief among these disputes was the rivalry between Guy of Lusignan and Conrad of Montferrat for the kingdom of Jerusalem. Guy had become king only because he had married Sibylla, the heiress to the kingdom. After Sibylla and her

THE FOUR HUSBANDS OF QUEEN ISABELLA

The youngest child of King Amalric of Jerusalem (died 1174) and four times married, Isabella or Isabel of Jerusalem (1172–1205) was depicted by Saladin's secretary Imad ad-Din as a beautiful, idealized woman, mistreated by the barbarous Christians.

With the death of her elder sister, Queen Sibylla, in summer 1190, Isabella became heiress to the kingdom of Jerusalem. In November, crusade leaders opposed to King Guy forced the eighteen-year-old Isabella to divorce her husband Humphrey IV, lord of Toron, and marry Marquis Conrad of Montferrat, so that Conrad could become king. Because Conrad already had two wives and there were no good grounds for Isabella's divorce, the clergy and many others condemned the marriage.

Bad luck dogged all Isabella's later husbands. Conrad was assassinated before being crowned. Imad ad-Din reported that Henry, count of Champagne, then compelled her to marry him so that he could claim the throne. Five years later Henry died in a fall from a high window. Then Isabella had to marry Amalric of Lusignan, king of Cyprus, who was chosen as king. He died in 1205 of food poisoning. Isabella died a few months later.

In 1213 a judicial inquiry into the rights of Isabella and Henry's children to inherit Champagne heard evidence that she had married Conrad against her will. This meant that her last three marriages were arguably illegal, and that none of her descendants on the throne of Jerusalem was truly legitimate.

daughters died in the summer of 1190, Conrad controversially married Sibylla's younger half-sister Isabella (see box) and claimed the crown. He was supported by Philip II, the powerful dukes of Swabia and Austria (successive leaders of the German contingent after the death of Frederick I), and the Genoese. Guy was supported by Richard I (the liege lord of the Lusignans and a cousin of Sibylla), and the Pisans. Both men had their supporters among the Frankish nobles.

The dispute seriously hindered the crusade. Almost from his first arrival in the East in 1187, Conrad refused to cooperate with Guy (whom many Franks blamed for the disasters of that year) and negotiated on his own behalf with Saladin. Even when leading crusaders thought they had persuaded Conrad to assist the crusading effort, he continued to act in his own interests, and not to aid Guy. The dispute was eventually decided in Conrad's favor, but he did not live to be crowned (see page 92).

Meanwhile, Saladin had his own problems. He usually relied on members of his own family as administrators, but quarreled with his nephew Taqi ad-Din, who left the war. He ran short of money and food for his troops, and at Jaffa on 5th August 1192 his army refused to fight. He could play the crusader factions off against each other, but he was not able to defeat them and had to settle for a stalemate.

AN UNEASY ALLIANCE

Richard and King Philip II had been allies against Richard's father, King Henry II of England, in an attempt to force Henry to acknowledge Richard as his heir. Richard had been betrothed to Philip's elder sister Alice, but Henry had never allowed the marriage to take place. When Richard became king, he and Philip agreed to go on crusade as allies, working together and sharing all their gains. But they quarreled in Sicily when Richard decided to abandon Alice and marry Berengaria, daughter of the king of Navarre, whose lands adjoined Richard's territory in Aquitaine. Richard married Berengaria at Cyprus, thereby breaking the alliance with Philip. He then compounded the rift by refusing to give his ally any share in his conquest of Cyprus. According to the contemporary French writer Rigord, Philip even feared that Richard would try to murder him. He returned to Paris soon after Acre fell (see page 87) and then invaded Richard's Norman lands.

THE END OF THE ENTERPRISE

A disguised Richard I is taken captive (top) and is led before the emperor Henry VI to answer for the murder of Conrad of Montferrat (bottom); according to the accompanying Latin text, Richard begs Henry for mercy and is released. An illustration from the Liber ad Honorem Augusti (Book in Honor of the Emperor [Henry VI]) by Peter of Eboli, written 1195–96.

On 2nd September 1192 Richard I and Saladin concluded the treaty of Jaffa. Under its terms, the Franks held the coastline from Jaffa to Tyre, but Saladin retained some towns. The fortifications of Ascalon would be demolished. Christian pilgrims could travel to Jerusalem, and trade could be conducted freely. There would be a truce, on land and at sea, for eight months and three days that covered the kingdom of Jerusalem, Tripoli, and Antioch. The Franks of the East, including Count Henry of Champagne, the king-elect of Jerusalem following the murder of Conrad, also agreed to this treaty.

Many of the crusaders took advantage of the truce to travel to Jerusalem to visit the Holy Sepulcher, the object of their pilgrimage. For security reasons Richard himself did not go, but he sent his friend Hubert Walter, bishop of Salisbury, as his representative. Instead, Richard prepared to depart for home, hoping to return to the East after the truce ended.

That same September and into October, many crusaders sailed for home. At the end of September, Richard sent his wife Berengaria, his sister Joanna, and their households on ahead of him. He took ship ten days later, but already the winter storms were coming on. Although Berengaria and Joanna reached Italy safely, Richard's ship was forced ashore by bad weather in the Ionian islands. He decided to continue his journey across central Europe by land.

Some contemporary accounts state that Richard knew he had enemies in the area and that he duly disguised himself as an ordinary knight. But on reaching Vienna around Christmas 1192 he was recognized and became a prisoner of Duke Leopold V of Austria, who had not forgotten Richard's refusal to give him a share in the booty of Acre. He also blamed Richard for capturing his relatives, the "emperor" Isaac of Cyprus and his wife, and for the murder of Marquis Conrad. Leopold sold Richard to the emperor Henry VI, a political rival to Richard in Europe, and for some months the king's whereabouts were unknown. Then, in spring 1193, he was located near Worms in Germany by two English envoys (not, as legend states, by a minstrel; see box), who received an exorbitant ransom demand of 100,000 marks, roughly 65,000 lbs (29,500kg) of pure silver. The emperor had tried to set a sum that could not be paid, but the English raised it and in February 1194 Richard was freed (see sidebar).

It is a tribute to the strong administration bequeathed by his father, King Henry II, that Richard I's government in England continued to operate throughout his long absence and his authority was never

MINSTRELS

According to legend, King Richard I was discovered in an Austrian prison by a minstrel called Blondel. The story is not true, but it does illustrate Richard's interest in singing and the importance in this period of the minstrel (called a *troubadour* in southern France, a *trouvère* in northern France, and a *minnesinger* or *minnesänger* in Germany). Most rulers and prominent nobles had their own court minstrels (minstrel itself is from the Latin *ministerialis*, "attendant"), and also composed their own songs. Richard's only surviving song complains about the length of his captivity and Philip II's invasion of his lands. Most familiar to us are the wandering minstrels who traveled from court to court. Friedrich von Hausen, who died on the Third Crusade, wrote a song about those who vowed to go on crusade but did not go:

"They think that they've avoided death
Who cheat God of their journey.
But it is my belief
That they are acting against their own interests.
Whoever takes the cross and does not set out,
Will see God appear to him at last
When to him the door [of Heaven] is closed,
Which He opens to His chosen ones."

A 14th-century English citole, an instrument popular with troubadours and similar to a lute. This example was later converted into a violin.

in real danger, despite his brother John's plotting. However, King Philip II of France had invaded Richard's lands in Normandy, and a campaign to recover them occupied the rest of Richard's reign until his death in 1199. He was never to return to the East (see page 100).

After the departure of the crusaders, Saladin intended to go on pilgrimage to Mecca, but then had to postpone his plans because of the need to rebuild Jerusalem and to keep an eye on the Franks of the East. However, in February 1193 he fell mortally ill and on 4th March 1193 he died. His sons succeeded him in Aleppo, Damascus, and Cairo, but between 1193 and 1202 Saladin's brother al-Adil overthrew them and seized power himself (see page 145).

As for the emperor Henry VI, he had not participated in the Third Crusade but in 1195 he began planning a new venture to fulfill the ambitions of his father, Frederick I Barbarossa (see pages 84–85). He pressured the Byzantine emperor Alexius III, brother and successor of Isaac II Angelus, into contributing mercenary troops that were paid for by a tax that made Alexius highly unpopular—but his regime was saved by the death of Henry on 28th September 1197, before he could set out on crusade. Fellow German crusaders, though, did reach the East where they recaptured Beirut and Sidon.

RANSOM

It was a convention of warfare at the time of the Third Crusade that important prisoners would be held until their relatives or vassals paid for their release—the size of any ransom being set to reflect the importance of the prisoner. Money had to be raised by selling property, raising loans, or taxing tenants. Large ransoms were often paid in instalments, with the prisoner being released after the first payment provided he left hostages as a guarantee. This happened when Richard I was released from captivity by Henry VI in 1194. His hostages included two of his nephews and his brother-in-law, as well as the archbishop of Coutances and the bishop of Bath. In November 1195 Henry VI let Richard off the small balance of his ransom and freed the hostages.

THE FOURTH CRUSADE

A TRAGIC MISFIRE

THOMAS F. MADDEN

A NEW POPE, A NEW CRUSADE

A 13th-century fresco of Pope Innocent III in the Sacro Speco monastery at Subiaco near Rome. One of the strongest and most effective of medieval popes, he intervened throughout Europe to assert papal authority. Innocent's most cherished goal was the restoration of Jerusalem and the True Cross to Christendom.

The failure of the Third Crusade to recapture Jerusalem and recover the relic of the True Cross (see Chapter Four) was a bitter disappointment to European Christians. However, in 1198 a young and energetic pope was elected, and almost immediately he called a new crusade. Pope Innocent III (1198–1216) was convinced that all of Christendom would need to be mobilized for the effort and that those who could not fight should instead fast and pray. The pope also ordered collections for the sake of the crusade to be taken up in every church, and even the clergy and monasteries were instructed to donate a portion of their income. He intended his new crusade to overshadow all others—to succeed where they had failed.

Two papal legates were appointed to make the crusade a reality. Cardinal Peter Capuano was sent to France to broker peace between King Richard I ("the Lionheart") of England and King Philip II Augustus of France. The task was far from easy: Richard had cut short his involvement in the Third Crusade in part because of Philip's attacks on his dynastic lands in France (see page 95). Now the pope wanted a truce struck despite the fact that Philip still held some of those territories. Richard was so furious when he heard the pope's request that the cardinal fled, fearing the king would carry out his threat to castrate him. In time, though, Richard and Philip agreed to the pope's request and signed a five-year truce. However, in spring 1199 hopes for a new crusade were dealt a blow when Richard died from a crossbow wound during the siege of a castle in France (see box).

The other crusade legate, Cardinal Soffredo, was sent to Venice, which indicated that Innocent expected his crusade to follow the example of the previous one and sail directly to the East rather than make the long and dangerous march overland. A large crusade would need a large fleet and the Venetians could supply one. The city's elderly but still capable leader, Doge Enrico Dandolo, suggested that his people might be willing to help—provided that an army ever materialized.

That, indeed, was the problem. Richard I's death had cast a long shadow over the plan. To dispel it, the pope sent preachers, such as the German abbot Martin of Pairis (see sidebar) across Europe to stir up the faithful.

THE DEATH OF THE LIONHEART

King Richard I (1189–99), the great champion of the Third Crusade, made no secret of his desire to return to the East, but whether or not he would have joined the next crusade we shall never know. Shortly after making his truce with King Philip II Augustus of France (see main text), Richard made his way to Chalus-Chabrol in the Limousin region, where he besieged a castle held by the rebellious viscount of Limoges. On 26th March 1199, Richard came out of his tent to survey the situation and noticed a defender using a frying pan for a shield, who would occasionally pop his head up to fire off a crossbow shot. Richard applauded the bravery of the man, who responded by hitting him in the left shoulder. Not wishing to alarm his men, Richard ignored the wound and returned to his tent. A surgeon removed the bolt, but the wound became gangrenous and within two weeks the Lionheart was dead. It was a blow to the morale of the burgeoning crusade, as expressed by Gaucelm Faidit in the only surviving lament (*planh*) by a troubadour for his patron:

"Saracens, Turks, Pagans, and Persians,
Who dreaded you more than any man born of woman
Will so greatly increase their arrogant attitude
That the Holy Sepulcher will [only] be conquered much later.
But God wills it; for, if he had not wanted this,
And if you, Lord, had lived, without fail
They would have had to flee Syria.
Henceforth there is no hope that they will go there,
Kings and princes who might know how to recover it!"

Their efforts successfully spread pious zeal among commoners and nobility alike. One of those who answered the pope's call was the powerful Count Thibaut (Theobald) of Champagne, whose brother Henry had ruled the kingdom of Jerusalem until 1197 (see page 92). On 28th November 1199, Theobald hosted a tournament at his castle at Ecry-sur-Aisne near Rheims. During the knightly revelry, he announced that he would henceforth place his weapons in the service of the Lord. He was joined immediately by his cousin, Count Louis of Blois, and the pledge of these two influential men fired the enthusiasm of the nobility. In February 1200 the illustrious Count Baldwin of Flanders took the cross, together with his wife, Marie, Theobald's sister. The three most powerful lords in France, all still in their twenties, were eager to finish the work of the Lionheart in the East. At last the crusade was coming to life.

A CRUSADE SERMON

Abbot Martin of the Cistercian abbey of Pairis in Alsace not only preached the Fourth Crusade at the behest of the pope, but joined it as well. One of his fellow monks, Gunther, heard Martin's sermon and later wrote it down:

"Today Christ addresses you in his words through my mouth. It is he who grieves before you over his wounds. Christ has been expelled from his holy place—his seat of power. He has been exiled from that city which he consecrated to himself with his own blood. Oh, the pain!...The Holy Land, which Christ impressed with his footprints, in which he cured the lame, caused the blind to see, cleansed lepers, raised the dead—that land, I say—has been given over into the hands of the impious. Its churches have been destroyed, its shrine polluted, its royal throne and dignity transferred to the gentiles. That most sacred and venerable Cross of wood, which was drenched with the blood of Christ, is locked and hidden away by persons to whom the word of the Cross is foolishness, so that no Christian might know what was done with it or where to look for it. Virtually all of our people who used to inhabit that frontier have been eliminated, either by the enemy's sword or an already prolonged captivity.

"And so now, true warriors, hasten to help Christ. Enlist in his Christian army. Rush to join the happy ranks. Today I commit you to the cause of Christ. I give him into your hands, so to speak, so that you might labor to restore him to his patrimony, from which he has been so unmercifully expelled."

VENICE JOINS THE CRUSADE

THE SEEDS OF RUIN

No one could see it at the time, but the contract that was sealed with the Venetians would have disastrous consequences. By greatly overestimating the size of their forces, the crusade envoys had ordered a fleet that they simply could not afford. This miscalculation drove all subsequent events in the crusade. The crucial portion of the treaty states:

"And so the aforesaid envoys requested that we [the doge] provide for you [the Frankish crusaders] vessels to transport 4,500 well-armed knights and as many horses, and 9,000 squires…and 20,000 infantry well armed, with provisions for up to one year, which we promised to give to them.

"Provisions for each and every man will be thus: for each man six sextaria [110 gallons/500 liters] of bread, flour, grain, and legumes and a half amphora [75 gallons/340 liters] of wine. For each horse three modia [35 cubic feet/1 cubic meter] [of grain] according to the measure of Venice, and of water there will be sufficient amounts. To transport the aforesaid horses we will provide enough horse transport galleys so that they will be sufficiently comfortable. Also we will provide enough vessels to transport the men according to our discretion and that of our barons in good faith.

"And this aforesaid fleet will be handed over on the next feast of the holy apostles Peter and Paul [29th June 1202] for the honor of God and St. Mark the Evangelist and Christendom for up to one year…."

At a meeting at Soissons in Champagne in early 1200, the barons of the crusade agreed to follow a strategy proposed earlier by Richard I of England (see page 93). The crusaders would sail directly to Egypt, the source of Muslim power in the region: only once Egypt was in Christian hands, they believed, could Jerusalem be made permanently safe. Because none of the barons possessed a fleet it would be necessary to hire vessels. Counts Theobald of Champagne, Louis of Blois, and Baldwin of Flanders each appointed two men and gave them full powers to make contracts in their names with whatever port seemed best. One of these men was Geoffrey of Villehardouin, the marshal of Champagne, whose memoirs provide one of the most valuable sources for the crusade.

The envoys selected Venice because it was a great maritime city and had long experience trading in the East. Also, perhaps, there was the fact that the Venetians had already expressed to the pope an interest in joining the enterprise (see page 100). In Venice the six men were welcomed personally by Doge Enrico Dandolo, a man who made up for his complete blindness and extreme old age—he was probably in his nineties—with extraordinary intelligence and energy (see box).

The envoys told the doge about the great crusade that was forming across Europe and they begged the Venetians to help avenge the

injuries of Christ. After negotiations, the Republic of Venice agreed to provide provisions and transport—see sidebar—for one year for 33,500 knights, squires, and footsoldiers in return for 85,000 marks of Cologne, roughly 55,000 lbs (25,000kg) of pure silver. The Venetians further promised to supply fifty manned war galleys at no cost, provided that they received an equal share of the booty. The fleet would be ready to sail on 29th June 1202. The envoys enthusiastically signed the treaty and the pope ratified it.

The fleet that the crusaders had ordered was one of the largest assembled in the period and the citizens of Venice put enormous resources into the effort—they purchased thousands of tons of provisions, suspended all overseas trade, and built and fitted out war vessels at an amazing rate. Venice met its obligations to the letter; unfortunately, the northern crusaders did not do the same.

Opposite: *The Bacino San Marco in Venice, showing a highly stylized representation of the doge's church of San Marco, visible to the top left with the four bronze horses that Enrico Dandolo would acquire in Constantinople after the conquest. To the right is the ducal palace. Venetian wealth was acquired through trade and commerce at a time when agricultural feudalism dominated. From a French manuscript of* The Travels of Marco Polo, *ca. 1399.*

DOGE DANDOLO: HERO OR VILLAIN?

Few participants in the Fourth Crusade are as controversial as Doge Enrico Dandolo. A Byzantine senator, Nicetas Choniates, describes him as "a sly cheat…madly thirsting after glory as no other," who diverted the crusade for his own evil ends. For a long time historians tended to accept this judgment, casting Dandolo as a beguiling trickster with no religion save greed. However, modern research has caused historians to revise that view. To begin with, Choniates never met Dandolo and his description is based on little more than conjecture, doubtless colored by his experience of seeing his beloved city of Constantinople sacked (and his own palace destroyed); and most Byzantines were suspicious of Catholics and loathed Italians in general and Venetians in particular.

Those who did know the doge spoke very differently. Geoffrey of Villehardouin described him as "very wise, brave, and vigorous," while Robert of Clari judged him "most worthy" and "wise." The Cistercian abbot Martin of Pairis (see page 101) called Dandolo "perceptive of mind;" one who "compensated for physical blindness with a lively intellect…." The powerful baron Hugh of St. Pol praised the doge, describing him as "prudent, discreet, and skilled in hard decision-making." New research has also shown that Dandolo came from a family known for its piety and commitment to crusading. There is no reason, therefore, to accept Choniates description of the doge's character and motives.

Emperor Alexius IV Angelus asks Doge Enrico Dandolo for help to free his father, Isaac II. Andrea Vicentino's painting of 1578 shows the doge as a relatively young man.

BROKEN PROMISES

The crusade sailed out of Venice in early October 1202, arriving at Zara in late November. The fleet spent the winter there and in spring 1203 they sailed via Dyrrachium (modern-day Durrës) to Corfu, where they remained for several weeks. In May the crusaders rounded Cape Malea and entered the Aegean Sea, heading toward the Dardanelles. They finally cast anchor before Constantinople in late June 1203.

One of the crusade leaders, Theobald of Champagne, died shortly after the treaty with Venice was signed in 1201. Nevertheless, enthusiasm for the crusade remained high in France and Germany. The crusade barons successfully recruited a commander-in-chief for the enterprise in the shape of the powerful Italian magnate Marquis Boniface of Montferrat, whose family had close connections with the crusader states and the Byzantine empire.

In June 1202 crusaders began arriving in Venice and setting up camp on the Lido—at the time a largely uninhabited sand bar not far from the city. Exactly as promised by the treaty, on 29th June the Venetians had everything in readiness. Hundreds of manned vessels stood at anchor prepared for departure and tons of provisions were dockside. However, on the Lido only about 11,000 crusaders had arrived—fewer than a third of the projected number. The gap between the size of the army and the size of the fleet spelled trouble.

Hoping for late arrivals, the crusaders waited a month. A few more troops came, but not many. By the end of July Doge Dandolo could delay no longer. Venice was no place to contain a large feudal army and he insisted that the crusaders pay what they owed so that the fleet could get underway. Yet with only a third of the expected forces, even when the crusaders gave over all the money they had they were still short by 34,000 marks—almost nine tons of pure silver. They simply could not afford the fleet they had ordered. The situation grew increasingly tense, with the crusaders resentful at having to pay for ships and provisions that they did not need while the Venetians were equally upset because the broken promises of the crusaders had cost them dearly in terms of effort and resources.

Dandolo diffused the tension by crafting a compromise. Zara (modern Zadar) on the Dalmatian coast had years earlier rebelled against Venice. If the crusaders would help the Venetians to restore the city to obedience, the people of Venice would loan the crusaders 34,000 marks until they could acquire it in booty from the conquest of Egypt. Since it was already too late in the year to sail to Egypt, the crusaders would be able to spend the winter at Zara before departing the following spring.

There was only one problem with this idea: Zara was under the protection of King Emeric of Hungary, who had taken the crusader vow himself some years earlier. While Emeric had no intention of joining this particular crusade, he insisted that his lands enjoyed church protection so long as he wore the cross. The pope agreed.

However, the crusaders only had the Zara option, which offered both a loan and a place to spend the winter. The alternative was the dissolution of the crusade. The barons accepted the compromise.

The papal legate, Cardinal Peter Capuano who had joined the crusade at Venice in late July, was placed in a dilemma. He was aware that Zara was under papal protection, but he also knew that unless he let the crusaders proceed the compromise would collapse and with it the crusade—it called for a little subterfuge. When several churchmen asked him what they should do, Capuano ordered them to remain with the crusade and only when the army was safely at Zara should they speak out against the plan. By then the Venetians would no longer be in a position to refuse the crusaders anything.

Only Dandolo and Capuano knew that the pope had forbidden an attack on Zara, and the legate's silence must have raised the doge's suspicions. Dandolo would not allow any more broken promises and he informed Capuano that he would be permitted to accompany the crusade only if he renounced his legatine authority. Unwilling to do that, and equally unwilling to forbid the attack on Zara while the fleet was still being prepared, Capuano left for Rome.

In September 1202 the aged and blind Dandolo took the cross himself, vowing to lead the Venetians on their holy mission. The magnificent fleet, consisting of approximately fifty large transport ships, 100 horse transport galleys, and sixty war galleys, sailed out of the Venetian lagoon in early October. At last the crusade was underway.

THE FALSE TREATY WITH EGYPT

It was a great disappointment to the Christians of the Holy Land that the crusade never arrived to help them. Because Venetians were concerned with commerce, which was generally distrusted at the time, they were in some quarters suspected of treachery. A late chronicle written in the crusader kingdom suggested the Venetians had previously made a treaty with the sultan of Egypt to divert the crusade away from his lands. However, no contemporary source mentioned such a treaty and in 1877 the French scholar Gabriel Hanotaux demonstrated conclusively that it simply did not exist. Although historians have long ago rejected it, many popular authors continue to include the fictitious "false treaty" in their histories of the Fourth Crusade.

Venice was a city of merchants. Its wealth derived from a lucrative trade with numerous cities in the eastern Mediterranean and this affluence resulted in opulent buildings and decoration. This late 16th-century Flemish view shows St. Mark's square and the two columns representing the city's patron saints, Theodore and Mark (symbolized by the lion).

THE CONQUEST OF ZARA

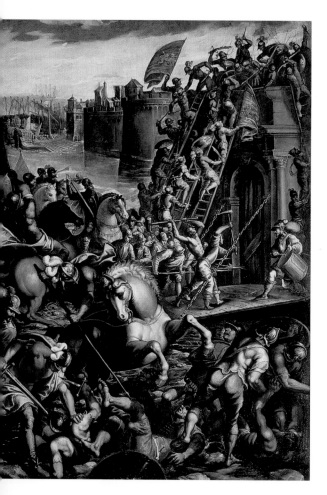

Doge Enrico Dandolo and his crusaders storming the city of Zara in 1202, a painting by Andrea Vicentino (1542–1617). Prior to the assault, the inhabitants had draped crosses on the walls to signify that theirs was a Christian city, protected by the pope—but it made no difference to the attackers. Within a week the crusaders had stormed Zara and helped themselves to anything of value. Although the Franks were remorseful, the Venetians were not and continued to believe that they had acted within their rights.

On 11th November 1202 the crusaders landed at Zara on the Adriatic and quickly made camp. The citizens saw the large army and its siege engines and knew that resistance was impossible, so they promptly sent out a delegation offering to surrender the city if their lives were spared. This was agreeable to Dandolo, who asked the delegates to remain in his tent while he went to confer with the barons.

In Dandolo's absence, Simon de Montfort the Elder (1160–1218), the leader of a small faction of crusaders opposed to the detour to Zara, informed the Zarans that the crusade leaders had a letter from Pope Innocent III threatening to excommunicate anyone who raised a sword against Zara. Simon insisted that if the citizens could defend themselves against the Venetians they would be safe from the Frankish (non-Venetian) crusaders, who would not disobey the pope. The delegates thanked Simon and returned to their city. When Dandolo and the crusader barons returned they were outraged by these actions. A peaceful surrender had been thwarted.

The pope's stern letter forced the crusade's leaders to choose between excommunication, for attacking a city under church protection, and the end of the crusade. Believing that God could not desire the latter, most chose to keep their word to the Venetians as a matter of honor. Simon and his men withdrew from the army, but the majority of the crusaders attacked Zara, capturing it on 24th November—as a result, the Fourth Crusade was excommunicated.

The Frankish leaders sent a delegation to Innocent III, begging forgiveness. He granted them the absolution they sought, but reaffirmed the excommunication of the Venetians. The pope was now convinced that the Venetians had deliberately taken over the crusade for their own ends. In a letter to the crusade leaders he said that once the Franks had been delivered to the Holy Land, they should have nothing more to do with the Venetians.

The crusade had other problems too, with huge debts, no money, and a shortage of provisions. According to the contract (see page 103), Venice supplied each man with enough to sustain him at low activity levels for about nine months. Since they had begun eating their provisions in late June 1202 the crusaders would have been out of food by late March 1203, when the fleet was again ready to sail from Zara. There were insufficient resources to keep the army and fleet together, let alone support it on its mission to fight in Egypt.

It was at this moment that a group of envoys arrived at Zara led by a Byzantine prince, Alexius Angelus, who had recently fled to the

West. His father, the emperor Isaac II Angelus, had been blinded and deposed by his own brother, Alexius III, in 1195. The young man asserted that he, not his usurping uncle, was the rightful emperor of Constantinople. If the crusaders would help him to his throne he would provide them with food, pay them 200,000 silver marks, join their crusade with 10,000 soldiers, place a permanent garrison in the Holy Land, and restore the obedience of the Greek church to Rome. For the crusaders this offer was extremely attractive. But it would, of course, necessitate a further diversion of the troubled crusade.

These mosaics in the basilica of St. John the Evangelist in Ravenna, Italy, depict the conquest of Zara (left) and a Venetian galley with a seaman blowing a horn (above). They are the only surviving artistic representations of the Fourth Crusade from the Middle Ages. The crusade is depicted in the mosaics from a decidedly Venetian point of view, closely following the story told by the Venetian Martino da Canal in the 13th century.

VENICE AND THE PAPACY

The excommunication of Venice on the Fourth Crusade marked the end of an exceptionally close relationship with the papacy. Venetians did most of their business in the East, but remained devoted to the church of Rome, supporting it during various disputes. In 1077, Pope Gregory VII spoke of the "uniquely close relationship" between Venice and Rome, and in 1177 the republic helped to end a struggle between the pope and the German emperor.

Venetians were also strong supporters of the crusades—indeed, no state in Europe so often and so vigorously took up the cross. Venice's fleet was the largest single contribution to the First Crusade, and in 1122 the doge in person led thousands of Venetians to the Holy Land, where they crushed the Fatimid navy and helped to conquer Tyre. That Innocent III should turn to Venice for help with the Fourth Crusade was unsurprising, but circumstances outside anyone's control made him regret that choice.

AN ERRAND OF MERCY

There was considerable debate among the crusaders concerning the offer made by Alexius Angelus. The majority of the troops wanted no more detours or delays. They had made vows to fight for Christ, not a Byzantine pretender. However, the crusade leaders favored helping the young man. They saw that with only a few months left on the fleet's lease, no food, and crushing debt, the crusade simply could not survive without replenishing its resources. It would have made little sense to transport an impoverished army directly to the East. They also saw the detour to Constantinople as an errand of mercy to free the Byzantine people from the oppression of a tyrant. Alexius Angelus assured them that his uncle, the emperor, was so hated in the city that he would be overthrown as soon as the crusaders arrived with the rightful heir.

The crusade leaders accepted, informing the pope shortly afterward: "lacking all foodstuffs and supplies, we appeared to be bearing a burden to the Holy Land…rather than bringing some sort of aid; nor did we believe that, given such extreme poverty, we could effectively land in the territory of the Saracens." When the rank-and-file soldiers learned of the leaders' action, many of them abandoned the crusade, making their own way to the East to fulfill their vows. Only

Crusaders arriving at the land and sea walls of Constantinople, from a Venetian manuscript (ca. 1330) of La Conquête de Constantinople *by Geoffrey of Villehardouin, who took part in the Fourth Crusade. When the Venetian force's entry into the city was pushed back by the imperial bodyguard, they set fire to a number of buildings and burned a large section of an affluent suburb. It was a harbinger of worse destruction to come.*

by swearing that the stop in Constantinople would be brief were the leaders able to win the grudging acceptance of the other crusaders.

The crusade left Zara in April 1203, made its way through the Aegean and arrived at Constantinople in late June. Mismanagement had reduced Byzantium's once proud navy to a few worm-eaten vessels incapable of challenging the enormous crusade fleet. In several dramatic displays, the crusaders let the people of Constantinople know that they came as friends, having brought them their rightful lord. The Byzantines responded with insults, rocks, and bare backsides. They wanted nothing to do with the Westerners' pretender.

Reluctantly, the crusaders at last accepted that they would have to attack. The massive city had enormous fortifications that no enemy had ever breached before and a garrison three times the size of the crusader force. Nevertheless, on 17th July the crusaders attacked the northeastern area of the city, the Franks assaulting the land wall and the Venetians the seawall. After fierce fighting the Venetians captured a portion of the wall and entered a short distance before being pushed back by the élite imperial bodyguard.

Discontent at Alexius III's ineffectiveness made him fearful of a coup and he fled. His brother, Isaac II Angelus, was freed and restored to the throne. He ordered the gates to be opened so that Prince Alexius could enter. The crusaders were dutifully acclaimed as heroes and within days the young man was crowned co-emperor Alexius IV.

THE MAJESTY OF CONSTANTINOPLE

Few of the Frankish crusaders had any experience of a city like Constantinople. The ten largest cities of western Europe could have fitted easily within its walls. The enormous fortifications, massive churches, and magnificent palaces were an awe-inspiring sight. Some of the crusaders remembered their first impressions of the great city and have left a record. Geoffrey de Villehardouin, the marshal of Champagne, wrote: "Those who had never before seen Constantinople looked upon it very earnestly, for they never thought there could be in all the world so rich a city; and they marked the high walls and strong towers that enclosed it round about, and the rich palaces, and mighty churches—of which there were so many that no one would have believed it who had not seen it with his eyes—and the height and the length of that city which above all others was sovereign." The poor knight Robert of Clari was no less impressed: "It was reckoned that there were in the city a good thirty thousand priests, both monks and others. Now about the rest of the Greeks, high and low, rich and poor, about the size of the city, about the palaces and the other marvels that are there, we shall leave off telling you. For no man on earth, however long he might have lived in the city, could number them or recount them to you. And if anyone should recount to you the hundredth part of the richness and the beauty and the nobility that was found in the abbeys and in the churches and in the palaces and in the city, it would seem like a lie and you would not believe it."

RELATIONS SOUR

CONSTANTINOPLE: A TOURISTS' VIEW

Before moving to Galata, the men of the Fourth Crusade had the opportunity to tour Constantinople. Escorted by Greek guides, they were shown exotic wonders and told tall tales. Here are just a few of the "marvels" recorded by the knight Robert of Clari:

"Now there was elsewhere in the city a gate which was called the Golden Mantle. On this gate there was a golden globe which was made by such enchantment that the Greeks said as long as it was there no thunderbolt would fall in the city.... There was an open place … called the Games of the Emperor. … Around this place there were fully thirty rows of seats or forty, on which the Greeks used to mount to watch the games… Along this open place there was a wall which was a good fifteen feet [4.6m] high and ten feet [3m] wide. Upon this wall there were figures of men and women, and of horses and oxen and camels and bears and lions and many other kinds of animals, all made of copper, and all so well made and formed so naturally that there is no master workman in heathendom or Christendom so skillful as to be able to make figures as good as these. And formerly they used to play by enchantment, but they do not play any longer."

The size and magnificence of Constantinople was beyond the conception of most western Europeans. This illustration from the Luttrell Psalter of ca. 1340 depicts Constantinople as an English walled city, with church—complete with weathercock—in the center, thatched houses, inns, and alehouses. At each end is a towered gateway and portcullis. On the left, musicians and garlanded dancers emerge from the gates, watched from the battlements by a lady and four men.

All seemed to be going well as the newly crowned emperor Alexius IV began fulfilling his promises to the crusaders. He ordered the patriarch of Constantinople to submit to the authority of the pope in Rome and he paid the crusaders half of the 200,000 marks he had promised. This in turn allowed the crusaders to pay their debt to the Venetians and even have a little money left over. But Alexius began to experience difficulty in coming up with the other half. Among the ordinary people of Constantinople anti-Western hatred was already commonplace, and the emperor's attempts to raise the large sum of money to pay the crusaders only inflamed that hatred and made him increasingly unpopular.

To give himself sufficient time to raise the additional funds and help safeguard against a palace coup, Alexius asked the crusaders to spend the winter at Constantinople. To compensate them for the lost time, the emperor agreed to extend the lease on the Venetian fleet for an additional year at his own expense.

Reluctantly, the crusaders agreed to stay. The emperor moved them out of the main city to the suburb of Galata just across the harbor. However, as the months passed, Alexius realized that further payments to the crusaders would make him so hated by his own people that he would certainly be overthrown. The anti-Western feeling was now at a fever pitch, particularly after a devastating fire set by Westerners in the main city in the summer of 1203 (see box).

THE GREAT FIRE

On 19th August 1203 Flemish, Pisan, and Venetian renegades crossed the Golden Horn and set fire to a mosque. A strong wind whipped the blaze into a massively destructive fire that cut a wide path across the great city's most populated and opulent areas, making thousands homeless and inflicting staggering material losses. Nicetas Choniates, whose own palace was destroyed in the inferno, wrote that "while in the past many conflagrations had taken place in the City…the fires ignited at this time proved all the others to be but sparks." Looking at it from across the harbor, the crusade leaders were horrified. Geoffrey de Villehardouin recorded that they were "extremely grieved and filled with pity, seeing the great churches and the rich palaces melting and collapsing, the great streets filled with merchandise burning in the flames, but they could do nothing."

A view of Constantinople, from an Ottoman manuscript of 1537.

Realizing that they would never be paid their due, the crusaders formally defied the emperor and began pillaging his lands to "pay ourselves," as Robert of Clari put it. With no support either from his own people or the crusaders, in January 1204 Alexius was overthrown, imprisoned, and killed by a palace functionary, who took the crown himself as Alexius V Mourtzouphlus.

THE SACK OF CONSTANTINOPLE

"SACRED SACRILEGE"

Constantinople suffered the loss of countless relics during the sack of 1204. Most writers either ignored the theft or explained it away. One exception is the account of the actions of Abbot Martin of Pairis (see page 101) during the sack, as recorded by Gunther, a monk in Martin's abbey:

"While the victors were rapidly plundering the conquered city, which they had made their own by right of battle, Abbot Martin began to think about his own booty and, lest he remain empty-handed while everyone else got rich, he resolved to use his own consecrated hands for pillage. But because he thought it improper to touch secular spoils with those same hands, he began to plan how he might scrape together for himself some portion of those relics of the saints, which he knew to be in great quantity there.... Martin, thinking it improper to commit sacrilege except in a holy cause, sought out a more remote spot, where the very sanctity of the place seemed to promise that it was possible to find there those objects he so greatly desired. [Martin then threatened an old priest, who showed him a chest filled with relics.] On seeing it, the abbot hurriedly and greedily thrust in both hands, and, as he was girded for action, both he and the chaplain filled the folds of their habits with sacred sacrilege."

Right: *The conquest of Constantinople; a mosaic in the basilica of St. John the Evangelist, Ravenna, Italy. Feelings were running high on either side by the time hostilities erupted. The crusaders were disgusted with the Byzantines, who they believed had failed to keep their promises and had murdered their rightful lord. Nicetas Choniates tells of the bands of Greek captives whose hands were bound before they were led out of the city.*
Opposite: *A crusader wields a spear; a mosaic in the basilica of St. John the Evangelist, Ravenna.*

The death of Alexius IV put the crusaders in a difficult situation. In addition to their food and money problems they now had no fleet (the lease having long since expired) and were in hostile land. In short, they could not go forward, backward, or stay where they were.

The knights were informed by their clergy that the sins of the Greeks against the army of Christ and His Church had made them a legitimate target of a crusade. Although this ruling was at variance with the pope's instructions, the clergy saw no other option. The rank-and-file crusaders were told that they would not be leaving for the Holy Land in the spring. Their mission was now at Byzantium.

On 9th April 1204 the crusaders launched a seaborne attack on the harbor walls, which was repulsed. They tried again on 12th April, this time with more success. The fall of the city was the direct result of the actions of one man. During the assault a small group of men managed to land on the shore below the seawalls and dig out a small hole in a walled-up gate. Despite the presence of a large number of Greek soldiers on the other side, one of the men, a priest named Aleaumes of Clari, demanded to squeeze through the hole and be

the first to enter the city. His brother, the chronicler Robert of Clari, tried to stop him but he wriggled through, drew his sword and ran, roaring, toward the Greeks—who panicked and fled, triggering a chain reaction of abandonment across the city's fortifications. Soon the city's defenses had collapsed utterly.

That night, Alexius V Mourtzouphlus did his best to convince his people to fight. But the Greeks could not accept the idea of warfare inside the walls of the great city. They preferred to offer the crown to the chief of the crusaders, Boniface of Montferrat. Mourtzouphlus fled and on the morning of 13th April 1204 the city was formally offered to Boniface, He wanted nothing more than to accept it, but he could not, because in March the crusade leaders had agreed to elect a new emperor after the city had been taken and secured. The Byzantines, it seems, had miscalculated. What they had read as a coup by the crusaders was, in fact, an outright war of conquest.

Presented with one of the richest cities in the world, now completely defenseless, the crusaders embarked upon three days of looting and destruction. By medieval standards, it was acceptable to sack a city that had resisted capture. The crusaders had previously sworn to leave Byzantine churches, monasteries, and women unmolested, but very few of them kept their oaths.

The sack of Constantinople, a city crammed with ancient treasures and holy relics, was one of the most destructive and profitable in history. In time, a feeling of betrayal would manifest itself among the Greeks, thus slamming shut a door between the Catholic west and the Orthodox east that still remains closed today.

THE DECLINE OF CONSTANTINOPLE

Beautiful, wealthy, and populous, Constantinople was by far the greatest city in Christendom. It is ironic that its ruin was caused by an army of Christians who had set out to save it. The city endured great physical damage at the hands of the crusaders. Three fires had raged across one-sixth of the city's area and destroyed approximately one in three of its dwellings. During the chaos of the sack, great works of ancient art were destroyed or melted down for coin. The Byzantine senator Nicetas Choniates lamented, "O City, formerly enthroned on high, striding far and wide, magnificent in comeliness and more becoming in stature; now your luxurious garments and elegant royal veils are rent and torn; your flashing eye has grown dark and you are like an aged furnace-woman all covered with soot."

In the decades that followed the decline of the city continued. The Latin emperors (see pages 114–115) had no funds to repair or maintain the city's amenities, which fell into disuse and decay. In 1203 the population of Constantinople stood at more than 500,000; when the Byzantines reclaimed the city in 1261 there were only about 35,000 inhabitants left.

THE FOUNDING OF THE LATIN EMPIRE

The conquest of Constantinople shattered the Byzantine empire, which the crusades had originally been designed to save. Imperial claimants quickly arose in various parts of Greece and Asia Minor, carving out for themselves their own governments-in-exile.

The crusaders in Constantinople fashioned themselves as heirs of the empire, having seized control of its capital city. The crusade leaders had agreed in March 1204 that a committee of Venetians and Franks would elect a new emperor after the city's fall. In addition, the rank-and-file crusaders agreed to remain to defend the new Latin empire for one year in order to fulfill their crusade vows.

Contentiously, the electoral committee passed over the official leader of the crusade, Marquis Boniface of Montferrat, in favor of Count Baldwin of Flanders. In May 1204 the count was crowned emperor in the church of Hagia Sophia (see box). Constantinople and the empire were then divided up, with one-quarter (two-eighths) going directly to the emperor, three-eighths to the Franks, and three-eighths to the Venetians (who also bought the island of Crete from Boniface). The final division, made on 1st October, was a paper exercise because the territories still had to be conquered. The crusaders then set out in all directions to seize Greek lands.

The departure of most of the crusade's forces left Constantinople in a vulnerable position that did not go unnoticed by its enemies.

AN IMPERIAL CORONATION

On 16th May 1204 Baldwin of Flanders was crowned the first emperor of the Latin empire of Constantinople. The ceremony in Hagia Sophia, the great church built by the emperor Justinian in the sixth century (see illustration), was a mixture of both western and eastern practices that combined the magnificent pomp and splendor of a traditional Byzantine coronation with Latin rites. Robert of Clari, who was in attendance, described the spectacle:

"When the emperor was come before the altar, he knelt down…then all the bishops went and took hold of the crown all together and blessed it and made the sign of the cross on it and put it on his head. And then to serve as a clasp they hung about his neck a very rich jewel which the emperor Manuel had once bought for 62,000 marks. When they had crowned him, they seated him on a high throne, and he was there while the mass was sung, and he held in one hand his scepter and in the other hand a golden globe with a cross on it. And the jewels which he was wearing were worth more than the treasure of a rich king would make. When the mass was heard, they brought him a white horse on which he mounted. Then the barons took him back to his palace of Boukoleon and seated him on the throne of [the Roman emperor] Constantine [the Great]."

Ioannitsa, king of the Vlachs and Bulgarians, made an alliance with Byzantine lords in Thrace aimed at overthrowing the crusaders. After Ioannitsa captured Adrianople (present-day Edirne), Emperor Baldwin I rode out with Hugh of St. Pol and about 140 other knights to take it back. But in a rout of the Westerners, Hugh was killed and Baldwin taken prisoner and later killed. Baldwin's brother Henry was named regent and he later took the imperial crown.

In April 1205 the Fourth Crusade finally ended and most of the ordinary crusaders went home, leaving the leaders with a mere skeleton force to hold on to Constantinople. The following month Doge Enrico Dandolo died and was buried in Hagia Sophia.

Pope Innocent III had opposed the diversion of the crusade to Constantinople, but he accepted its conquest in the hope that the Latin empire would bring together eastern and western Christians against a common Muslim foe. But it was not to be, because the creation of the Latin empire on the ruins of the Byzantine world only drove Greeks and Latins further apart. Always teetering on the brink of destruction, the new empire merely siphoned off European crusade energy that would otherwise have been used in the Holy Land.

Above: *The great domed church of Hagia Sophia (Holy Wisdom) was designed by its architects, Isidorus of Miletus and Anthemius of Tralles, to allow a mystical quality of light to illuminate its interior. The church was built from 532 to 537 by the Byzantine emperor Justinian (527–65) on the site of a church that had twice burnt down. The former seat of the patriarch of Constantinople, the Hagia Sophia once had a personnel of 600, including 80 priests. Following the conquest of Constantinople by the Ottoman Turks in 1453 the church became a mosque, and today it is a museum.*

Opposite: *Baldwin of Flanders (1171–1205) is crowned Baldwin I, the first Latin emperor, in 1204 (top). This historiated initial "R" shows both his coronation and his generosity toward a woman sending her child off to the crusades. From a 13th-century French manuscript of the history of the crusades by William of Tyre (ca. 1130–86).*

THE SPOILS OF WAR

"The booty gained [from Constantinople] was so great that none could tell you the end of it: gold and silver, and vessels and precious stones, and samite, and cloth of silk, and robes vair and grey, and ermine, and every choicest thing found upon the earth. And well does Geoffrey of Villehardouin, the marshal of Champagne, bear witness, that never, since the world was created, had so much booty been won in any city."

Villehardouin's assessment was no exaggeration. Constantinople was a wealthy place and within its walls were the riches of an empire. However, few of the crusaders had much interest in the artistry of exquisite chalices and other ecclesiastical items, preferring the monetary value of their gold and precious gems. Nicetas Choniates, a Byzantine senator heartbroken at the destruction, left depictions of items such as a monumental statue of the Greek goddess Hera, whose "head could barely be carted off by four yokes of oxen."

The Venetians had a greater appreciation for Byzantine culture. Greek artists and sculptors had probably worked on Venice's great church of San Marco (completed in 1071), which, with its five domes, rich mosaics, and Greek-cross plan, is notably Byzantine in style—and in San Marco's treasury one can view the rich chalices, icons, crowns, and other items looted from Constantinople. However, these are but a small part of the treasures that Doge Enrico Dandolo acquired. The entire church of San Marco was decorated inside and out with Byzantine spoils, including most of the marbles and relief sculptures now found in the basilica. On a corner of the church façade stand four stone figures of emperors that once adorned the great Philadelphion Square in Constantinople, symbols of the imperial tetrarchy instituted by Emperor Diocletian. But the most famous item carried back to Venice is the Quadriga, a group of four bronze horses originally mounted over the starting gates of the hippodrome, where chariot races were held. It is ironic that in a city without horses these gilded steeds became the symbol of Venetian power for centuries.

Material riches were not the only loot; as Abbot Martin of Pairis makes clear (see page 112), the crusaders also took countless religious relics. Although, from a medieval perspective, relic theft was not necessarily wrong, since it was generally believed that relics could only be stolen if the holy figure wished them to be, many of Europe's most famous relics were looted in 1204. The supposed head of John the Baptist, pieces of the True Cross, hair of the Virgin, and innumerable body parts of various saints went westward. Other relics were later sold by the Latin emperors of Constantinople—in 1240 King Louis IX of France purchased the Crown of Thorns in this manner and built the Sainte-Chapelle in Paris to house it. The Shroud of Turin was also almost certainly taken during the sack of Constantinople. Robert of Clari recorded that there was a church "called My Lady Saint Mary of Blachernae, where was kept the shroud in which Our Lord had been wrapped, which stood up straight every Friday so that the features of Our Lord could be plainly seen there. And no one, either Greek or French, ever knew what became of this shroud after the city was taken." It reappeared, in the West, in 1357.

Top: *A Byzantine chalice adorned with pearls and jewels, now in the church of San Marco.*
Right: *A detail showing two of the Four Horses of San Marco, magnificent gilded bronze statuary dating from the 2nd or 3rd century CE.*
Opposite: *A 10th-century Byzantine plaque with gold, enamel, and precious stones, depicting the Crucifixion.*

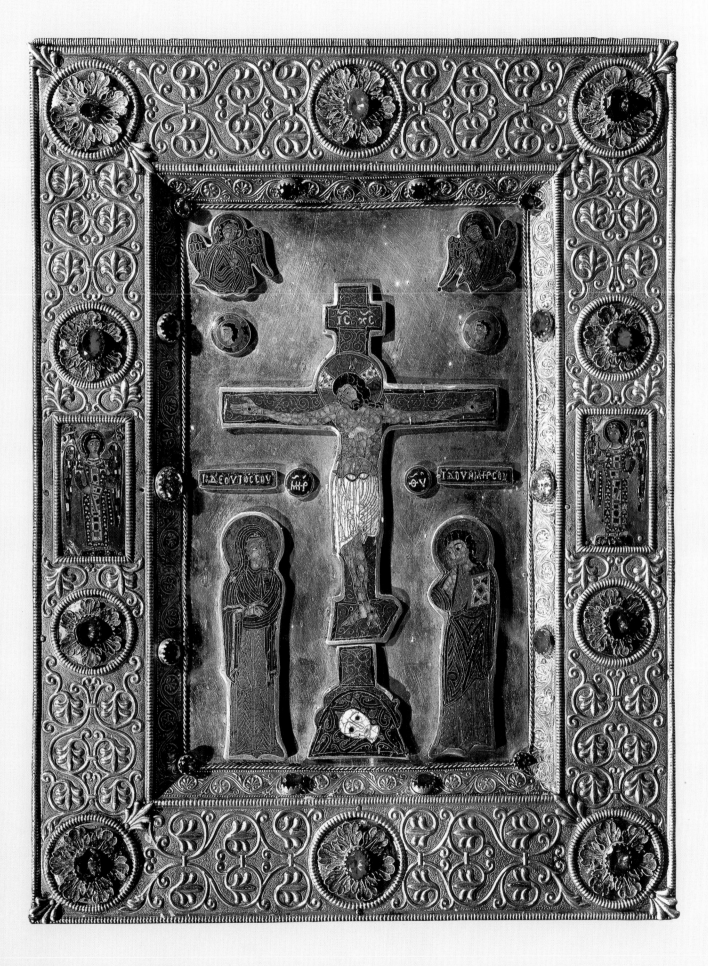

6

CRUSADES IN EUROPE
INFIDELS, PAGANS, AND HERETICS

WILLIAM L. URBAN

THE RECONQUISTA

Before the First Crusade to the East, the church had lent its support to Christian rulers who fought wars of conquest and conversion against non-Christians in Europe. The oldest of these conflicts was against the Muslim rulers of Spain and Portugal and is known by the Spanish term Reconquista (Reconquest). It began nearly three centuries before the First Crusade and ended in 1492 with the fall of Granada. If the name suggests a systematic advance against the Iberian Muslims, or Moors, in reality it was a piecemeal, intermittent process of wars and frontier skirmishes. At times, the personal ambitions of individual rulers were more important than religion.

In 711 Tariq ibn Ziyad, the Muslim governor of Tangiers, landed at Gibraltar (Jabal al-Tariq, Tariq's Mountain) and overthrew the Christian kingdom established by the Visigoths in the fifth century. By 716 all of the peninsula was in Muslim hands except for parts of the far north and northwest. Muslim forces crossed the Pyrenees into Gaul (France), and in 732 a raiding party reached Poitiers on the Loire, but it was repelled by the Franks under Charles Martel.

After the bloody overthrow of the Umayyad caliphs in Damascus in 750 (see page 21), the last surviving Umayyad prince, Abd al-Rahman, fled to Spain and in 756 established his own caliphate at Córdoba. In 759 Charles Martel's son, King Pepin I (741–768), finally drove the Muslims back across the Pyrenees into Spain.

This painted ceiling in the Hall of the Kings in the 14th-century Alhambra palace, Granada, depicts scenes of chivalry and romance, perhaps legends of the Muslim kings of Granada. The scenes were painted by Christian (possibly Italian) artists, probably owing to Islamic strictures against depicting living beings. The small kingdom of Granada was the last Muslim territory in Spain, falling to the Christians in 1492.

Pepin's successor, Charlemagne (768–814), was renowned as a great enemy of the Moors, and legends such as the twelfth-century French epic *Song of Roland* certainly encouraged the practice of assisting Spanish Christians against the Muslims. However, Charlemagne's involvement in Spain was more complex. In 778 he intervened in Christian Asturias as an ally of Muslim Barcelona, and attacked the Christian Basque city of Pamplona. Charlemagne never returned to Spain, but from 788 his forces carved out the Spanish March, a Spanish enclave that included Barcelona (which fell in 800).

It was from Christian Asturias and Barcelona that the Reconquista began. A key moment came in 844, when Ramiro I of Asturias (842–50) defeated a Muslim army at Clavijo (see box on page 123).

In 1031 the caliphate of Córdoba broke up into twenty or so petty states, and there was little resistance to Christian advances in this period. Also in the eleventh century, an expanded Asturias became the kingdoms of León and Navarre, and Barcelona became Aragon. However, the fall of Toledo in 1085 to Alfonso VI of León-Castile (1072–1109) brought Castile, a powerful state in the center of the peninsula, to preeminence among the Christian kingdoms.

In Muslim Spain, al-Andalus, Christians and Jews were generally tolerated, some achieving high status. In the early centuries of the reconquest, Christian rulers similarly allowed conquered Muslims to worship freely and manage their own affairs, even to raise their own taxes and military units. They also found it more convenient to accept tribute from neighboring Muslim rulers than to fight them.

THE CID

The great Spanish literary classic of the Reconquista age is the anonymous twelfth-century epic poem *Cantar del mio Cid* (*Song of my Cid*). It centers on the heroic exploits of an eleventh-century warrior, Roderigo Díaz, called the Cid ("Lord"), who was among the foremost vassals of King Alfonso VI of León-Castile (1072–1109). In an era of shifting loyalties, he fought not only for his lord, but also for the Muslims. In 1094 Roderigo conquered the city of Valencia for himself and subsequently extended his holdings at the expense of the Almoravids. Following his death in 1099 in Valencia, his widow was forced to abandon the city.

In the poem, the Cid's enemies at court turn Alfonso against him, and in many lines he endeavors to make the king understand the concepts of loyalty and fidelity. In real life, the Cid was unable to reform Alfonso or his court. Today Alfonso's success in the Reconquista is attributed to Muslim weakness at a time of general Islamic decline after the incursions by Turks into the Arab world.

Above: *A natural defensive citadel protected to the north by the Sierra Nevada range, Granada— dominated by its Alhambra palace (seen here)— held out for two and a half centuries after the rest of Muslim Spain had been conquered.*

Below: *Symbols of royalty and death in the 13th-century Knights' Cloister of the Cistercian monastery of Santa Maria de Huerta, Castile. Cistercians played a central role in establishing the influential Order of Calatrava. The monastery also contains the tomb of Archbishop Jimenez, who fought at the great battle of Las Navas de Tolosa.*

This changed in the mid-twelfth century when the Almohads, fundamentalist Berbers, conquered al-Andalus and transformed the Muslims' defensive wars against the Christians into a *jihad*. The Almohads ended Muslim disunity, but also the era of tolerance and cultural exchange; there was even persecution of non-Muslims. The newcomers' fanaticism alienated local Muslims and made Christian rulers determined to eliminate the threat of *jihad* once and for all.

Meanwhile, French pilgrims to the tomb of St. James at Compostela had occasionally joined Spanish expeditions against the Muslims. After 1095 the popes approved the perception of these wars as crusades, conferring remission of sins on participants. The military orders founded in the twelfth century were important in these intermittent conflicts, since only they could provide garrisons for exposed castles. In general, Spanish orders (see sidebar) were based on the frontier, while the Templars, Hospitallers, and even the Teutonic Knights occupied neutral areas between the Christian states.

Portugal, separated by mountains from Spain and difficult to reach overland, received crusader assistance only occasionally, and usually by sea. In the summer of 1147, a fleet en route to the Second Crusade from Germany, Flanders, England, and Normandy helped the count (later king) of Portugal, Alfonso-Henry I (1128– 85), to capture Lisbon. In 1189, en route to the Third Crusade, two fleets from Denmark, Frisia, Flanders, Germany, and England assisted the Portuguese against the revived Almohad forces (see page 82).

The Reconquista made its greatest advances in the thirteenth century, when Christian Spain experienced economic and population growth, while Muslim Spain stagnated and military reinforcements from North Africa became sporadic and insufficient. Backed by the papacy, crusading enthusiasm reached a peak.

SAINT JAMES THE MOOR SLAYER

The shrine of Santiago de Compostela in northwest Spain has supposedly held the body of the apostle St. James (Santiago in Spanish) the Greater, the elder brother of St. John the Evangelist, since the early ninth century. As the Reconquista began to get underway in the same century, Santiago metamorphosed into a warrior saint, Santiago Matamoros, "St. James the Moor Slayer." Tradition records that the transformed saint first appeared in 844 at the battle of Clavijo, where he killed thousands of Muslims.

In combining penitential pilgrimage with a holy war (see pages 22–23) against Islamic enemies, the cult of Santiago anticipated by two and a half centuries the First Crusade, or armed pilgrimage, called by Pope Urban II. Those who prayed at St. James's shrine were entitled to wear the pilgrim's seashell insignia. From the twelfth century the journey to Santiago became the third most popular Christian pilgrimage, ranking closely behind Jerusalem and Rome.

The greatest battle of the Reconquista was fought on 12th July 1212 at Las Navas de Tolosa in southern Spain, when the Almohads were defeated by a huge Christian force including the kings of Aragon, Castile, and Navarre, the military orders, and as many as 70,000 French crusaders. This battle was decisive, but did not appear so at first because few of the heavily-fortified Muslim cities in the south were taken immediately. James I of Aragon (1213–76) conquered Valencia between 1229 and 1245, and Ferdinand III of Castile (1217–52) took Córdoba in 1236 and Seville in 1248, pushing the Muslims back to Granada in the far south. As Castile and Aragon advanced, they gradually imposed tighter controls over their growing Muslim populations, responding to insurrections by seizing Muslim lands and resettling them with Christians.

The reconquest of Portugal ended in 1249. Thereafter, its military orders led attacks on Muslim Africa, and Prince Henry the Navigator (1394–1460) used the resources of the Order of Christ for voyages that were to lead Portuguese explorers around Africa to India and the Far East.

In 1469 the marriage of Ferdinand of Aragon and Isabella of Castile created a united Spanish kingdom and made possible the conquest of Granada, the last Muslim state, in 1492. In that same year, Jews were ordered to convert to Christianity or leave Spain, and heavy strictures were imposed on Muslims. Ten years later, the remaining Muslims were forcibly converted.

THE IBERIAN MILITARY ORDERS

In the early twelfth century the Christian monarchs of Spain endowed the Templars and Hospitallers with estates and castles in the peninsula. Both military orders participated in the Reconquista, but their primary focus on the Holy Land meant that they could not be the force that their royal patrons had envisioned. In the face of the Almohad invasion (see main text), from 1146 Christian Spaniards found it desirable to create their own military orders, most of them modeled on the Templars. The three most important were the Order of Calatrava, founded in 1158, the Order of Santiago (1170), and the Order of Alcántara (1176). Santiago was the largest and most widely diffused.

Around 1166 Portugal created the Order of Évora, later known as the Order of Aviz. It was Portugal's sole military order until 1319, when the Order of Christ was established with confiscated Templar properties. A number of smaller Iberian orders, such as the Aragonese Order of Monte Gaudio (Mount Joy), founded in 1173, were absorbed by one or other of the four great orders: Santiago, Calatrava, the Templars, and the Hospitallers.

Spain's native military orders provided the core of the victorious army at Las Navas de Tolosa in 1212, and the fall of Granada in 1492 was facilitated by the border castles of the orders of Santiago, Calatrava, and Alcántara, which strangled this last Muslim outpost in Iberia.

THE FRUITS OF THREE FAITHS

Muslim Spain, or al-Andalus as it was known in Arabic (hence the name of the modern region of Andalusia), was for some time the core of an independent Muslim state, the Umayyad caliphate of Córdoba, that stood, until its break-up in 1031, in opposition to the rest of the Muslim world. Established in 756, the caliphate became a center of Muslim culture, a place where the great cultures of the East—Arabic, Persian, and Greek— were planted, absorbed, and altered in the far west of Europe.

The Andalusians were Spaniards, Visigoths, Arabs, Berbers, and Syrians; and they were Christians, Muslims, and Jews. The mutual toleration of such ethnic and religious diversity, known as *convivencia* (living together), was unprecedented in medieval Europe and fostered a rich cultural and intellectual exchange that was possible nowhere else. For centuries Córdoba had

great libraries and scholars, and boasted architectural marvels such as the Great Mosque (see illustration pages 118–19) as well as public baths and indoor plumbing. The urban sophistication of al-Andalus existed nowhere else in western Europe.

Many of Spain's Muslim rulers surrounded themselves with poets and scholars who wrote on every imaginable topic. (Paper, unknown in the rest of Europe at this period, was produced and widely available in Spain.) Ibn Hazm (died 1064), for example, wrote numerous works, including a famous tract on love entitled *The Ring of the Dove* and a monumental history of religions. The poet-king al-Mu'tamid (1078–95) established an academy of arts in Córdoba that attracted the best minds in the West. Lesser rulers did the same, thus further promoting the cultural development of Spain.

Scientific and philosophical thought also flowered in al-Andalus, and it was the principal channel through which many important ideas and concepts passed into Christendom in the fields of mathematics, science, medicine, and philosophy. It is through Spain, for example, that the use of arabic numerals (which are actually of Indian origin) caught on in Europe.

Scholars in al-Andalus were particularly interested in astronomy, and worked on a simpler and more elegant description of the solar system than the ancient Ptolemaic one prevalent in Christian Europe. This had practical applications, as when az-Zarqali (died 1100) invented the *azafea* (astrolabe), a navigational instrument used by sailors for centuries. He also maintained—six centuries before Kepler demonstrated it—that planetary orbits were elliptical rather than circular.

Medicine was another interest of Andalusian scholars, who contributed to the *Materia Medica*, an enormous compendium of medical knowledge that remained a work-in-progress for centuries. Originally an Arabic translation of an ancient Greek work by Pedanius Dioscorides, it was revised and augmented

Left: *The 11th- or 12th-century* hammam *in Jaen is the largest surviving Arab bathhouse in Spain.*
Opposite, above: *An azafea, or astrolabe, made in Muslim Spain ca. 1430. Invented by az-Zarqali (see main text), this ingenious device was widely used throughout Europe for navigation and surveying.*
Opposite, below: *A page from a 14th-century manuscript of Maimonides' great work* Guide for the Perplexed, *written in 1190.*

by numerous Muslim, Jewish, and Christian scholars, and by the thirteenth century it described more than 1,400 medicinal plants and their uses.

The greatest Andalusian-born philosopher was Moses ben Maimon (Maimonides, 1135–1204), a Jewish physician and rabbi who was born in Córdoba. Maimonides was greatly influenced by Arab philosophers, who were in turn influenced above all by the ancient Greek philosopher Aristotle. Maimonides, author of the *Guide for the Perplexed*, maintained that there can be no contradiction between the logical truths of the physical world and the spiritual truths of God. Reason and the study of nature could help humankind come closer to understanding the eternal. These ideas, like those of Aristotle himself, had a profound impact on Christian scholars such as St. Thomas Aquinas (1227–74), laying the ground for medieval scholasticism.

Spain's lasting cultural impact was as a window for Europe onto the intellectual fruits of the Arabic, Persian, and Greek civilizations. Because of Spain's ethnic diversity, translation was an important activity. Arabic versions of Greek philosophers were in turn translated into Latin, and it was by this path that western Christendom rediscovered the majority of Aristotle's works. This would have far-reaching effects on western thought and culture, influencing the establishment of Europe's first universities in the thirteenth century, and ultimately the great revival of Classical culture in the Renaissance.

THE WENDISH CRUSADE

The Germanic tribes who migrated southward and westward in the early centuries CE left areas of northern Germany largely unoccupied. Into these regions came Slavic migrants from further south and east, who by the eighth century had settled in villages and towns close to the Baltic between the Elbe and Oder rivers. There were various groups, speaking similar dialects, who were known collectively as the Wends by their Saxon and Danish neighbors.

Like the Saxons and Danes at this period, the Wends were pagans (see sidebar). Conflict among these peoples did not have any expressly religious motive until after the Saxons had been conquered and converted to Christianity in a series of wars waged (772–804) by Charlemagne. In the tenth and eleventh centuries there were terrible wars between Saxons and Wends along the Elbe river, which served as a natural frontier; the Saxons won peace by paying tribute.

In the eleventh century Scandinavia underwent conversion to Christianity, increasing the pressure on the pagan Wends. As the balance of power continued to shift in favor of their Christian neighbors, the Wends were no longer able to collect tribute from the Saxons or keep them west of the Elbe. From 1110 the Wends were forced to pay tribute to the Saxons, and in 1111 their rulers had to

THE "EASTWARD URGE"

Nineteenth-century German nationalists coined the phrase *Drang nach Osten* (Eastward Urge) to describe what they saw as an inexorable eastward expansion of the Germans in the Middle Ages. The Nazis used the term to justify the Third Reich's own eastward expansion, linking it to Nazi theories of the "superior" German race that naturally needed greater *Lebensraum* ("living space").

However, the so-called *Drang nach Osten* in the Middle Ages was less military than economic, and less German than international. German rulers of newly conquered lands attracted immigrants with promises of lower taxes and fewer feudal services; and once they had demonstrated that the frontier lands were safe, settlers came in great numbers. But Polish dukes and churchmen also invited German knights, peasants, and merchants, as well as many Jews, to their own sparsely populated eastern lands. Reality in medieval east-central Europe was a colorful mixture of ethnicities and languages.

BALTIC PAGANISM

Baltic paganism, with its pantheon of powerful deities and lesser supernatural beings, was sufficiently similar to Viking beliefs and practices to be both easily grasped and easily misunderstood. The most important deity was Perkunas, the god of lightning and thunder, who was worshipped in forests under the open sky. At the other end of the scale were the household gods and deities of the fields, forests, and waters; these were called upon daily, and especially at the times of birth and death.

The role of the pagan priests was informal but powerful. On military campaigns they would listen to bird calls, observe the weather, and cast bones to determine the will of the gods. Otherwise promising campaigns would be called off if the omens predicted misfortune. What is known of pagan rites and practices is limited because the pagans were illiterate, and only scant information survives through old oral tradition and the biased accounts of Christian chroniclers. Even this has been distorted in modern times by efforts to tie this religion to ancient ones predating the Greeks and Romans, and to nineteenth-century folklore, and to modern nationalism.

assist German lords in attacking pagan Vikings on the island of Rügen. In the following decades Saxon migrants moved into Wendish Holstein and the missionary Vicelin (died 1154) made some converts among the Wends. In 1143 Saxony, Denmark, Brandenburg, Holstein, and other states seized lightly populated Wendish lands.

Despite this encroachment, the Wends continued to be fiercely independent and to practice paganism. Bernard of Clairvaux, in Germany preaching the Second Crusade (see pages 60–61), saw the Wends as ripe for conversion by arms. In 1147 he easily persuaded north German and Danish nobles to launch a campaign against them, and convinced Pope Eugenius III to declare it a crusade. In that year, a Saxon-Danish force besieged the Wendish fortress at Dobin and German and Czech prelates led an attack on Demmin, while Danish ships harassed the coast. The Wends saved themselves by a combination of fierce fighting and accepting baptism.

Although the Wends relapsed into paganism almost as soon as the crusaders had left, the new monasteries established in their lands became centers for immigrants and missionaries, and there were further Danish and German invasions that ended only in 1185. The Wendish princes then agreed to become Christian vassals of their more powerful neighbors. With the help of new bishops and abbots they gradually converted the rural population, transformed their lands along western feudal lines, and attracted more immigrants. This eventually made the Wends as prosperous as the northern sandy soils would allow, and they were able to regain considerable independence. Soon they would be participating in crusades themselves, in Prussia, Livonia, and the Holy Land.

Above: *The island of Rügen off the north German coast was one of the last outposts of Wendish and Viking paganism in the Baltic. Rügen was a major center of the cult of Svantovit, recorded by western chroniclers, such as Helmold of Bosau and Saxo Grammaticus, as the god of gods whose prophecies were much sought after.*

Opposite: *This image of an unknown Baltic deity on Rügen survived the destruction of the island's pagan shrines, which included the important center of worship at Arkona. The wooden idol of Svantovit, whose temple at Arkona survived until 1168, is known to have been multiheaded and to have held a drinking horn filled with wine—but other pagan gods are known to have been depicted in this manner so this deity's actual identity remains unknown.*

CRUSADES IN THE EASTERN BALTIC

THE BATTLE ON THE ICE: THE NOVGOROD CRUSADE

In the thirteenth century, in the wake of the Fourth Crusade (see Chapter Five) the Catholic polities of the Baltic became involved in conflicts with the Russian principalities, which were both Orthodox Christians as well as military and commercial rivals.

In 1240, following the devastation of Russia by the Mongols, a papal legate organized a crusade against the last important independent Russian state, Novgorod. Although the crusaders had some initial successes, the Russian prince Alexander destroyed the Swedish prong of the attack on the banks of the frozen Neva river, earning him the title Nevsky. In 1242 he recovered Pskov and defeated crusaders from Danish-occupied parts of Estonia, the bishopric of Dorpat, the former Swordbrothers, and some Teutonic knights. Alexander Nevsky's victories did not end the ambitions of Swedish and German rulers, but they did effectively set a limit on their eastward expansion.

The crusade against the Wends set a precedent for later attacks on Baltic pagan peoples by Christian rulers such as Waldemar I of Denmark (1157–82). The Poles also strove to impose their influence in the area, while further east the Swedes moved into pagan Finland. In 1171 Pope Alexander III declared all wars against the pagans of the north equal to crusades to the Holy Land. Later popes attempted to control these wars by sending legates, but even then legates and bishops could call crusades without obtaining specific papal approval in advance. This enabled Danish kings to create a Baltic empire and supported Polish expansion into Prussia and Russia, while the Teutonic knights exploited it for their ongoing crusading operations.

Prussia and the Teutonic Order

In the twelfth century the Baltic coast was sparsely populated and Poland's rulers assumed that they could easily conquer and convert the pagan tribes of Prussia. King Boleslaw IV's (1146–73) campaign in 1173 began well, but support for it among the Polish nobles ebbed away after his death. Furthermore, the Polish church lacked missionaries to proselytize among the Prussians, and it was not until after 1215 that the newly appointed bishop of Prussia—supported by Conrad of Masovia, Poland's most powerful duke—began a mission that it was hoped could convert the entire region. Such an approach had succeeded in Pomerania, but it failed in Prussia, probably because there was no single local ruler to work through. In the 1220s Prussians overran Culm, the one Prussian province Conrad had been able to conquer, and attacked Polish villages and abbeys, seizing people to be sold as slaves or put to work on the warriors' farms.

Conrad approached several military orders for aid, offering them lands if they would build castles, provide garrisons, and bring in farmers to produce food. He would help as much as he could, especially in raising crusader forces to assist them. The Templars, Hospitallers, and even the Spanish order of Calatrava sent small units, and Conrad founded a military order of his own—but they were all ineffective. The Prussians could be pacified only by larger and better organized armies, and then held down by permanent garrisons. To this end, in 1225 Conrad invited in the Teutonic Order, which had close ties to the emperor Frederick II. When the order was invited to Prussia, Frederick gave it generous grants of rights and all the lands its knights could conquer. The church encouraged them as well and attempted to protect the rights of Prussian converts.

The first units deployed, in 1231, were small, and had to raise additional forces in Poland, Germany, and Pomerelia (West Prussia). By the end of the thirteenth century the Teutonic Order had conquered all of East Prussia. Polish and German migrants eventually outnumbered the Prussian converts, and behind the dense wilderness that divided Prussia and Poland an autonomous state was set up. The order subsequently defended its independence from both Polish and papal efforts to influence its military and political decisions.

The Teutonic Order relied largely on Germans for its crusading armies, but Poles and even Russians aided the order in crusades against pagan Lithuania. This cooperation ended in 1309, after a dispute over the order's occupation of Pomerelia and Danzig (Gdansk), which the Poles claimed. The ensuing conflict with Poland disrupted the Lithuanian crusade until the Peace of Kalish in 1343.

Around this time the Polish kings and the archbishops of Riga called for the Teutonic Order to be suppressed. However, unlike the Templars, who were subject only to the pope, the Teutonic knights were subject to both the pope and the emperor. By skillfully playing off one overlord against the other, the order succeeded in avoiding a similar fate to the Templars (see page 175). The refusal of the Prussian regional masters of the order to deal with papal legates meant that subsequent generations heard only one side of the order's quarrels with the Poles and the archbishops of Riga. As a result, the order acquired an exaggerated reputation for brutality.

Under grand master Winrich von Kniprode (1352–82), the crusade against the Lithuanians became a spectacle of chivalry that attracted nobles from all parts of the Holy Roman empire, as well as from France, England, and Scotland. The climax of every campaign, apart from raids and sieges (there were very few battles), was the celebration of the Round Table, a magnificent chivalric display involving the most important knights. They compared themselves to the Arthurian knights and heaped praise upon the noble chosen to bear the banner of St. George into battle.

Climate and practical considerations determined the seasons for campaigning. High summer and fall were the best times for crusaders to travel overland and by sea. But in December and January crusader armies could also

Opposite: *The German troubadour Tannhäuser (ca. 1220–ca. 1270) is depicted in this 14th-century manuscript as a Teutonic knight, wearing the order's uniform of a white cloak with a black cross. The knights of the Order of the Hospital of St. Mary of the Teutons (Teutonic Order) were essentially tough warriors, but even those who hated and feared them respected their skill, piety, dedication, and discipline. The order's Prussian masters and grand masters practiced power politics, but backed their diplomacy with fasts, processions, and continual prayer, and made periodic inspections of the spiritual life of their convents. When not on campaign the order devoted much time to peaceful business, encouraging agriculture and trade.*

Below: *Central and east-central Europe were the scene of much crusading activity: the Wendish Crusade along the west Baltic coast; crusades in Prussia, Livonia, and Lithuania; the Hussite Crusade in Bohemia; and the march of the Children's Crusade up the Rhine river and over the Alps into Italy.*

march across the frozen rivers, lakes, and swamps of the uninhabited frontiers; consequently, winter became the favorite time of year for expeditions up the Nemunas (Memel) river into Lithuania, despite short days, unpredictable storms, and dangerous thaws.

In 1386–87, following the marriage of Duke Jogaila (Jagiello) of Lithuania to Jadwiga of Poland, Lithuania underwent conversion, bringing this "eternal" crusade to an end. In 1399 the Poles and Lithuanians joined the Teutonic Order in pacifying the Samogitians, the last Lithuanian pagans. But eleven years later relations between these regional rivals had deteriorated into war. The conflict reached a climax at the battle of Tannenberg (Grünwald) in 1410, where the Poles and Lithuanians crushed a seemingly invincible crusader army led by the Teutonic knights. The order soon recovered its lost territories, but its power was severely dented (see sidebar).

Livonia and the Swordbrothers

Further north, Livonia, roughly the region occupied by modern Latvia and Estonia, was ethnically diverse and had no single powerful ruler who could lead its Christianization. By the end of the twelfth century Russians were moving in from the east and Lithuanians raiding from the south, while pirate ships of pagan Estonians and Kurs were plaguing the villages and shipping of Germany and Scandinavia.

In 1188 an elderly German priest, Meinhard, traveled on a mission of conversion to Livonia's Daugava (Düna, Dvina) river. He was

The Teutonic Order's architecture was designed to impress. The great headquarters of the order at Marienburg in West Prussia (below; present-day Malbork, Poland), founded in 1274, was a combination of military fortress, monastery, and walled town, and was described in terms of both admiration and envy. From 1309, amid fears that the Teutonic knights would suffer the same fate as the Templars, the fortress became the seat of the order's grand masters, who had been based in the Holy Land until the fall of Acre in 1291.

subsequently made the first bishop of the region (his successors became archbishops of Riga), but conversion was slow and in 1195 Pope Celestine III authorized a crusade, reaffirmed in 1198 by Innocent III. The first crusaders to Livonia, led by the second bishop, Berthalt, were merchants from the Baltic island of Gotland. They returned home before ice closed the Baltic Sea, and the third bishop, Albert, despite having a good base in Riga, was unable to garrison his castles properly. By establishing a military order, the Swordbrothers, in 1202, he made possible a rapid expansion of his domains. The bishop was supported by native peoples seeking revenge on traditional enemies, and by crusaders from Germany and Denmark. They crushed the pagans in Estonia, warded off Russian and Lithuanian attacks, then made a peaceful conquest of Kurland.

In time the Swordbrothers saw that the bishop intended to cast them aside once their task was accomplished and they ceased to cooperate with him. Albert appealed to the pope, and a compromise in 1227 divided Livonia between the bishops and the Swordbrothers—but left the key issue of the order's sovereignty unresolved. After the Swordbrothers were defeated in Samogitia in 1236, they were absorbed into the Teutonic Order as the semiautonomous Livonian Order. Albert's successors sought to assert their authority over the order. The pope upheld the verdicts against it, but did not enforce them, seeing the order as Livonia's only effective defense against Orthodox Russians or pagan Lithuanians. In effect, Rome treated the order as *de facto* rulers of Livonia.

The Livonian Order assisted the campaigns of the Teutonic Knights in Prussia by striking into Lithuania and Samogitia from castles along the Daugava and in Kurland. There were also conflicts with the Russian cities of Novgorod and Pskov, including a crusade (see sidebar on page 128), especially after 1300, when these commercial states were usually governed by hostile Lithuanian princes.

After the battle of Tannenberg (see above), the Livonian Order invaded Lithuania repeatedly, but in 1435 the order's army of Lithuanians, Germans, Russians, and Tatars was routed by its Polish and Lithuanian opponents. Afterward power in Livonia was exercised by the Livonian Confederation, an assembly composed of the master of the Livonian Order, the bishops, three abbots, and delegates of the cities of Riga, Dorpat (Tartu), and Reval (Tallinn).

In 1500 the Livonian Order won a tough victory at Pskov over Ivan the Great of Russia (1462–1505). But with the coming of the Reformation the order's days were numbered (see sidebar).

Statutes of the Teutonic Order, dated sometime after 26th August 1442, a period when the order was still recovering from the disaster at Tannenberg.

THE LATER HISTORY OF THE TEUTONIC ORDER

Following the disaster at Tannenberg (see main text) in 1410 there were proposals to relocate the Teutonic Order to the Ukraine or along the Danube river, but the grand masters found it impossible to support garrisons at such a distance from their Prussian and German bases. In 1525 the last grand master in Prussia, Albrecht von Hohenzollern, margrave of Brandenburg-Anhalt and duke of Prussia (1525–68), became a Protestant and secularized the Prussian lands. He made some knights and prelates into vassals, let others leave for German convents, and pensioned off the rest. This was the end of the Teutonic Order in Prussia.

When Prussia became a Protestant state the Livonian knights lost their most valuable ally and source of recruits. Dependent on mercenaries, the order declined in numbers and vigor. In 1557 the Russian armies of Ivan the Terrible invaded Livonia and in 1559 the order's small army was defeated. When Sweden, Denmark, and Poland entered the war, Livonia was divided among them.

THE ALBIGENSIAN CRUSADE

(see page 97)

(see pages 60–61)

In the twelfth century, the Languedoc (Provençal-speaking southern France) was the home of a vibrant and prosperous culture. Its pleasant climate produced abundant crops which provided the nobles of the region with the wealth and leisure to cultivate love poetry (see page 97) and courtly manners. The region's rugged hills, meanwhile, made it easy for nobles and burghers to defend their independence.

This region was also home to an ascetic sect known as the Cathars (literally "pure ones" from Greek *katharos*, "pure"), whose beliefs (see box) linked them with a wider movement that flourished in parts of France and Italy from the eleventh to thirteenth centuries. The origins of this movement are not entirely clear, but some of its beliefs resemble those of the Manichaeans, a Near Eastern sect condemned as heretical by the early church. The French Cathars were commonly referred to as Albigensians (Albigenses), from the Languedoc town of Albi, although the biggest center of the heresy was the city of Toulouse. How many followers the sect had among the general population is unclear, but it enjoyed wide support among the fiercely independent Languedoc nobility. The Albigensians probably owed their popularity to a widespread contempt (see sidebar) for the often worldly, corrupt, and poorly educated Catholic clergy.

The council of Tours in 1163 was one of a series of attempts by the church to stamp out the heresy. These had included dispatching a papal legate, Cardinal Alberic of Ostia, to Languedoc to preach against the Cathars in 1145, followed by the indefatigable Bernard of Clairvaux (1090–1153). The collaboration of these forceful churchmen proved to no avail and they were soon turning their attention to preaching the Second Crusade (see pages 60–61). In 1148, at the council of Rheims, the church excommunicated all protectors "of the heretics of Gascony and Provence," and in 1163 the council of Tours decreed that Albigensians should be imprisoned and stripped of their property. In 1179 the third Lateran council called on secular rulers to use force against the heretics, but this was made difficult by the fact that many of the nobles who were being asked to implement the decree were Albigensian supporters. The Albigensians received a further boost when the Catholic count of Toulouse, Raymond V, was succeeded by the Albigensian-friendly Raymond VI (1194–1222). It has been estimated that the sect had followers in as many as 1,000 Languedoc towns and cities at this time.

Almost as soon as Innocent III became pope in 1198 he authorized the Fourth Crusade to the Holy Land (see Chapter Five) and

THE WALDENSIANS

The wealth, moral laxity, and poor education of much of the clergy in southern France sowed the seeds for the growth of the Albigensian heresy. Toward the end of the twelfth century it also prompted the rise of another group: the Waldensians, named for Peter Valdès (Waldo), a wealthy merchant of Lyons. In ca. 1173 gospel passages in which Jesus tells a rich young man to give his wealth to the poor and follow him (Matthew 19.21, Mark 10.21–22) inspired Peter to give away all his own wealth, mostly to the poor, and adopt a life of poverty and preaching. So that he could communicate the gospel directly he had part of it translated into the vernacular.

Peter collected a following, the "Poor Men of Lyons," who were devoted to ascetic piety as the means to salvation. In 1179 Pope Alexander III confirmed Peter's vow of poverty but forbade him to preach, an activity reserved for the clergy. But Peter claimed that his duty was to God not men, and continued his preaching. In 1184 Pope Lucius III excommunicated the Waldensians, condemning them as heretics. What became of Peter himself is unknown, but the Waldensians were greatly persecuted and their itinerant preachers forced to teach in secret. During the Reformation they reemerged as a Calvinist Protestant church and survive as such to this day.

CATHAR BELIEFS AND RITUALS

While they professed to be Christians, the Cathars or Albigensians adhered to a theology that differed radically from Catholic orthodoxy. They were dualistic, believing that there were two Gods, one a spiritual being associated with good and the other a material creature associated with evil. In the world, indeed inside every human being, these two forces wrestled for domination, and good would triumph only when the spirit vanquished the flesh.

Cathars also taught that Jesus was a pure spirit and therefore could not have been crucified or resurrected, and they therefore followed an ascetic lifestyle, disdaining the inferior material world. Those who learned to live with minimum food and comfort and to abstain from sex were eligible for the *consolamentum* (consolation), a special sacrament that designated them as *perfecti* (Latin, "complete" or "perfect"). Ordinary believers (*credentes*) were not held to such strict standards, but they were assured either that reincarnation would ultimately place them in a position to become *perfecti*, or that taking the *consolamentum* just before death would transform them immediately.

Above: *The castle of Peyrepertuse was the largest Cathar stronghold and one of the last to fall, holding out until 1240.*

---

another to the Baltic (see pages 130–131). Also, he did not hesitate to act against internal threats to the church and took up the task of either converting or repressing the Albigensians. In 1204 he sent Abbot Arnaud-Amaury, the head of the Cistercians, as legate to the Languedoc. He also sent a request to the French king, Philip II, asking him to compel the regional lords, especially Raymond VI, to disown and suppress the heresy. But Philip was preoccupied trying to dispossess England's King John of his lands in France, and the pope himself soon became distracted by the Fourth Crusade. Innocent

THE INQUISITION

In order to bring order and justice to the treatment of heretics, in 1184 Pope Lucius III (1181–85) defined two heresies, the Cathars and Waldensians (see page 132), and established many of the principles, based on Roman law, by which individuals could be identified, tried, and sentenced. In 1227–31, in the wake of the Albigensian Crusade, a papal Inquisition was formally established specifically to deal with heresy.

Most inquisitional tribunals were run by friars of the Dominican and Franciscan orders. Both orders had recently been created to preach to a public that in some areas, such as southern France, was being subverted by heretics who were usually more than a match for the local clergy.

Modern research suggests that the Inquisition's popular reputation for harshness derives largely from Protestant (specifically Dutch and English) propaganda. In fact the Inquisition, which still exists, was probably the most humane and merciful tribunal in medieval Europe.

later dispatched the Spanish friar Domingo (Dominic) Guzman (St. Dominic, the founder of the Dominican Order, ca. 1170–1221) to employ his friars in public debates against the Languedoc heretics.

The Church Adopts Force

Such peaceful methods as Dominic's had been tried unsuccessfully before—and yet again they failed, although Dominic did institute reforms aimed at ridding the local Catholic church of abuses. In 1207, the pope called upon Philip II, as feudal overlord of the county of Toulouse, to suppress the heresy by force. In 1208 another papal legate, Peter of Castelnau, formally excommunicated Raymond VI and the two exchanged bitter words. As Peter rode from Raymond's castle he was attacked and murdered. Whether Raymond was directly to blame or not, the legate's death was the final straw. On hearing the news, Innocent proclaimed a crusade against the Albigensians.

Two legates were charged with raising an army, and up to 20,000 took the cross, including nobles from Germany and England as well as France. Among them was Raymond VI, who had submitted to the church in the hope of saving his lands. The crusade was launched in 1209 and the first towns besieged and captured were Béziers and Carcassonne, which fell in July that year to the Norman knight Simon de Montfort the Elder, who had been involved in the Fourth Crusade (see page 106). Simon's sack of Béziers and the accompanying brutal massacre of its inhabitants—in which many more Catholics than Albigensians died—shocked contemporaries.

Led by Simon de Montfort, the crusade took town after town, usually against fierce resistance from the local population, both Catholic and Cathar, who considered this a patriotic war against foreign aggression rather than a religious matter. Meanwhile, Raymond VI had again been excommunicated for not meeting the terms of his reconciliation, and in 1211 he was declared an enemy of the church, his lands granted to anyone who could seize them. King Peter II of Aragon, Raymond's brother-in-law and the hero of Las Navas de Tolosa (see page 123), tried to intervene with the pope. When he failed he took up arms on Raymond's behalf. At the battle of Muret on 12th September 1213, Peter was killed and Raymond VI fled to England. In 1215 he was once more reconciled with the church, but his lands were given to Simon de Montfort. King Philip II sent his son, Louis, with an army to assist Simon to seize Toulouse.

When Raymond and his son arrived in Provence in 1217, they were welcomed joyfully. He and his son, Raymond VII, immediately made plans to renew the war against Simon de Montfort. In 1218 it seemed that the war might finally end when Simon died besieging

Toulouse, but the new pope, Honorius III, persuaded the French king to accept leadership of the crusade. Philip II again sent his son south with an army, but that brief effort brought no end to the war.

After Honorius III called for another crusade in 1225, Philip II's son and successor, Louis VIII, made some gains before he fell ill and died. In 1229 Louis's widow, Blanche of Castile, at last negotiated an end to the conflict which effectively saw the Languedoc incorporated into the French kingdom. Indeed, the chief beneficiary of the crusade was France's ruling dynasty; next came the papacy, which had doggedly pursued its goal of rooting out the Cathar heresy. This insistence on Catholic orthodoxy went hand in hand with reform: in 1215 the fourth Lateran council (see pages 146–147) instituted measures aimed at improving the education and probity of the clergy.

The losers were not only the Albigensians, but the entire Languedoc, which had been devastated and impoverished by the protracted conflict. When the final revolts had been suppressed, the once prosperous and flourishing Provençal culture lay in ruins. The heresy had not disappeared either (the last Cathar outpost fell in 1255), but after 1231 the suppression was entrusted to a new papal institution: the Inquisition (see sidebar). Most of those it tried recanted and did penance in return for their freedom, but a few were burned at the stake. The last Cathar burning was in 1321, and the Albigensians had probably ceased to exist as a sect by the end of the fourteenth century.

Opposite: *The burning of heretical books, a detail of* The Entombment of Christ and Scenes of St. Dominic *by the Dominican friar and painter Fra Angelico (1387–1455). Dominic's experiences in the Languedoc inspired his foundation of a new order of well-educated friars to combat heresy and spread the word of God. The first Dominican convent was established in 1215 at Toulouse, the seat of the Albigensian heresy, a year before the pope officially confirmed the order.*

Below: *The death of Simon de Montfort the Elder on 25th June 1218 while besieging Toulouse during the Albigensian Crusade. From a 13th-century manuscript.*

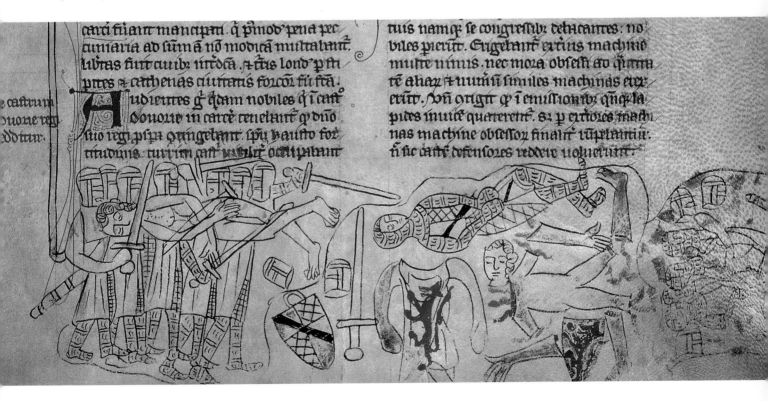

POPULAR CRUSADES

Nothing illustrates the widespread popularity of crusades better than the various efforts of common people to participate in the defeat of the enemies of Christ. There were no papal summons for these mass movements, which are distinct from the so-called People's Crusade (see page 37) and from the mass followings of ordinary folk who accompanied the armies on "official" crusades.

In the spring of 1212, a crowd of youths gathered near Cologne in Germany and started south, gathering followers along the way. Soon Nicholas, a boy who said that he had been told by an angel to liberate the Holy Sepulcher from the Saracens, emerged as their leader. As he and his youthful supporters made their way up the Rhine valley, an unprecedented hot spell caused many to die or return home. A difficult crossing of the Alps reduced their numbers farther, and only about 7,000 made it to Genoa in the late summer.

Disappointed that the Mediterranean did not part as they had expected, the "children" dispersed. Some may have gone to Rome to try to meet the pope; there is a tradition that others went to Marseilles, where they were enticed onto ships supposedly sailing for

The "Children's Crusades" of 1212 do not appear to have attacked Jews, but this was not the case in the "Shepherds' Crusades" of 1251 and 1320. This scene from a 14th-century French manuscript depicts peasants burning down a tower in Verdun-sur-Garonne in the Languedoc, where around 500 Jews committed suicide rather than be massacred. In their desperation, they are said to have thrown their children from the tower. The victims are identifiable by the red and white badge that all Jews were obliged to wear. In general churchmen and rulers tried to protect the Jews, from whom they derived important tax revenue (see page 60).

Jerusalem, only to be sold into slavery. Most probably found work wherever they could and remained in Italy. Few returned home.

A second group sprang up in north-central France in the early summer of 1212. A shepherd boy, Stephen, displayed a letter claiming to be from Christ to the king of France, Philip II (1180–1223). Stephen led perhaps 30,000 persons to Paris to speak with the king, a former crusader (see Chapter Four), and presumably to ask him to return to the Holy Land—some of the crowds were heard to chant "Lord God, restore to us the True Cross." It seems that after scholars had confirmed the letter's inauthenticity, the king told the crowd to go home. Most did so and the "crusade" dispersed, though there is evidence that a few joined the Albigensian Crusade.

Movements like this were born in a time and in a culture in which crusade sermons, religious enthusiasm, and predictions of the end of the world abounded. Innocent III seems to have been greatly impressed by the popular response. Until this time, popes had discouraged the poor from taking crusading vows—poor, hungry, ill-clad, and untrained people were merely a hindrance to an effective army of well-equipped knights. But in 1213 Innocent III openly invited the general population to participate, a move that may have reflected the previous year's demonstration of popular enthusiasm.

Another popular crusading movement that arose in France was the so-called "Shepherds' Crusade" of 1251. It was inspired by a mysterious preacher called the "Master of Hungary" to go to the aid of King Louis IX of France in the East (see pages 158–159). Queen Blanche of Castile, Louis's mother and regent in his absence, was initially impressed with the fervor of the "crusade," but as anticlerical riots and massacres of Jews became commonplace, she ordered its suppression. This was accomplished with some difficulty, because the mobs had dispersed in various directions. The Master of Hungary died in a riot with the citizens of Villeneuve-sur-Seine.

A similar "crusade" began in Normandy in 1320 when "shepherds and simple men" claimed to have seen visions ordering them to help the Holy Land. Marching behind the banner of the cross, they reached Paris and demanded that King Philip V (1314–28) lead them against the infidels. Philip, who had taken the cross in 1313 but had not fulfilled his vow, failed to appear. The throngs then wandered southward, and it soon became clear that this was less a crusade than an uprising by disaffected peasants, who took the opportunity to attack wealthy clergy and Jews and to burn town halls and taxation records. Pope John XXII (1316–34) threatened to excommunicate anyone who supplied the participants with food, and authorized the secular authorities to disperse them by force.

Carcassonne in southern France, where rampaging peasants were destroyed during the second Shepherd's Crusade of 1320. Another group was crushed in Aragon, yet another at Avignon (where they had terrorized the pope), and some at Genoa.

THE "CHILDREN" OF 1212

Each of the popular crusades of 1212 has been called a "children's" crusade because contemporary and later chroniclers described the participants as *pueri* ("youths" in Latin). They do not appear to have been armed, and did not persecute Jews, unlike mass followers of other crusades. The term *puer* commonly meant a boy who was unmarried or below the age of maturity (14), but there is some debate as to whether the participants were really so young. It has been claimed that *puer* was also used to denote someone of low social status, such as a shepherd, irrespective of age. Many of the *pueri* were indeed shepherds, but boys as young as seven might be given charge of the flocks, so this argument is inconclusive.

POLITICAL CRUSADES

Even before the crusades popes had blessed armies that purported to be serving the church. Alexander II (1061–73) sent William the Conqueror (1066–87) a consecrated banner to carry on his invasion of England in 1066. Still, there were no crusades against Christian rulers until 1199, when Pope Innocent III (1198–1216) declared crusades against a minor German noble in order to recover church lands in Italy. This and a similar action were precedents used by all Innocent's successors to justify their own use of force for political goals.

As well as being Holy Roman emperor, Frederick II (emperor 1220–45) had inherited the kingdom of Sicily, which included Naples and southern Italy. His enormous domains formed a ring of territories around the Papal States, and clashes with the pope were inevitable. Gregory IX (1227–41) preached the crusade against Frederick II in 1239, ostensibly on the grounds of his supposed atheism and heresy, but mostly because his recent victories threatened the independence of the papacy. Gregory called a council for 1241 to discuss more extreme actions, but Frederick captured many of the prelates traveling by sea to the meeting. After Gregory died that same year, Frederick prevented the election of a successor for two years.

But the papacy proved more resilient than Frederick expected. With the support of Frederick's German opponents, Innocent IV (1243–54) issued a decree at the council of Lyons in 1245 deposing Frederick as emperor and king of Sicily. Frederick did not abandon his conflict, but by the time he died in 1250 he was confined to

CALLS FOR CHURCH REFORM

The political crusades of the papacy were to have far-reaching consequences. Through the turbulent years of the fourteenth century, discontent with the church grew until many Catholics became persuaded that it should be divested of its enormous wealth and excluded from politics. Those advocating that the church return to its roots and practice apostolic poverty included Marsiglio of Padua (see sidebar), William of Occam, and other critics associated with the emperor Louis IV, but also some of the papacy's own devout supporters. The question came to the fore in the period of the Great Schism (see page 141), and was to be a central issue of the Reformation of the sixteenth century (see pages 192–193).

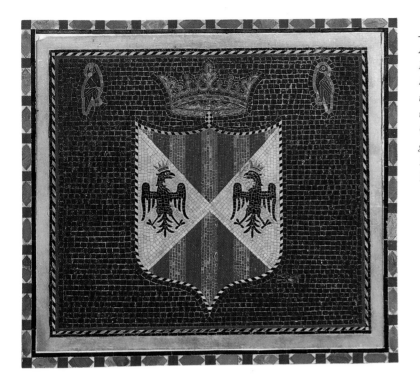

A mosaic with the coat of arms of Frederick II of Hohenstaufen, Holy Roman emperor and king of Sicily, in the Palatine Chapel, Palermo. Frederick's territories constituted the largest area of Europe under a single ruler since Roman times. The Catalan bars are derived from one of Frederick's granddaughters, Constance, who was married to Peter, king of Aragon and Valencia and count of Barcelona in the 13th century.

southern Italy and parts of Lombardy. Innocent IV tried to eliminate Frederick's descendants from power, but was unsuccessful, and the struggle with Frederick's dynasty, the Hohenstaufens, ended only in the reign of Urban IV (1261–64). Urban backed Charles of Anjou (see Chapter Seven) against Conradin, the Hohenstaufen claimant to Sicily, whom Charles captured and executed in 1268.

Pope Clement V (1305–14) raised the use of the crusade as a political weapon to a new height in his conflict with Venice (1308–09), granting Catalan mercenaries and other supporters the spiritual rewards of crusaders. As the escalating disorder in Italy required him to seek safety in Avignon, the pope found himself increasingly reliant on French protection; this was one reason he was unable to protect the Knights Templar from arrest (see page 175).

Pope John XXII (1316–34), who lived in exile in Avignon but still hoped to reassert papal leadership in Italy, refused to recognize the election of Louis IV of Bavaria (1314–47) as Holy Roman emperor in 1314. In 1324 John excommunicated Louis, who in 1327 invaded Italy, had himself crowned emperor by the people of Rome, and briefly established a rival pope, Nicholas V (1328–30). John countered in 1328 by declaring a crusade against Louis. The dispute was ended only in 1346, when Clement VI (1342–52) persuaded the electors (the group of rulers who chose the emperor) to depose Louis and elect Charles IV of Luxemburg (1355–78) as his successor. In the Golden Bull (1356), Charles carefully defined the imperial election process in such a way that future papal interference was impossible.

MARSIGLIO OF PADUA

Marsiglio (Marsilius) of Padua (1270–1342) took Aristotle's precept that a state is composed of its citizens, not its rulers, to argue for popular representation in both church and state. After Pope John XXII (1316–34) and the Holy Roman emperor Louis IV quarreled in the 1320s (see main text), Marsiglio wrote the *Defensor Pacis* (*Defender of Peace*), in which he argued that the state must be superior to the church: "The whole body of citizens, or its majority, alone is the human 'legislator'." He argued that no bishop, council or even pope could coerce or punish any secular person except when so authorized by the people or their representatives.

Marsiglio won the friendship and protection of the emperor and an excommunication from the pope, who said that he had never read a worse heretic. In 1328 the pope declared a crusade against Louis IV (see main text) and thereafter Marsiglio's influence declined, but he remained under imperial protection until his death.

THE HUSSITE CRUSADE

A battle between the Hussites and the crusaders, from an early 16th-century Bohemian manuscript. The Hussites fight under a red banner bearing a chalice, a symbol of the core Hussite belief that worshippers should receive communion in both kinds, that is, the wine (which the Catholic clergy reserved for themselves) as well as the bread. The Hussites also called for the church to give up its property, its wealth, and its monopoly on preaching.

In the fourteenth and early fifteenth centuries Bohemia was the most powerful state in the Holy Roman empire, especially under the Luxemburg kings Charles IV (1347–78), Wenceslas IV (1378–1419), and Sigismund (1419–37), who were also emperors. As the kingdom's economy and culture bloomed, so too did the rivalry between the country's Czech and German populations. The Luxemburg rulers preferred to appoint Germans to senior church positions, and the Czechs' complaints led them to advocate church reform, an important issue at a time of the Great Schism of 1378 to 1417 (see box).

The foremost Czech spokesman for reform was Jan Hus, a scholar and chancellor of the Charles University of Prague. Hus wanted a simpler and more understandable faith, and church services conducted in Czech. The German majority in the church hierarchy, reacted predictably, eventually obtaining papal instructions to destroy heretical writings at Charles University.

In 1411 Wenceslas resigned his claim to the imperial crown in favor of his half-brother, Sigismund of Hungary. Following a failed attempt to end the papal schism in 1409 there were now three popes, and Sigismund was determined to resolve the issue. To this end he persuaded one of the popes, John XXIII (1410–15), to call a council at Constance in southern Germany. The council (1414–18), which eventually won the support of all the major European powers, succeeded in deposing all three popes and electing a new pontiff, Martin V (1417–31), in their place. The council also acted to suppress the views of John Wycliff (see box), Hus, and others. In 1415 Hus went to Constance to defend his beliefs with the promise from Sigismund of an imperial safe-conduct. However, Sigismund was advised that Hus must be condemned as a heretic or the council might dissolve, and reluctantly allowed him to be tried and burned at the stake.

Hus's followers, the Hussites, were outraged, and the most radical of them began to organize new communities, the most important being at Tabor, where a military genius, Zizka (1370–1424), began to train peasants and artisans to fight. In Prague in the summer of 1419 a Hussite mob threw city magistrates to their deaths out of the city hall windows. This was followed by violence against the Catholic clergy and church buildings, and Catholic miners and nobles then carried out acts of revenge. In 1420, as civil war engulfed Bohemia, Pope Martin V declared a crusade against the Hussites.

Sigismund had now succeeded Wenceslas as king of Bohemia and went to Prague for a hasty coronation. He then fled the kingdom, promising to pay his mercenaries with lands confiscated from the rebels. In 1421 and 1422 crusaders from Germany and Hungary entered the Czech lands; one army alone contained as many as 125,000 troops. But the effectiveness of these forces was hindered by the steep Bohemian hills and forests, stoutly defended fortifications, and Hussite military ingenuity.

Between 1428 and 1431 a Hussite offensive ravaged Silesia, Saxony, the Upper Palatinate, and Hungary. The Hussites' most resolute enemy was the Teutonic Order, based in West Prussia; in 1433 a Hussite force raided West Prussia with the tacit agreement of King Jagiello of Poland (a Catholic but a lifelong enemy of the order), and reached the Baltic Sea. So completely did the Hussites rule the battlefield that they called these raids "beautiful rides."

At length the ageing Sigismund tired of the struggle and the churchmen who had been most vocal in denouncing all reforms admitted that they had failed. At the council of Basel (1431–49) the church came to an understanding with moderate Hussite representatives, permitting them to conduct church services in their own language and to receive communion in both kinds (see illustration, opposite). These were essentially the same concessions made to the Greek Orthodox church at this time in an effort to achieve Christian unity in the face of the growing Ottoman threat. In 1436, after the moderate Hussites had prevailed against the radical Taborites in a brief civil war, Bohemia reentered the Catholic community.

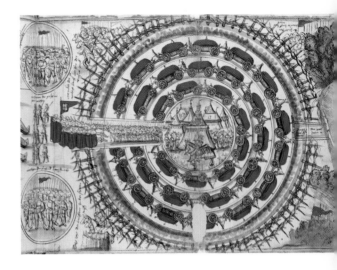

A Hussite war camp, from a manuscript of ca. 1450. The tents are surrounded and protected by a Hussite military innovation—wagons chained together and bearing light cannons. In battle, after the crusaders had exhausted themselves attempting to break through this barrier and had been decimated by the gunners, the Hussite cavalry would make a devastating charge into their ranks.

THE GREAT SCHISM AND REFORM

The election of Pope Urban VI (1378–89) proved to be unfortunate on account of his unpredictable and sometimes violent behavior: he once publicly struck a cardinal who had annoyed him. A group of disaffected cardinals thereupon elected a new pope, Clement VII (1378–94), who took up residence at Avignon, a city owned by the papacy in the south of France. Two rival papal courts came into being, each with its own pope and college of cardinals. European states were split in their allegiance: France, Scotland, and the Spanish kingdoms supported Avignon; England and the Italian and German states supported Rome.

The existence of two men claiming the apostolic crown, each having his own supporters and appointing his own cardinals, naturally brought the whole issue of papal power and patronage to the fore. Some radical reformers, such as the Oxford scholar John Wycliff (1320–82), had even questioned the very legitimacy of the papacy's leadership of the church. Wycliff declared, for example, that the supreme authority for Christians must always be the Bible, which should be translated into the language of the people and thereby be made available to all, not just the priesthood. To this end, Wycliff made an English translation of the Bible. Wycliff's ideas and those of his followers, the Lollards, were condemned but not entirely suppressed. They spread from England as far as Prague, where they were a key influence on Hus and his supporters.

tentozu$ in insidus manebat. de p[...]
Exercitus autem x̄ cū ducibus inte[...]
usu petriaru̅ z trebuculo5 alia[...]
machinau̅ muros ciuitatis subuc[...]
n̅ q̄eq̄ pfeciss̅ent a prudencioribz ip[...]
su̅ z ueracit̅ intellectu̅ n̅ sola n̅ un[...]
mictam fore capiendam. Vn̅ int̅ r[...]
mur murac̄o i̅ cast̄s co̅munibz enig[...]
cordie fomentis. Nam q̄uida̅ fuit p[...]
dano q̄ n̅o longe xanoy fixis tento[...]

ūt. l; peditu̅
i. fecerant etu̅
ad cautelam
llent icos.hui'
impetu facto
con̅ xanos
s 'tribili fos
ue po̅tē tem
mictis defende
tibz suis ab eos

7

THE FIFTH CRUSADE TO 1291

THE LOSS OF THE HOLY LAND

JAMES M. POWELL

THE CRUSADER STATES

In the early thirteenth century, the major crusader powers consisted of the kingdom of Cyprus, the principality of Antioch, and the Latin kingdom of Jerusalem. The Latin kingdom chiefly controlled some coastal cities, the most important being Acre and Tyre; Jerusalem itself remained in Muslim hands. The death of Saladin in 1193 had focused the attention of his heirs on internal affairs (see box), but the diversion of the Fourth Crusade against Constantinople and the foundation of the Latin empire of Constantinople in 1204–05 (see Chapter Five) had divided western European interests and weakened support for the crusader states.

The kingdom of Acre, as the Latin kingdom of Jerusalem became in fact if not in name, lacked the resources to support the monarchy and the nobility, yet it remained relatively stable due largely to the respite it enjoyed from external attack during these years. However, the tradition of strong royal leadership, which was so important in the twelfth century, entered a long decline following the rule of such figures as Henry of Champagne and Amalric of Lusignan, both of whom were king only by virtue of being married to Queen Isabella of Jerusalem (see page 94), and John of Brienne, who became king by marrying Isabella's daughter and heiress, Maria. Following the Fifth Crusade of 1217–21 (see pages 148–151), the papacy encouraged the emperor Frederick II to marry the daughter of John and Maria, also named Isabella, in order to persuade him to fulfill his crusade vow. As ruler of the Latin kingdom, Frederick attempted to centralize and strengthen royal authority, but he was an absentee monarch who faced strong opposition from the barons of the kingdom, led by John of Ibelin and other members of his family. Consequently, much of Frederick's effort merely exacerbated the growing tensions in the kingdom and ultimately contributed to a weakening of the crown in the second half of the thirteenth century.

However, until that time the situation for the crusaders in the region was actually better than it had been following the victorious campaigns of Saladin, due largely to the Third Crusade and the recapture of Acre. King Richard I had also taken most of the coast as far south as Jaffa, while to the north Tyre had held. Moreover,

THE AYYUBIDS AFTER SALADIN

The death of Saladin in 1193 influenced the development of all the lands that extended from Egypt to the Tigris and Euphrates rivers. Saladin's successors were his sons and other members of the Ayyubid family: al-Afdal Ali ruled in Damascus, al-Zahir Ghazi in Aleppo, and al-Aziz Uthman in Cairo. The northern territories, including the Kurdish homeland of the Ayyubids, were left to Saladin's brother, al-Adil Sayf ad-Din, while al-Adil's son, al-Muazzam, controlled Transjordan. Family members also governed less important areas. Other clans, such as the Artukids, Zengids, and Seljuks, ruled neighboring territories.

Clan rule by its nature encouraged divisions. Within a decade of Saladin's death, al-Adil emerged as the dominant figure in Egypt and southern Syria. He deprived Saladin's remaining sons of power and put his own sons in their places, making his son al-Kamil his deputy in Egypt and entrusting Syria to al-Muazzam. This was not an end to clan rule, but a shuffling of the

players that meant a stronger government, which, under al-Adil and al-Kamil, lasted for more than fifty years.

Yet the Ayyubid regime never attained full stability. Its relations with the crusader states and the way in which it met the challenges of the Fifth Crusade (see pages 148–151), the crusade of the emperor Frederick II (see pages 154–155), and the first crusade of King Louis IX of France (see pages 158–159), were entirely defensive, aimed at protecting its position. The achievement of al-Adil and al-Kamil lay in their preservation of the legacy of Saladin. Twice they turned back crusader attacks on Egypt at al-Mansurah. Al-Kamil made a treaty with Frederick II in 1229 that cost him little and gave him a free hand to consolidate his power in Transjordan and Syria.

The days of the Ayyubids came to an end in 1250 at the hands of the Mamluk ("slave") troops who had been recruited by the Turkish sultan as-Salih, al-Kamil's son (see pages 160–161).

under Henry of Champagne and Amalric of Lusignan, truces with the successors of Saladin (see box) provided the crusaders with a measure of security and time for rebuilding their defenses.

Meanwhile, in the West, Pope Innocent III was preparing to summon another crusade, aimed at accomplishing the goals that the Fourth Crusade had failed to achieve. The diversion of that crusade and the Frankish conquest of the Byzantine empire had seriously jeopardized his plans for church unity, but he remained committed to the fundamental aims of his pontificate: the summoning of a general council of the church to promote church reform, and a new expedition to the East. Innocent's ambitious agenda for the Fourth Crusade was now scaled down to meet reality.

Opposite: *The tomb of John of Brienne (ca. 1148–1237). An illustrious French knight, Count John of Brienne was chosen by King Louis VII of France to marry the heiress of the kingdom of Jerusalem, therby becoming king in 1210. He played a key role in the Fifth Crusade and ended his remarkable career as Latin emperor of Constantinople (1228–37).*

Right: *A Turkish steel helmet inlaid with gold, with Arabic inscriptions. From the 11th century the Islamic Near East was dominated by non-Arab dynasties. The hegemony of the Turks, in the form of the Seljuks, Mamluks, and Ottomans, endured until 1918.*

COUNCIL AND CRUSADE

In April 1213 Pope Innocent III announced his intention to summon a general council of the church in 1215 to deal with the reform of the church and also the planned crusade. In the fifteen years of his papacy, Innocent had experienced the many problems that had confronted the church as well as the debacle of the Fourth Crusade. It is not surprising, therefore, that he laid out detailed plans both for the organization of the crusade and for preaching.

His plans were contained in three letters, usually known by the first words of their Latin text, *Quia maior*, *Pium et sanctum*, and *Vineam Domini*. Taken together, these letters constitute the most complete plan for a crusade and church council undertaken by any pope up to this time.

Quia maior, the call for a new crusade, opens with a sense of urgency that can only reflect the pope's frustration at the failure of previous efforts. He seems obsessed by the evil of the times, and points to the recent Muslim capture of Mount Tabor. He promises full forgiveness of sins not only to those who go on crusade, but also those who provide support. Indeed, one of the more notable

Below: *The valley of Jezreel, looking toward Mount Tabor, traditionally the site of the Transfiguration of Jesus. Pope Innocent III's call for a new crusade was prompted by the capture and fortification of Tabor by the Ayyubids, although this action did not immediately pose a threat to the Latin position in the East.*

THE REFORM OF CHRISTIAN LIFE

On the surface, there was little to link the seventy main decrees of the Fourth Lateran council with the planned new crusade to the East. But from Pope Innocent III's point of view, the reform of Christian society was essential to the success of any crusade, and this connection had been developing with increasing force ever since the failure of the Second Crusade.

The majority of the council's decrees dealt with the regulation of the clergy. Among the most notable measures were those aimed at raising educational and moral standards among the priesthood and at promoting preaching by competent clerics. While the faithful were required to confess their sins to their parish priest at least once a year, any priest who revealed a sin heard in confession would be stripped of office and confined to a monastery.

characteristics of *Quia maior* is its emphasis on the importance of money and material assistance. In *Pium et sanctum*, Innocent spells out in detail the requirements of those selected to preach the crusade. Finally, in *Vineam Domini*, Innocent announces his plans for a general council of the church. Thus, for the first time, the crusade was fully integrated into the program of the reform papacy.

The general council that assembled at the Lateran basilica in Rome in November 1215 was the largest gathering of its kind in the history of the church to that time. Attending the Fourth Lateran council were more than 412 bishops and archbishops and 800 abbots, as well as envoys from many European monarchs.

The council promulgated seventy decrees touching on almost all aspects of church life (see box). The new crusade is dealt with specifically in the text *Ad liberandum*, which makes clear that preachers were to link the act of going on crusade with personal reform. With the events of the Fourth Crusade in mind, it stresses the obligation of crusaders to fulfill their vows unless there is a valid impediment. Recalling how disputes among western rulers had hampered earlier crusades, *Ad liberandum* calls for a general peace (see sidebar) and emphasizes the degree to which the church was prepared to provide support for the crusaders. *Ad liberandum* also forbids all Christians, on pain of excommunication, to trade in war materials with Muslims. Finally, the pope promises a full pardon of all sins that crusaders have confessed—a promise clearly linked to the council decree on confession (see box).

A CALL FOR PEACE IN THE WEST

The Fourth Lateran council took up various disputes that involved secular rulers, such as the attempt by Raymond of Toulouse to recover lands lost in the Albigensian Crusade. The settlement of such disputes formed part of Innocent III's extensive efforts to secure an unprecedented general peace throughout Christendom in advance of a new crusade. The peace is specifically called for in the council decree *Ad liberandum*:

"Since, moreover, in order to carry on this matter it is most necessary that Princes and the people of Christ should mutually observe peace, the holy universal synod urging us: we do establish that, at least for four years, throughout the whole Christian world, a general peace should be observed, so that, through the prelates of the churches, the contending parties may be brought back to observe inviolably a full peace or a firm truce."

THE FIFTH CRUSADE

THE FALL OF DAMIETTA

The Iraqi historian Izz ad-Din ibn-al-Athir (1160–1233) produced a famous account of the crusades in which he reports on the fall of Damietta to the Fifth Crusade in 1219:

"The Franks laid siege to Damietta and attacked it by land and by sea. After a prolonged struggle the defenders reached the end of their resources. They were almost without food, and exhausted by unending battle. The Franks were sufficiently numerous to take turns at the fighting, but Damietta lacked the soldiers to make this possible. In spite of this they held out amazingly and suffered great losses from death in battle, wounds, and sickness. The siege lasted until [5th November], when the survivors, so few in number and without provisions, were unable any longer to defend their city. Some left, some stayed, unable to move; the city's inhabitants were scattered."

On 16th July 1216, shortly after the Fourth Lateran council, Pope Innocent III died in Perugia. However, preparations for the new crusade were continued by his successor, Honorius III. By the following spring the first crusaders were ready to set out, and on 29th May 1217 a Frisian and Rhineland contingent left Vlerdingen in the Netherlands. At Dartmouth in England they elected leaders and were joined by some English crusaders before making their way along the coasts of France and Spain. They stopped at the pilgrimage shrine of Santiago de Compostela and again in Portugal, where they aided the bishop of Lisbon to capture the Muslim fortress of al-Qasr. They finally landed in Acre in April and May 1218.

In the meantime, contingents led by King Andrew II of Hungary and Duke Leopold VI of Austria had sailed to Acre from the Venetian port of Spalato (Split), arriving respectively in August and September 1217. They scouted around Mount Tabor, recently fortified by al-Adil, crossed the Jordan, and traveled up the east side of the Sea of Galilee before returning to Acre. They besieged Tabor in early December, but for reasons that are unclear soon gave up. After King Andrew had returned home in January 1218, the crusaders focused on restoring the fortifications at Chastel Pelerin and Caesarea.

The spring of 1218 brought the Rhenish, Frisian, and English contingents. The crusade leadership (comprising contingent leaders,

FINANCING THE CRUSADES

The First Crusade relied almost entirely on financing by the crusaders themselves, who were expected to support themselves in much the same way as vassals serving their lord. The cost to a knight of maintaining himself for even a relatively short period was very high, and the cost of crusading forced most to borrow money by mortgaging lands or borrowing from monasteries or Jewish moneylenders, with a negative effect on Christian-Jewish relations (see page 60)

Greater royal involvement in the Second and Third crusades brought systematic taxation. Louis VII of France imposed the first royal tax in support of a crusade, and Philip II of France and Richard I of England did likewise (see page 81). The church became directly involved in crusade financing under Pope Innocent III, who in 1199 called upon the clergy to pay one-fortieth of their incomes for this purpose, pledging a larger proportion from himself and his cardinals. This met with only limited success, and in 1215 the Fourth Lateran council decreed a tax of one-twentieth of clergy income for three years to finance the Fifth Crusade.

Reports produced for Pope Gregory X (1272–76) reveal an increasing concern about the misuse of the various crusading taxes that by that time had become a fact of life. Such criticisms grew in the fourteenth century, despite the increasing Ottoman threat.

bishops, and others) now made plans for the coming campaign in Egypt, which had been decided, following an existing strategy, at the Fourth Lateran council. The first objective was to be Damietta in the eastern Nile Delta. On 27th May 1218, the crusaders landed near the city and elected the king of Jerusalem, John of Brienne, as their overall leader when he arrived from Acre.

Damietta commanded the most direct route to Cairo and was easily reached from ports in Palestine. However, it was protected by the Nile river and three walls with numerous towers; in addition a chain stretched across the river from the city to a tower on an island near the west bank. A bridge of ships in turn protected the chain. The channel between the bank and the tower was unprotected, but too shallow for ships and too wide for effective attack from land.

In August the crusaders seized the tower and destroyed the chain, but their army was too small to move against Damietta itself. Many German and Frisian crusaders made plans to return home, but then a large contingent of English, French, and Italians arrived, as well as the papal legate, the Portuguese cardinal Pelagius of Albano.

The crusaders attack the "Turris Damiate" (Tower of Damietta), from a contemporary account in Latin by the English chronicler Matthew Paris. The tower is probably the one that stood near the west bank of the Nile and was linked to the city on the east bank by a protective chain and a pontoon bridge. To take the tower the crusaders built a siege machine mounted on two ships.

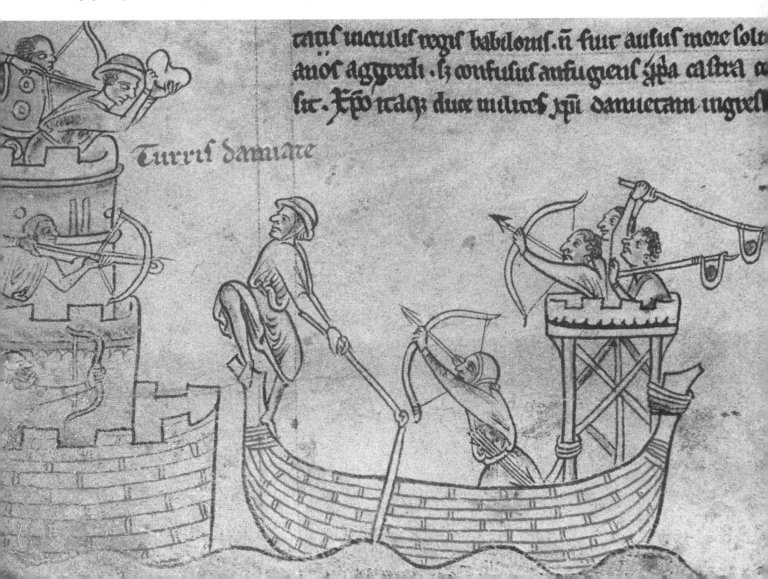

Before the crusaders could advance, the sultan of Egypt, al-Kamil (the son of al-Adil, who had died a few weeks earlier), attacked their camp, but was forced back. In order to surround Damietta, the crusaders now enlarged a canal that entered the Nile south of the city. However, their work was almost destroyed by a heavy storm.

Sometime before January 1219, al-Kamil learned of a plot to overthrow him and abandoned his camp at al-Adiliya. The crusaders crossed the Nile to take it over, and subsequently resisted al-Kamil's attempt to retake it with the help of al-Muazzam, the ruler of Syria and Palestine. Damietta was now cut off, but the crusaders were unable to follow up this success by seizing the city.

The summer of 1219 saw a stalemate. Al-Kamil had superior forces, but chose to remain in his new camp at Fariskur rather than take risks. The crusaders were expecting the arrival of the emperor Frederick II and they maintained a defensive position. Frederick had taken the crusade vow in 1215, but had so far been delayed by matters in Germany. At the end of August—when Francis of Assisi was in the camp (see box)—a crusader attack on the Egyptians ended in failure.

The stalemate dragged on and living conditions in the crusader camp deteriorated. But on 5th November 1219 Damietta finally fell (see sidebar on page 148). Out of a population of 60,000, only 10,000 remained. The city was put to the sack.

Al-Kamil withdrew to al-Mansurah. His main aim was for the crusaders to leave Egypt so that he could pursue his Syrian ambitions. He proposed a truce, offering to exchange Jerusalem and other holy sites for Damietta. But his terms did not include fortifications beyond the Jordan, without which Jerusalem would be vulnerable. Besides, the crusaders were confident that once the emperor arrived they would be able to complete the conquest of Egypt. On behalf of pope and emperor, Pelagius rejected al-Kamil's offer.

The emperor renewed his crusade vow in 1220, but a rebellion in Sicily delayed his departure yet again. The pope and some of the crusade leaders were growing anxious about his continued delay, but their immediate concern was keeping the crusader army together. In early 1220 al-Muazzam had attacked Caesarea and Chastel Pelerin in Palestine, and partly in response to this threat John of Brienne had returned to Acre with a large number of troops.

Cardinal Pelagius was left in charge in Egypt, where some crusaders sought to move at once against al-Kamil, although others wanted to wait for the emperor. By the spring of 1221 Frederick was

FRANCIS OF ASSISI ON CRUSADE

The reputation of Francis of Assisi (ca. 1180–1226), the founder of the Franciscan order (ca. 1210), is largely based on his charismatic personal appeal. His life is surrounded by myth and legend, a process that began while he was still alive and continues even today. In August 1219, at the height of the Fifth Crusade, as the crusaders were encamped outside Damietta, Francis arrived with a single companion. He received permission to preach, and his sermon warned the crusaders that they would lose the battle they were about to fight. Francis may well have gone further and warned them that they would lose the war, but contemporary accounts preferred not to stress this. At any rate, the crusaders suffered a significant defeat on the following day, 29th August, when they launched an attack on the Egyptian camp

It was probably during the ensuing truce that Francis gained permission to cross to the Muslim side—the Muslims perhaps regarded him as an envoy. He was well received by al-Kamil, but refused his gifts. The sultan listened to his message, which seems to have called for a peaceful solution through conversion to Christianity. The basic message of self-reform was probably in essence the same as he addressed to the crusaders. The episode captured the imagination of artists and those seeking alternatives to war. Although its immediate impact was not obvious, it may have encouraged al-Kamil to continue truce negotiations.

still not ready to come, but in May he sent Duke Louis of Bavaria with 500 knights. Pelagius urged him to act immediately; the duke, however, insisted on a proper reconnaissance and the army was not prepared to move against al-Kamil until July 9th. The annual Nile flood was nearly due and al-Kamil, knowing that his brothers were bringing troops from Syria, had renewed his offer of truce. Pelagius again rejected the offer and pressed the crusaders to attack.

Leaving a large force to defend Damietta, the crusaders advanced by land and water. On 18th July they reached Sharamshah, where mounted Turkish archers employed their usual harassing tactic of shooting without engaging the knights. John of Brienne, who had returned, advised withdrawal, but Pelagius refused.

At the end of July, the crusaders had reached the triangle of land opposite al-Mansurah. Al-Kamil was ready for them. He sent ships down the al-Mahallah canal behind the crusader fleet to block their escape by river and, with the support of his brothers, closed the route to the northeast. On 26th August the crusade army was forced to retreat. The Nile flood had begun, and that year the river was high. Al-Kamil opened irrigation sluices to flood the fields. The crusaders were completely cut off and retreat became a rout. Their only choice was surrender, which they negotiated in exchange for Damietta. There was bitterness in the city, especially since reinforcements sent by the emperor Frederick had arrived under Count Henry of Malta. Victory had slipped away; only recriminations remained.

PROPHECY

During the Fifth Crusade, Francis of Assisi may well have prophesied defeat for the crusaders in the coming battle, if not in the entire war (see page 151). Moreover, in the months following the crusader capture of Damietta, various apocryphal prophetic accounts began to circulate in the crusader camp, most notably *The Revelations of the Apostle Peter edited in one volume by his disciple Clement*, or *The Book of Clement*. According to Oliver of Paderborn, who went on the Fifth Crusade, this book (which purported to be ancient but was certainly a near-contemporary writing) contained many prophecies that had

already come true, and it detailed how a mighty ruler from the East, "King David" (who was interpreted as the Mongol leader Genghis Khan, ruled 1206–27), would unite in Jerusalem with a king from the West (clearly intended to be the emperor Frederick II). *The Book of Clement* also prophesied the fall of a "watery city" (possibly Tanis, east of Damietta) to the crusaders as well as Damietta and Alexandria. The prophecies were taken seriously by the crusade leaders, and the bishop of Acre included an account of them in a letter to Pope Honorius III.

In an age in which the belief in prophecy was common, the popularity of *The Book of Clement* was not exceptional. Throughout the crusades there were prophetic incidents. Perhaps the first was the vision that led to the discovery of the supposed Holy Lance in Antioch on the First Crusade, which inspired a demoralized army to victory (see page 42).

To elicit support for the Second Crusade, Bernard of Clairvaux (St. Bernard) had quoted the biblical prophetic phrase "Now is the acceptable time" (2 Corinthians 6, echoing Isaiah 49.8). Around the time of the Fourth Crusade, Pope Innocent III would quote St. Bernard to the Byzantine emperor Alexius III, who argued that God would free the holy places when he was ready, not at man's behest.

In the thirteenth century, the prophecies attributed to the twelfth-century Italian abbot Joachim of Fiore aroused great controversy, but also touched the crusade. While King Richard I was in Sicily during the winter of 1190–91, he had met Joachim, who had interpreted the Bible to predict the future of the world. Joachim believed that the beast with seven heads in chapter 13 of the *Book of Revelation* referred to seven kings who would persecute the church: five were dead, one (Saladin) was living, and the seventh (Antichrist) was to come. Joachim foretold that Richard would defeat Saladin, but that his victory would be followed by the coming of the Antichrist, who would try to destroy all Christians and the church. Eventually he would be defeated and a golden age would dawn. King Richard disagreed with some of Joachim's calculations, and the interview ended with the parties still arguing.

Although Joachim's predictions of victory turned out to be optimistic and some of his work was later condemned as heretical, his ideas were influential. His belief that the

Antichrist's coming was imminent and that his downfall would be followed by a new age of the Holy Spirit, when God would reign, was very attractive to pious Christians of the twelfth and thirteenth centuries, when the church was challenged from within by heretics and from outside by Islam.

The coming of the Mongols also lay behind the popularity of the "Cedar of Lebanon" prophecy that circulated from ca. 1250 and presented a vision of the fall of Tripoli and Acre, and predicted dire happenings for the West. Interestingly, despite the continued importance of prophetic thought generally, there is no evidence that prophecy played any particular role in the actual events surrounding the fall of Acre in 1291 (see pages 170–171). The period after 1291 was more notable for various practical proposals aimed at mounting more effective crusades.

Opposite: St. Francis, with Scenes from his Life, *attributed to Bonaventura Berlinghieri (active 1228–74).*
Above: *Men prostrate themselves before the beast of the Apocalypse (Revelation 13, 11–14), from a 13th-century English manuscript.*
Right: *The discovery of the Holy Lance at Antioch during the First Crusade, from a 15th-century French version of William of Tyre's* History of Deeds done Beyond the Sea.

THE CRUSADE OF FREDERICK II

Detail of a relief on the marble pulpit made in 1229 for the great cathedral of Bitonto, Apulia (built 1198–1250), during the reign of Frederick II as king of Sicily. The figure on the right holding a scepter is the emperor himself. The kingdom of Sicily embraced not just the island of Sicily but all of southern Italy, including Apulia. Frederick was the grandson of King Roger II, the founder of the kingdom, and the emperor Frederick I.

The Fifth Crusade probably failed owing to the lack of effective leadership. As Pope Honorius III wrote to Frederick II, they shared responsibility for the failure, but the remedy lay in a new expedition. Frederick's treaty with the pope at San Germano in 1225 set out a plan for this crusade. The emperor agreed to leave for the East by the end of August 1227 or face excommunication. He would also marry Isabella II, the heiress to the throne of Jerusalem through her mother Maria, the late wife of John of Brienne. The pope believed the marriage would bind Frederick more closely to the crusade, while Frederick, already emperor and king of Sicily, gained another kingdom. John reluctantly surrendered his claim to the kingship.

But conditions were hardly conducive to a new crusade so soon after the last one. Experienced manpower was a problem, and Frederick had to rely chiefly on crusaders from Germany and the kingdom of Sicily. He left Italy on 8th September 1227, but was forced by illness to turn back. The new pope, Gregory IX, who had succeeded Honorius in March 1227, was determined to exercise papal authority over the emperor and excommunicated him at once. This meant Frederick was forbidden to crusade, but he was committed to going to the East and to his interests as king of Jerusalem. Success in the East was, he believed, the course most likely to restore him to papal favor. To prepare the ground he had already opened negotiations with the sultan al-Kamil, who was keen to avoid another conflict that would further disrupt his ambitions in Syria and the northern Levant. On 28th June 1228 Frederick set sail once more with about forty ships. In September he landed in Acre, joining those who had reached the East exactly a year earlier.

The death of his brother and rival al-Muazzam had removed the main

obstacle to al-Kamil's Syrian ambitions, but the presence of Frederick put them in jeopardy. Frederick moved with all the forces he could muster from Acre to Jaffa, clearly signaling his intention to attack Jerusalem itself, which was not fortified. Al-Kamil quickly offered terms and Frederick had little choice but to accept them. Under the treaty of Jaffa of 1229 Frederick gained Jerusalem, Bethlehem, Nazareth, some other sites, and a pilgrim route to Jaffa. Jerusalem would remain unfortified, while the Muslims kept control of the Temple area with its mosques. There was to be a ten-year truce.

Frederick quickly went to Jerusalem to affirm himself as king, although a coronation by a priest was impossible since Frederick was still an excommunicate. Shortly afterward, Frederick learned that the pope had invaded the kingdom of Sicily. Frederick returned to Acre and on 1st May 1229 left for the West, leaving imperial officials to try to impose his rule on the kingdom's Frankish barons.

The results of Frederick II's crusade make it clear that it was really the continuation of the Fifth Crusade. He was aware that the treaty of Jaffa gave the crusaders somewhat less than al-Kamil had offered during the earlier crusade (see sidebar), but it still meant that the Holy Sepulcher was in Christian hands for the first time in forty years. And in 1230 Frederick reached an agreement with Gregory IX that brought him the acceptance he had set out to regain.

WINNING THE PEACE

Al-Kamil and Frederick II both faced a difficult task in justifying the treaty of Jaffa to their supporters. Their propaganda played a key role in establishing the truce called for in the treaty, which was to remain in force for the next decade. Al-Kamil argued that the return of an unfortified Jerusalem to the crusaders was better than risking an all-out war with Frederick. The Islamic holy places remained in Muslim hands, and at some future date the city could be recovered. Al-Kamil portrayed Frederick sympathetically, both to keep him on his side and to justify making the treaty.

For his part, Frederick worked to shore up his support among the secular rulers of Europe. In a letter of 1229 to Henry III of England, he expresses the depth of his religious motivation and details his success in securing the treaty with al-Kamil. But, he assures the English king, this was due to divine intervention rather than his own efforts. Frederick stresses the limits that the treaty placed on the sultan's right to build fortifications, but omits to discuss his own similar constraints; in fact, he gives the impression that Jerusalem will indeed be fortified. Nor does he mention his excommunication.

DISORDER IN THE CRUSADER KINGDOM

The truce provided by the treaty of Jaffa offered the opportunity for both sides to pursue their interests in relative security until the treaty expired in 1239. After defeating the papal invasion of his Sicilian kingdom, the emperor Frederick II embarked on a period of cooperation with Pope Gregory IX that was to last for most of this time. Frederick's wife Isabella had died in childbirth in 1228 and he acted as regent for their son Conrad, the new king of Jerusalem. He remained in the West, leaving the administration of the kingdom to imperial officials who acted as *baillis* (deputies) for Conrad.

The determination of Frederick's men to govern the kingdom effectively brought about an internal conflict that consumed virtually the whole decade. Behind it lay the ambitions of John Ibelin, the powerful lord of Beirut, and his relatives and allies, to ensure their dominance of the kingdom, if not to secure the crown itself

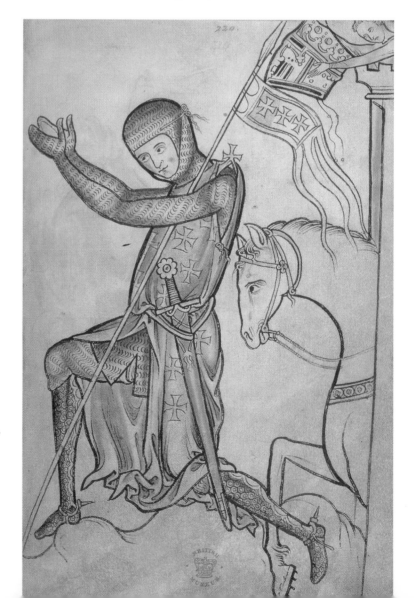

A crusader kneeling in prayer, from the Westminster Psalter, an English manuscript of the first half of the 13th century. The crowned helmet indicates the figure's royal or aristocratic status.

for one of their own, Queen Alice of Cyprus. Indeed, since many of these barons derived a large part of their incomes and military support from Cyprus, it is unlikely that they could have sustained themselves in any other way. Owing to their opposition, the efforts of pope and emperor to take advantage of the treaty of Jaffa to strengthen the kingdom were largely squandered.

In 1234 Gregory IX approached Count Theobald IV of Champagne, who was from one of the most distinguished crusading families, to lead a new crusade. Theobald, who was also king of Navarre, arrived at Acre in September 1239 at the head of many of the greatest nobles of France. They considered how best to exploit the disunity among the Ayyubids that had followed the death of al-Kamil in 1238.

An attempt to take Tripoli came to nothing. Theobald returned to Acre and began negotiations with the sultan of Damascus, who agreed to an alliance against Egypt, offering in return Jerusalem (which had been occupied by Muslim troops following the expiry of the treaty of Jaffa), Sidon, Tiberias, Galilee, and most of southern Palestine. Theobald advanced on Jaffa with his new allies, but many of them deserted when word came of an Egyptian advance. Still, Theobald was in a sufficiently powerful position to negotiate with the Egyptians in order to secure what Damascus had failed to deliver. Jerusalem was in Christian hands once more. After visiting the city to fulfill his pilgrim vow, Theobald left for home in September 1240.

Most likely, the concessions gained by Theobald would have melted quickly away had not Richard of Cornwall, the brother of Henry III of England, arrived with a large force in October 1240. Against baronial opposition, Richard upheld the agreement with Egypt and moved to fortify Ascalon. Richard concluded a treaty and crusader prisoners were released, but he returned home in May 1241.

Had he spent more time in the East, Richard's support for the imperial representatives in the crusader kingdom against the barons might have prevented the loss of Jerusalem in 1244 to the Kwarismians, Turkish mercenaries in Egyptian service. Never again was the city to be in Christian hands. There can be little doubt that the internal conflict in the crusader kingdom was an obstacle to any serious military effort in this period. The victory in the internal struggle went to the Frankish barons, led by the Ibelins. Acting on tenuous legal grounds, they suceeded in establishing Alice of Cyprus as regent in 1243. From that point the kingdom of Jerusalem was little more than an appendage to the kingdom of Cyprus.

The seal of Richard, earl of Cornwall and count of Poitou (1209–72). The crusading son of England's King John (and nephew of Richard the Lionheart) and younger brother of King Henry III is depicted on horseback as a knight in full armor.

THE FIRST CRUSADE OF LOUIS IX

King Louis IX embarks on crusade, from a 15th-century French manuscript.

THE CAPTURE OF LOUIS IX

The Muslim historian Ibn al-Furat (1334–1405) wrote an account of the capture of Louis IX. The following is an extract:

"[The Franks] set off with their horse and foot toward Damietta, while their ships began to go down the river opposite them. The Muslims crossed over to their bank and followed them in close pursuit. As dawn broke on the Wednesday [7th April], the Muslims had surrounded them.... [Louis] and the leaders from among the Frankish kings, may God Almighty curse them, withdrew to a hill where they halted, offering to surrender and seeking quarter. This was granted... and, relying on this, they came down and were surrounded. Louis was taken to al-Mansurah with the others, and there he was fettered by the leg and confined."

The loss of Jerusalem in 1244 provoked no immediate response in Europe. Although Pope Innocent IV proclaimed a new crusade at the council of Lyons in 1245, the chief business of the council was an attempt to depose the emperor Frederick II, who was embroiled in a struggle with the pope for dominance in northern Italy. Henry III of England was preoccupied with baronial opposition. Only in France was there a powerful, unchallenged ruler, King Louis IX. Against the opposition of his mother and former regent, Blanche of Castile, and of his chief advisors, Louis took the cross in 1244.

Louis combined religious idealism with a hard-headed practicality. There was no contradiction in his commitment to the crusade and to the French monarchy, as his mother claimed. He was also one of the wealthiest rulers of the time, although very careful when spending money. To fund his crusade, Louis secured from the council of Lyons the grant of one-twentieth of church revenues for three years, with the French clergy increasing this to one-tenth. This grant, subsequently extended for two further years, meant that about two-thirds of the total cost of Louis's crusade was born by the church, with barely anything coming out of his regular royal revenues.

In preparation for the crusade, the French king also built up huge stores of foodstuffs, which he sent to Cyprus as provisions for his army. His forces consisted of some 1,500 knights and their retinues, suggesting a total of more than 25,000, including about 5,000 crossbowmen. The crusaders were almost entirely French, with a sprinkling of English, Scots, Germans, and Norwegians.

In late August 1248 Louis and his army sailed from France and reached Cyprus in September, where the king decided to await more troops. He set off again in May 1249 and landed in Egypt near Damietta on 5th June. The crusaders overran the Egyptian position, forcing their retreat, and soon afterward the ailing sultan as-Salih died. The Egyptians moved to al-Mansurah to await the arrival of the sultan's successor, Turanshah, and his élite Mamluk (slave) troops.

The crusaders seized Damietta, but it was late November before the army left the city to begin a slow advance by land and water toward Cairo. Near the end of January 1250 they finally entered the triangular territory between the Nile and the al-Bahr as-Saghir canal, perhaps 50 miles (80km) south of Damietta. They crossed the canal to the al-Mansurah side on 7th February. The king's brother, Robert of Artois, quickly advanced into al-Mansurah itself, but the narrow streets favored the defenders and he was defeated and killed.

Louis, who had remained near the crossing point, drove off the Egyptians, but it was a brief victory, since with the arrival of Turanshah the crusaders now faced a stronger force than they had anticipated. In a tactic reminiscent of the Fifth Crusade, the sultan moved ships to a position on the Nile behind the crusaders, barring their retreat by water. They were forced to surrender and Louis was taken prisoner (see sidebar). Thanks in part to his queen, Margaret, who vigorously defended Damietta, he was able to negotiate terms for himself and his nobles. Half of Louis's ransom of 400,000 *livres tournois*—his annual revenues were around 250,000 *livres tournois*—was paid at once to secure his release. The rest was never paid.

Louis refused to return to France immediately but instead sailed to Acre. There, for nearly four years, he worked to strengthen the defenses of the kingdom of Jerusalem and to provide it with effective government. When Louis finally departed in 1254, he left a garrison of 100 knights as defenders of Acre.

THE MONGOLS: THREAT OR ALLY?

In the early 13th century Christendom and the Islamic world both faced a new threat on their eastern flanks: the Mongols. A nomadic northeast Asian people known as superb warriors and horsemen, the Mongols had conquered northern China before sweeping westward. By the late 1230s they were ravaging southern Russia and moving on to Poland and Hungary. Pope Gregory IX proclaimed a crusade against them in 1241, as did Innocent IV in 1243.

In 1243 the Mongols defeated the Seljuks of Rum (Asia Minor), creating even greater instability in the Near East. Some Christian leaders, such as Louis IX of France, began to consider allying with these formidable newcomers against the Muslims. During his years in the East in the early 1250s (see main text), Louis entered into negotiations with the Mongols and promoted missionary efforts aimed at converting them to Christianity. The key to conversion lay in the fact that their leader, the Great Khan Mongka (1251–59), had numerous Nestorian Christians at his court.

Mongka agreed to an alliance as long as Louis became his vassal, a condition the French king naturally rejected. Still, as the Mongol advances on Islam continued, the potential for a Christian-Mongol alliance remained and was later pursued by Lord Edward of England (see page 167).

The fall of Baghdad in 1258 to the Mongols under Hulagu, the grandson of Genghis Khan, from a 14th-century Persian miniature. The brutal destruction of the city stunned Muslims and Christians alike and ended the Abbasid caliphate, although the caliphs of Baghdad had long been rulers of Islam in name only.

THE MAMLUK SULTANATE

THE MURDER OF TURANSHAH

The pro-Mamluk historian Ibn al-Furat's account of Turanshah's murder masterfully exposes the conspiracies that formed an important part of politics in Egypt. Writing more than a century after the event, Ibn al-Furat offers three versions of the murder. This is an extract from the first:

"When the fighting against the Franks was ended and they had been beaten...the Bahriya Mamluks heard such menaces and threats [from Turanshah] as led to estrangement and revulsion. As a result, these Mamluks united against him, and decided to kill him. ... in the year 648 [1250]...he sat on his throne, and the table was spread in the customary way. Then one of the Bahriya Mamluks came up and struck him with his sword. He met the blow with his hand and some of his fingers were severed. He got up to flee and went into his tower, where he shouted: 'Who wounded me?' They said 'The Assassins.' He said: 'No, by God, it was the Bahriya. By God, I shall not spare any of them.' Then he called the barber-surgeon, who sewed up his hand, while he went on threatening the Bahriya. So they said to one another: 'Finish him off, or he will destroy you.' Then they went in against him with their swords."

Turanshah's victory over King Louis IX at al-Mansurah in 1250 was one of the greatest achievements by a Muslim leader against the crusaders. Why then was the sultan murdered that same year (see sidebar)? While western historians have tended to emphasize the role of the crusades in shaping the direction of Muslim societies, internal dynamics were much more important. Turanshah was an Ayyubid, with strong roots among the Kurds of Mesopotamia. Ayyubid rulers had long relied for their security on Mamluk (slave) troops forcibly recruited among the Kipchak Turks of the steppes. Captured young and reared as Muslims, these élite troops were the bodyguard of the sultan of Egypt. Under as-Salih (1238–49) their importance grew, especially of the regiment stationed on the island of Bahriya in the Nile, which effectively controlled the capital, Cairo.

The Mamluks were chiefly responsible for the victory over Louis IX. However, they felt threatened by Turanshah's policy of bringing large numbers of his supporters from Mesopotamia to Egypt to play key roles in government. Although the Mamluks formed a military aristocracy, their sons could not inherit their status, since only former slaves could be Mamluks, and their sons, as Muslims, could not be enslaved. Their power rested on their relationship to the sultan, and his power in turn rested on their support. When these mutual ties broke, it meant the end of the Ayyubid sultanate.

Turanshah was murdered on 2nd May 1250 (see sidebar) by a Bahriya Mamluk conspiracy that included al-Zahir Baibars Bunduqdari (Baibars), who was later to prove devastatingly effective against the crusader states. Under Aibek, the first Mamluk sultan (1250–59), the Kurds were largely forced from power in Egypt and their place was taken by Turks. A war between the Mamluks and the Syrian Ayyubids ended in 1253 when both sides agreed terms, under which the Mamluks retained southern Palestine and Egypt and the Ayyubids northern Palestine and Syria.

In September 1260 the Mamluk sultan Quduz and his general Baibars defeated the Mongols at Ain Jalud in Syria. It was a stunning victory, ending the myth of Mongol invincibility. That same year, Baibars himself became sultan following the murder of Quduz.

The rise of the Mamluk sultans could not have come at a worse time for the crusader states. Following the departure of King Louis IX in 1254, their continued internal power struggles left them ever more dangerously weak and disunited. With the Mongol threat diminished, Baibars had one principal ambition: to drive the crusaders into the sea. His motive seems to have been strictly a military one, to reinforce his personal hold over his domains, and there is no indication that Baibars or his successors were committed to the Muslim idea of *jihad*.

In 1263 Baibars took the poorly defended town of Nazareth and threatened Acre. The crusaders were able to offer very little resistance when, in 1265, the sultan launched a devastating full-scale campaign against their positions. Baibars' offensive culminated in 1268 with the fall of Antioch, the greatest Christian city in Syria, which had been held by the crusaders since 1098.

Four Mamluk horsemen, from the Treatise on the Art of War *by Muhammad ibn-Isa ibn-Ismail al-Hanafi al-Aqsarai, 14th century.*

THE END OF THE LATIN EMPIRE

While the Fourth Crusade (see Chapter Five) was a traumatic experience for the Byzantines, its impact has perhaps been exaggerated. However, the creation of the Latin empire of Constantinople was certainly very damaging to the crusades. Had it been successful, it might have benefited the position of the Latins throughout the East. But the Latin empire proved to be every bit as much of a drain on crusading resources as Pope Innocent III and others had warned. At the very time when King Louis IX was attempting to raise funds for his first crusade (see pages 158–159), for example, the Latin emperor Baldwin II was persuading the pope to divert support to his own rather futile effort to prop up the Latin empire.

From its inception, the Latin empire was an anomaly. Elected emperor in 1204, Baldwin I immediately began to seek aid in the West and enticed people from the Holy Land with the promise of generous fiefs. Many of these lands, however, remained in Greek hands and would have to be conquered. In fact, the emperor controlled only Constantinople and a small area around it. Boniface of Montferrat was building a power base in Thessaly, having sold Crete to the Venetians. Baldwin was also confronted by opposition from King Ioannitsa of the Vlachs and Bulgars, who had recently promoted the union of the Bulgarian church with Rome and received a crown from Pope Innocent III. In 1205 Ioannitsa and Byzantine

Below: *Map showing the division of influence between different Christian and Muslim powers in the Near East in the mid-13th century.*

Byzantine

Latin [Frankish Influence]

Latin [Venetian Influence]

Sultanate of Rum

Kingdom of Armenia

Ayyubid Sultanate

THE END OF THE LATIN EMPIRE 163

rebels defeated Baldwin near Adrianople (Edirne); the emperor was captured and died shortly afterward. It was an inauspicious start.

Baldwin was succeeded by his energetic and talented brother Henry, who pushed the Bulgarians back and secured a treaty with Theodore Lascaris, the Byzantine ruler of Nicaea. But these gains scarcely outlasted Henry's death in 1216. There followed a period of ineffective Latin rulers, while various Byzantine warlords built up rival power bases and established their own claims to be emperor.

In the face of the weakness of Peter of Courtenay (1216–19) and his sons Robert (1218–28) and Baldwin II (1228–61), the Latin barons turned in 1231 to the elderly ex-king of Jerusalem, John of Brienne, who had lost his throne to Frederick II (see page 154). John was made co-emperor with the fifteen-year-old Baldwin II. He brought 500 knights and a large contingent of infantry, as well as the support of Pope Gregory IX. John was able to defeat an alliance of Bulgaria and Nicaea before his death in 1237, but the Latin empire by this time consisted of little more than Constantinople itself and stumbled on chiefly because of new support from the West. Baldwin II canvassed Europe for funds and aid. He even pawned the relic of Christ's crown of thorns to the Venetians; they then sold it to Louis IX, who built the Sainte Chapelle in Paris to house it.

Meanwhile, the death of John III Ducas Vatatzes (1222–54), the ruler of Nicaea, opened the way for Michael Palaeologus to come to power there. In 1261 he overthrew Baldwin II in Constantinople and assumed the restored Byzantine throne as Michael VIII (see box).

The Arimondi Fountain in Rethymnon, Crete, built during the island's occupation by the Venetians, which lasted from the time of the Latin empire until its capture by the Ottomans in 1669.

THE RESTORATION OF BYZANTIUM

Among the fragments of the Byzantine empire that opposed the Latin emperors, Epirus and Nicaea played the leading role. Under John III Ducas Vatatzes, the empire of Nicaea gradually asserted its dominance in opposition to the Latins. His most successful general, Michael Palaeologus, became regent in 1258 for the seven-year-old John Lascaris and within a year had proclaimed himself emperor. In 1261 Michael's general, Alexius Strategopulos, seized an unexpected chance to break into the weakly-defended Constantinople. Baldwin II fled and Venetian resistance crumbled.

As ruler of a restored Byzantine empire, Michael employed his military and administrative skills as well as his considerable wealth to consolidate his power. He crushed a coalition led by William of Villehardouin, prince of Achaia, a Latin state in southern Greece, and defended the empire against Epirus and the Bulgarians. However, these efforts seem to have exhausted his treasury and forced him to take a more conservative stance. Nevertheless he successfully thwarted the ambitions of the new king of Sicily, Charles of Anjou, to restore the Latin empire (see pages 166–169). Michael died in 1282. The reign of his son, Andronicus II, began a long decline in Byzantine fortunes that saw successive Palaeologus emperors chiefly interested in preserving their dynasty's hold on the throne.

A KINGDOM WITHOUT A KING

LOSING TOUCH WITH REALITY

There is ample evidence that many of the Frankish leaders did not fully grasp the seriousness of their situation in the wake of the devastating conquests of Baibars. One incident illustrates this. Following the loss of Antioch in 1268, Baibars sent envoys to Tripoli to discuss a truce with Bohemond VI, prince of Antioch and count of Tripoli. Baibars himself, traveling incognito, was among the delegation.

In a dramatic scene, the sultan's envoys addressed Bohemond as "count" but he insisted that they use his title of "prince." The envoys refused, on the grounds that he no longer ruled Antioch, but Baibars surreptitiously kicked one of the envoys and told him to do as Bohemond wished. When he returned to his camp, the sultan jokingly declared "To the Devil with the prince and the count!"

When King Louis IX left Acre in 1254 the kingdom of Jerusalem was, for all practical purposes, leaderless. In that year the absentee king Conrad II (Conrad IV of Germany, 1250–54), the son of the emperor Frederick II and Isabella of Brienne, had been succeeded by his two-year-old son Conrad III (1254–68).

The Mongols were now the dominant force in the region and the Mongol threat actually created a brief period in which the crusader states enjoyed relative peace with their neighbors. Unfortunately, the internal political situation prevented them from taking advantage of this to strengthen their position. The absence of royal authority and the relative freedom from external threat allowed the various factions within the kingdom to give full vent to their grievances.

These included the Venetians and Genoese, who were vying for dominance in the eastern Mediterranean. More crippling, however, was the contest for control of the regency for Conrad II between two factions of the Ibelin family. Their machinations finally led to a state of affairs in which one child, King Hugh II of Cyprus, became regent for another, Conrad III. Hugh's mother, Plaisance, acted as the regent's regent. Clearly, in these years, the seat of real power in the crusader kingdom was no longer on the mainland, but in Cyprus.

SLAUGHTER AT ANTIOCH

On the fall of Antioch to the sultan Baibars in 1268 the city's inhabitants were either slaughtered or granted to Muslim commanders as slaves. Some leading figures simply disappeared in the chaos; a few were later ransomed. The amount of booty was enormous. Ibn al-Furat provides a vivid account of the city's capture:

"[The sultan] waited until the priests and the monks [a peace mission] had entered the city and then he gave orders for the advance. The troops surrounded the whole city and the citadel. The people of Antioch fought fiercely, but the Muslims scaled the walls by the mountain [Mt. Silpius] near the citadel and came down into the city. The people fled to the citadel, and the Muslim troops began to plunder, kill, and take prisoners. Every man in the city was put to the sword— and they numbered more than one hundred thousand."

The five years from 1265 to 1270 witnessed serious losses by the crusader states at the hands of the Mamluk sultan Baibars (see page 161). In the West, however, attention was focused on internal matters, especially the struggle between the Hohenstaufens and Charles of Anjou. In the critical period of Mamluk expansion, therefore, the crusader states lacked the new infusions of western manpower and money upon which they depended. The internal conflict in the crusader states was partly, or perhaps even mostly, due to the inability of the various factions to find security in a deteriorating situation.

In the mid-1260s another dispute arose over the regency for Hugh II of Cyprus between Hugh of Brienne and Hugh of Antioch-Lusignan. The Frankish barons favored Antioch-Lusignan, one of the most powerful men in Cyprus. They were already looking to Cyprus as the most likely source of their future security.

This was the situation when, in 1265, Baibars launched an offensive against crusader territories of the interior. One by one castles and towns fell, including Caesarea, Haifa, Toron, Arsuf, and, in July 1266, the great Templar fortress of Safad, the key to control of the lands around Acre. In that same year, a second Egyptian army devastated Cilician Armenia. In 1268, Baibars again moved north from Egypt, seizing Jaffa and Beaufort castle. He bypassed Tyre, which was well fortified, and on 14th May besieged Antioch. The city fell on 18th May and was put to the sack (see box).

Antioch, which had been in Christian hands since 1098, was one of the major centers of Christendom and its loss was a disaster for Christianity, removing a key base of support for the Armenians, and an ally of Baibars' Muslim enemies in the north. The loss alerted the West to the danger that confronted the crusader states. In France, King Louis IX had already taken the cross once more. Lord Edward of England, the future King Edward I, prepared to join him.

Opposite: *Remains of the ancient city walls of Antioch (now Antakya, Turkey). The sack of the city by Baibars in 1268 was particularly brutal.*

Below: *Montfort (Starkenberg) castle in Upper Galilee, the stronghold of the Teutonic Knights and one of the few inland fortresses to remain in crusader hands by 1268. However, it fell to Baibars in 1271 after a week-long siege.*

THE SECOND CRUSADE OF LOUIS IX

Having devoted the thirteen years since his return from Acre (see pages 158–159) to rebuilding his kingdom, King Louis IX of France renewed his crusader vow in 1267, when the Mamluk sultan Baibars was making swift advances against crusader positions. Louis was now the head of a family with wide interests in the Mediterranean. His brother, Charles of Anjou, had conquered the kingdom of Sicily from the Hohenstaufens, with papal support.

Louis secretly decided that before beginning his crusade he would sail first to Tunis in North Africa, where he believed the sultan was prepared to embrace Christianity. Although this possibility may seem far-fetched, rumors of conversion among both Muslims and Mongols were commonplace (see box on page 159). Moreover, seen against the context of the failure of Louis's first crusade, his decision to stop in Tunis makes a certain amount of sense: an alliance with the sultan of Tunis against Egypt would substantially increase the chances for success of the new expedition.

Louis's decision to go to Tunis was probably influenced by the missionary enthusiasm of the Dominicans rather than the political ambitions of his brother Charles. In fact as late as mid-1269 Charles had no knowledge of the king's decision, and no plans to join the crusade. It was almost a year later, in July 1270, on the very eve of the crusade, that Charles learned of the plan and pledged his

The crusaders under King Louis IX landing at Tunis. From the Chroniques de France ou de Saint Denis, *produced in France sometime between 1325 and 1350.*

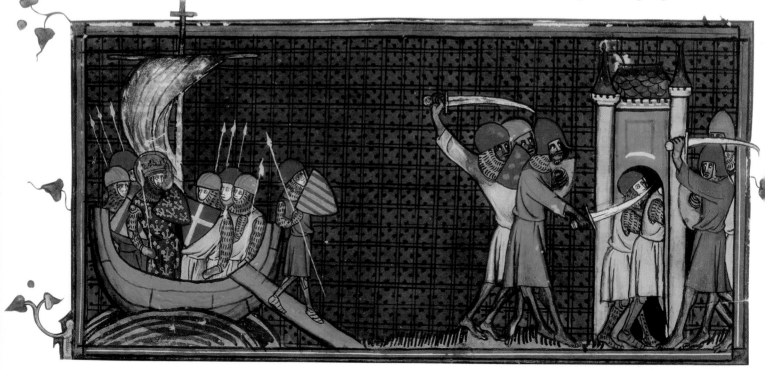

THE WEST REJECTS A NEW CRUSADE

Soon after his election, Pope Gregory X (1271–76) began preparations for a church council scheduled for Lyons, France, in 1274 to deal with pressing problems for the church. The crusade was of central importance to the new pope, but in the event the issue of church unity consumed most of his time. In order to head off the ambitions of Charles of Anjou, the Byzantine emperor Michael VIII Palaeologus (see page 163) initiated negotiations for the reunion of the Greek and Roman churches. This move, backed by Gregory and confirmed by the council, aroused great opposition in Greece. But it was a clever step that removed Charles's main pretext for a planned crusade to restore the Latin empire of Constantinople with himself as its head.

The pope's plan to win the council's support for a new crusade proved a thornier issue. Representatives of secular rulers and the military orders were unwilling to commit themselves to a new crusade, and although the council discussed plans for a crusade tax on church rents, no real progress was made.

Despite Gregory's labors, the climate for a crusade was quite unfavorable. Some scholars have stressed the unwillingness of anyone to take the lead in a new venture, but a more important factor is perhaps the simple lack of suitable leaders in the period following the failure of Louis IX's second crusade. It would be mistaken, therefore, to assume that there was any permanent alteration in the attitude of the West toward the idea of crusading. Nevertheless, the failure in support for a new crusade certainly played a part in the continued weakness of the crusader states in the period up to the fall of Acre in 1291.

support. He ordered supplies to be moved from Syracuse to the western Sicilian port of Trapani to support the Tunisian expedition.

Shortly after landing at Tunis, Louis IX became ill, and on 25th August 1270 he died. Charles of Anjou carried out a brief campaign, but withdrew in November. The crusade had come to nothing. Louis IX, canonized around thirty years later as St. Louis, was to be the last reigning western monarch to embark on crusade to the East.

A follower of Louis IX's second crusade was Lord Edward, the thirty-one-year-old son of Henry III of England (1216–72) and his eventual successor as Edward I (1272–1307). Edward arrived at Tunis too late but decided to continue to the East. He journeyed to Acre in 1271, just as Baibars was completing his capture of the northern crusader fortresses from the military orders. There was little he could do. He stayed in the East for more than a year, providing some stability for the remnant of the crusader kingdom and arranging a ten-year truce with Baibars that gave Acre a breathing space.

In Edward's retinue was the archdeacon of Liège, Theobald Visconti, who in 1271 was elected pope as Gregory X while in the East. Like his predecessors, Gregory championed the crusade, but his bid to secure a new expedition in 1274 was a failure (see box). However, the French monarchy provided the crusader kingdom with financial support until 1286 and maintained its garrison in Acre. Edward also continued to send aid after he became king.

THE DECLINE OF THE LATIN EAST

ARAGON AND THE CRUSADES

The Aragonese takeover of Sicily (see main text) had a profound impact on the crusades by diverting attention to the western Mediterranean. The next two decades were consumed in a struggle by the Angevins against Peter III and his successor, James II (1291–1327), to retake Sicily. In 1302 Charles of Anjou was taken captive by the Aragonese, and the settlement achieved in the treaty of Caltabellotta that year led to the election of James II's younger brother Frederick as king of Sicily for life. On Frederick's death in 1322, the Sicilians defied the papacy and the Angevins and chose his son Peter as their king.

On Easter eve, Saturday 30th March 1282, at the time of Vespers, a French soldier insulted a Sicilian lady outside a church in Palermo. The incident sparked a riot and a massacre of the French, and the ensuing "Sicilian Vespers" rising throughout the island led to the overthrow of Charles of Anjou as king of Sicily. While the riot was unplanned, the rising was not. The Byzantines had encouraged opposition to Angevin rule in the kingdom in order to frustrate Charles's expansionist ambitions.

The surprising player in the uprising, and its chief beneficiary, was King Peter III of Aragon (1276–85). In 1262 Peter had married Constance, the granddaughter of the Hohenstaufen emperor Frederick II. With papal support, Charles of Anjou had wrested Sicily from the Hohenstaufens, but Peter gave no assurances that he would accept the new status quo. When the Vespers revolt broke out, Peter was already pressing against the Tunisian coast with his fleet. Within a few months, he had landed at Trapani in Sicily to a hero's welcome from Hohenstaufen sympathizers, and by 4th December he had been proclaimed king in Palermo. Aragon was now a serious force in the western and central Mediterranean.

THE KINGDOM OF CYPRUS

In the declining years of the Latin kingdom, the kingdom of Cyprus took on a special significance. The last two kings of Jerusalem were members of the Lusignan family, Hugh I and Henry I, both of whom were also kings of Cyprus (Hugh III and Henry II). If Hugh seems always to have placed the interests of Cyprus ahead of those of Jerusalem, that is not surprising, since the barons of Cyprus were reluctant to fight on the mainland. Moreover, he faced considerable opposition on the mainland, not merely from the representatives of his rival, Charles of Anjou, but also from various baronial families. He arrived in Tyre in 1283 with 250 knights, but in the circumstances they were of little help. His most important initiative, a move to secure Tyre, failed because he lacked resources and the support of the barons and the military orders.

Hugh was succeeded by his son John in 1284, but he ruled for only a year and was succeeded by his brother Henry II of Cyprus (I of Jerusalem, 1285–1324). It is a kind of historical irony that the Latin kingdom gained one of its more capable rulers at the time when it faced its final hour. Henry worked to resolve the conflict between the maritime Italian cities, which prevented them from providing support to the monarchy. He installed his brother Amalric (Amaury) as lord of Tyre and later sent him with a force to relieve Tripoli. He himself arranged a truce to protect Acre and issued an appeal to the West. These energetic efforts were mostly inadequate and did nothing to stave off the final chapter in the history of the kingdom. But Cyprus proved to be an important key to maintaining a western presence in the East and keeping alive the idea of the crusade.

Meanwhile, in 1277 Maria of Antioch (granddaughter of Isabella I and Amalric of Lusignan; see page 94) had sold her strong claim to the crusader kingdom to Charles of Anjou. This had created a situation in which there were two kings. Hugh I (King Hugh III of Cyprus) ruled in Tyre and Beirut, while Charles, represented by Roger of San Severino, was recognized by Acre, Sidon, and Chastel Pelerin. Hugh's position depended on the Monfort family; when they withdrew support in 1283 he returned to Cyprus (see box).

However, the Sicilian Vespers fatally undermined Charles's ability to support Roger's government. Roger's main achievement was a ten-year truce with the sultan Qalawun of Egypt (1277–90), the successor of Baibars. The treaty applied only to Acre, Sidon, and Chastel Pelerin. Tyre concluded a truce in 1285, but with the fall of the Hospitaller fortress of Marqab that same year and the encroachment of Muslim power to the suburbs of the crusader cities, it was obvious that the Mamluk advance was not to be stopped by truces.

Charles of Anjou died in 1285 and in 1286 Henry I (II of Cyprus) was crowned king in Tyre. The lavish coronation festivities held in Acre were to be the last. In 1287 Qalawun took Laodicea (Lattakieh) and in 1289 Tripoli. While it would be rash to blame this string of misfortunes entirely on the Sicilian Vespers, it is clear that it was an important factor in the events leading up to the final disaster of 1291.

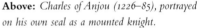

Above: *Charles of Anjou (1226–85), portrayed on his own seal as a mounted knight.*

Left: *Marqab (Margat) castle in Syria, the principal fortress of the Hospitallers. It was considered impregnable until its fall in 1285 to the Mamluk sultan Qalawun.*

THE FALL OF ACRE

After the fall of Tripoli King Henry I of Jerusalem renewed the ten-year truce with Qalawun. However, knowing that the sultan was unlikely to observe the truce for long, Henry also sent out envoys to seek help for Acre, the last important city in crusader hands. The crusade still had powerful supporters, such as King Edward I of England, but not even the pope was willing to devote much effort to a new one. Indeed, the force eventually sent by Pope Nicholas IV was ill-disciplined, and its bad behavior in Acre (including attacks on Muslim merchants) simply gave Qalawun grounds for breaking the truce.

The situation was so dire that some sought to buy the sultan off. But the citizens of the city refused; Acre was, after all, well fortified and even well defended. Qalawun's death in November 1290 seemed to justify this position, because the city expected the transition of power to give them a respite. But the quick succession of his son, al-Ashraf Khalil, spelled the end for the Christian kingdom.

On 6th April 1291 the new sultan placed Acre under siege. The defenders were no match for the Muslim forces and on 18th May the city fell. Many, including women and children of the upper classes, had already been sent to Cyprus and some of the defenders now escaped, but thousands were massacred (see box). Within a short time the entire coast of Palestine and Syria was under Mamluk rule.

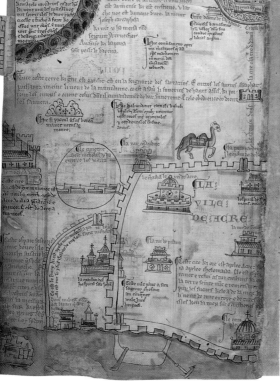

PANIC AT ACRE

When Baibars embarked on the conquest of Palestine, he never attempted to besiege Acre. Undoubtedly its importance as a commercial center where Muslim merchants traded with Europeans was a factor, as were the city's strong garrison and fortifications. In 1291 Acre had good reason to think that it would again be spared, and was unprepared for the disaster that overtook it between King Henry's attempt to make a truce on 8th May and the collapse of its defenses on 18th May.

It appears that Acre's various defenders sought refuge in their own castles and did not help one another, confirming that there was a breakdown in discipline, except among the military orders. One chronicler, the Templar of Tyre, describes people running to the port ahead of the Muslims: "Women and girls were frantic with terror, they went running through the street, their children in their arms...when the Saracens caught them one would take the mother and the other the child, they would drag them from place to place and pull them apart."

A Muslim writer, Abu al-Fida, relates how, when the city was nearly in al-Ashraf Khalil's hands, the sultan ordered those still resisting to come out. When they did so, he had them killed. The implication is that he had promised to spare them but did not.

In the harbor, there were too few vessels for all those trying to flee. But the king, his brother, and other leaders were among those who succeeded in escaping by ship. The Latin patriarch was drowned when he allowed too many aboard his boat, causing it to sink.

The story of the fall of Acre, which ended the crusader presence on the mainland of Palestine and Syria, is anticlimactic. In the West, almost nothing had been done to stave off its final demise. Why, after two centuries of Christian commitment to the crusade, did the final act ring down with such small clamor? The answer probably lies in the fact that most westerners had already adjusted to the loss of the Holy Land, seemingly accepting it as inevitable. For many, the reason for its loss lay in the sins of Christians and conflicts within the Christian ranks. The defenders of Acre were isolated and some commentators were quick to label them as lazy and cowardly. Writing in Parma at the end of the thirteenth century (perhaps after 1291), the Franciscan Salimbene of Adam even suggested that the recovery of the holy places was not God's will, since all efforts had failed.

However, it is also likely that many in the West did not view the fall of Acre as an ending. In the later thirteenth century there was an increasing realization that the huge investments of people and wealth in the crusades of Louis IX, for example, did not produce significant results. Some historians have perceived a lessening of support for the very idea of crusade, and there no doubt was in some quarters. There is also considerable evidence that, for the crusade to be successful, there would have to be important changes in strategy. While it was not clearly perceived by contemporaries, the fall of Acre therefore marks the end of the traditional approach to the crusades and the beginning of a quest for new approaches.

Opposite: *The end section of an itinerary from London to Jerusalem, produced in England ca. 1250–59 by the monk and chronicler Matthew Paris, consists of a map centered on the walled city of Acre. Jerusalem is at the top right and coastal cities are marked by castles and towers. Among the buildings shown within the walls of Acre are the royal palace (top left) and the headquarters of the Hospitallers (far left), the Templars (bottom), and the Teutonic Knights (top right).*

8

THE LAST CRUSADES

THE OTTOMAN THREAT

JONATHAN HARRIS

CRUSADING PROJECTS AND DREAMS

For centuries after the loss of the Holy Land in 1291 Christians continued to dream of recapturing Jerusalem and there was no shortage of schemes to accomplish that feat. In 1306 the Norman lawyer Pierre Dubois argued that future crusades should be led not by the pope, a cleric who should stick to the administration of the church, but by the king of France, who could recruit and equip a disciplined regular army. The Catalan scholar and mystic Ramon Lull had said much the same in 1305, but stressed that the crusade leader could be any man of royal blood, elected by the pope and the cardinals.

While the vision of royal leadership of the crusade to recover Jerusalem seemed practical and sensible, in the end it proved illusory. It is true that many monarchs and nobles professed great enthusiasm

The burning of Jacques de Molay, grand master of the Knights Templar, and Geoffrey de Charnay, one of his senior officers in 1314, from a 14th-century French manuscript. Following the suppression of the crusading order (see box), its leaders were ordered to make a public confession of their guilt; instead de Molay and de Charnay dramatically recanted their confessions. Both men were burnt at the stake, denying their guilt to the last.

THE FALL OF THE TEMPLARS

On 13th October 1307, without warning, all the Knights Templar in France were arrested on the secret orders of King Philip IV and charged with heresy, worshipping idols, and practicing magic. In trials marked by irregular procedures and torture, many Templars confessed to these and more bizarre crimes and in 1310 fifty-four who had recanted their confessions were burned as heretics. Most of those declared innocent were secularized or permitted to join other monastic orders.

The accusations had been prompted by the allegations of a few witnesses before a royal commission into the order's future. The commission itself was probably motivated by the powerful position that the Templars had come to occupy in France, particularly after the loss of the Holy Land in 1291.

The ensuing papal inquiry found the order innocent of the accusations in Germany, Italy, and most other countries. In England, members of the order escaped severe penalties when they freely acknowledged that they had mistakenly held a heretical belief—that the grand master could grant absolution.

In 1312 Pope Clement V abolished the order, but did not condemn it owing to the lack of evidence of heresy in most states. The secular powers confiscated the huge Templars estates, retaining some and redistributing the rest among other orders, in particular the Hospitallers.

---

for the idea and greatly admired the crusading heroes of the past. But in the end no ruler was prepared to leave his realm unprotected and march east with his army. King Philip IV of France (1285–1314), who initiated the spectacular fall of the Templars (see box), did take the cross in 1313, but he died before fulfilling his vow. Henry V of England (1413–22) is said to have longed to retake Jerusalem, but he spent his short reign fighting his Christian neighbors, the French.

The problem is encapsulated in the detailed plan for a crusade proposed in 1332 by Philip VI of France (1328–50). The pope was impressed and authorized Philip to levy a ten percent tax on the clergy for six years, and in 1333 Philip took the cross at an elaborate ceremony. The tax was gathered, but the expedition never materialized. Many contemporaries saw Philip's catastrophic defeat by the English at Crécy in 1346 as divine retribution for his breach of a crusading vow and misappropriation of crusading funds.

The possibility of organizing a crusade to recapture Jerusalem became even more remote during the Great Schism of 1378 to 1417, when there were rival popes in Rome and Avignon (see pages 140–141) and no prospect of European unity. Slowly the truth dawned. In the 1480s a German monk Felix Fabri of Ulm wrote sadly: "The Holy Land has been so utterly lost to us that now no one so much as thinks about recovering it, and there is no longer any way to recover it, unless it shall please God to work some miracle." By this time, the crusading agenda had changed rapidly as Christians realized that the pressing problem was no longer one of recovering what they had lost—but of retaining what they still had.

PILGRIMAGE TO JERUSALEM IN THE LATER MIDDLE AGES

In spite of the loss of Jerusalem, the flow of pilgrims from western Europe continued unabated. The Mamluk authorities by no means discouraged the traffic, which brought them revenues from tolls and customs duties. Nevertheless there could be tension between pilgrims and local Muslims. A German monk, Felix Fabri, who visited Jerusalem twice in the late 15th century, recalled an ugly confrontation in Bethany when a Muslim youth stole a pilgrim's haversack, containing his precious supplies of food. Peace was only restored after strenuous efforts by the pilgrim's guide and interpreter.

In spite of such annoyances, the sight of the Holy Places was an intensely emotional one for most pilgrims. An English pilgrim, Margery Kempe, was overwhelmed by the sight of Calvary and "had such great compassion and such great pain at seeing Our Lord's pain that she could not keep herself from crying and roaring though she could have died for it."

CYPRUS: THE NEW FRONTLINE

The Latin presence in the East was not extinguished completely when Acre fell in 1291. The Lusignan kings of Cyprus, who had ruled the island since Richard the Lionheart sold it to Guy of Lusignan in 1192, presided over a wealthy and flourishing kingdom. Its chief port of Famagusta became one of the richest cities in Christendom, largely owing to a papal ban on direct Christian trade with the Mamluks, which meant that commerce had to pass through Cyprus. The Lusignans, who still claimed the title of king of Jerusalem and underwent two such coronations, regularly sent ships to raid the coasts of Egypt, Syria, and Asia Minor, and urged the pope to use Cyprus as a staging post for a crusade to retake the Holy Land.

The Mamluk sultans planned to conquer Cyprus, but civil strife within Egypt prevented them from mounting an attack and allowed the Lusignans to take the initiative during the reign of Peter I (1359–69). He toured the courts of western Europe to gather money

CRUSADE INDULGENCES

Raising the money to finance crusading expeditions was a constant problem throughout the later Middle Ages. One method adopted by the papacy was to sell letters of indulgence in parish churches; the letters promised remission of sins and a reduction of the time that the buyer would spend in Purgatory after death.

The advent of printing in the fifteenth century meant that letters of indulgence could be mass-produced and circulated far more widely. However, the "pardoners" who sold the indulgences skimmed off much of the proceeds for themselves. The English poet Geoffrey Chaucer (died 1399) was among the critics of such practices. In his *Canterbury Tales* he has the pardoner declare: "But let me briefly make my purpose plain; I preach for nothing but for greed of gain."

and men, and the pope declared his planned expedition a crusade. Peter sailed from Cyprus with his fleet in October 1365 and launched an assault on the Egyptian port of Alexandria. The city's governor was absent on a pilgrimage to Mecca and the attack came as a devastating surprise to the Mamluks. The crusaders broke into the city and subjected it to a merciless sack.

At first sight, the capture of Alexandria was a triumph for Christendom. One of the greatest cities of the Islamic world had fallen into Christian hands and seventy ships were filled with the booty. Unfortunately, Peter and his army had made no plans as to what to do after taking the city and had no resources to face the relief army that would soon be upon them. So, on 16th October, the crusaders evacuated Alexandria and sailed back to Cyprus. The conquest had proved ephemeral, but it was to have one enduring consequence: the Mamluks were not to forget the humiliation of 1365 and thereafter were determined to take vengeance on the rulers of Cyprus.

The opportunity came in the 1420s, by which time the kingdom of Cyprus had declined in both wealth and power thanks to a disastrous war with Genoa in 1373–74. A pretext for an attack was offered to the Mamluks in 1424, when King Janus of Lusignan (1398–1432) raided the Syrian coast. Over the next two years, the Mamluks responded with a series of powerful attacks on Cyprus. On 3rd July 1426 they captured Limassol and a few days later won a complete victory over the Lusignan army at Khirokitia. Janus was taken prisoner and there was nothing that could be done to prevent the Mamluk army from entering Nicosia and rounding up 6,000 captives to be transported back to Egypt. Janus himself was only released in May 1427 when a ransom of 200,000 ducats had been paid. He returned to a bankrupt and ravaged island, which henceforth was obliged to pay an annual tribute of 5,000 ducats to the Mamluk sultan in Cairo.

Christian Cyprus would never again threaten the Muslim world. In 1489 the widow of James II (1464–73), the last Lusignan king, handed the island over to Venice. Venetian rule lasted until 1571, when Cyprus was conquered by the Ottoman Turks.

Opposite: *A tower and the winged lion of St. Mark, Venetian emblems on the citadel of Famagusta, Cyprus.*

Below: *The Venetian cathedral of St. Nicholas, Famagusta, now a mosque. The western Europeans who ruled Cyprus from 1191 to 1571 have left an indelible mark on the Cypriot landscape. The cathedrals of Famagusta and Nicosia, built in the western Gothic style, still stand, while monasteries such as the Lusignan-period Bellapais and the Venetian Ayia Napa bear witness to the one-time wealth and power of the Catholic church on the mainly Greek Orthodox island. Rule by a minority of western settlers was made possible by the construction of massive castles, such as those at Kantara, St. Hilarion, and Buffavento.*

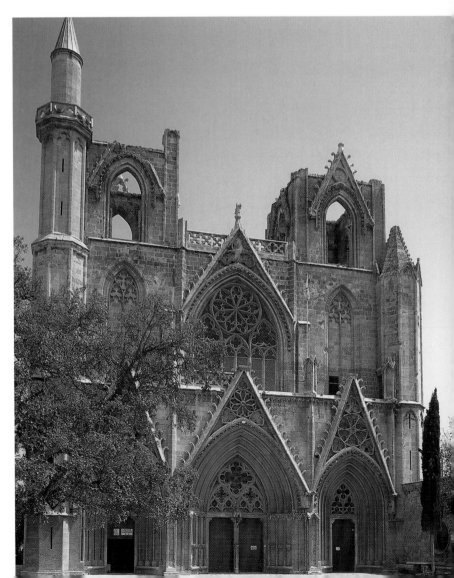

THE RISE OF THE OTTOMANS

The tiled minaret of the late 14th-century Green Mosque in Iznik, Turkey. Iznik, formerly Nicaea, was captured by the Ottoman Turks in 1331. Under Ottoman rule the city became famous for its tiles, which adorn many Turkish monuments (see page 197).

It is ironic that while the crusades were designed to combat the spread of Islam, they ultimately had the opposite effect, allowing a Muslim power to gain a foothold in Europe and to extend its control almost to the gates of Vienna. The process had begun with the capture and sack of Constantinople by the Fourth Crusade in 1204 (see Chapter Five). Although Constantinople was recaptured by Michael VIII Palaeologus in 1261 (see pages 162–163), the reconstituted Byzantine empire had a precarious existence. When news of the recapture reached Rome, the pope at once preached a crusade against Byzantium, promising that those who joined the expedition to recover Constantinople would receive the same remission of sin as those who went to the Holy Land.

The promotion of a crusade against Christians was seen as justified because the Byzantine church was still in schism with that of Rome, and in 1274 Michael VIII successfully thwarted the planned crusade by seeking a union of the churches, which was established at the second council of Lyons. But the union never really worked and was dropped after 1282, and as a precaution against the continued threat of a crusade from the West both Michael VIII and his successor, Andronicus II (1282–1328), had to move troops from the empire's frontier in Asia Minor.

At first, this diversion of resources did not matter too much, since the main Muslim power in the region, the Seljuk sultanate of Konya (Iconium), was too preoccupied with dynastic rivalry to present any threat to the denuded eastern Byzantine frontier. However, in order to gain support from their more powerful subjects during periods of civil strife, the Seljuk sultans made them grants of land on the edges of the sultanate, particularly along the border with Byzantium, in return for military service. As time went on, these Seljuk vassals tended to become semi-autonomous *amir*s who acted independently from their supposed overlords in Konya. They considered themselves *ghazi*s, or warriors of Islam, and not bound by any peace treaty that the sultan might have with the Byzantines. Consequently, from the 1260s, they mounted regular raids into Byzantine territory.

Resistance to these incursions was minimal, the Byzantine defenses, such as they were, being centered on the large towns of the region, such as Smyrna (Izmir) and Nicaea (Iznik), which left the countryside exposed to attack. As soon as this became clear, the Turks came no longer to raid, but to settle. The cities held out, but they became increasingly isolated in a countryside that was no

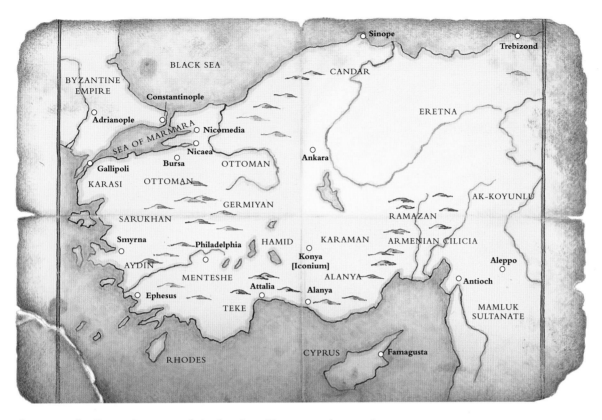

longer under Byzantine control. Andronicus II attempted to retrieve the situation and led a number of campaigns into Asia Minor, but he was hampered by his inability to remain for long in the region—the situation in the West always called him back. One by one, Byzantine cities fell to the Turks: Smyrna in 1329, Nicaea in 1331, Nicomedia in 1339, and finally Philadelphia, which held out until 1392.

What had once been Byzantine Asia Minor was now ruled by a number of small Turkish emirates. In the vicinity of Konya lay Karaman, which in 1316 had captured the city and ended the Seljuk sultanate. In western Asia Minor, the emirates of Menteshe, Aydin, Sarukhan, and Karasi were founded. But most significant for the future was an emirate in the far northwest, facing Constantinople, established by a *ghazi* called Osman or Uthman (1288–1326). It is from Osman that the name of his followers is derived: the Ottomans.

Osman defeated a Byzantine army at Bapheum in 1302, captured the city of Prousa (Bursa) in 1326, and established his capital city there. His son, Orhan (1326–62), consolidated Ottoman power in western Asia Minor and acquired the first Ottoman foothold in Europe (see pages 182–183). Orhan's position was recognized in 1346 when he married the daughter of the Byzantine emperor. Later generations of Turks regarded Osman and Orhan as the founders of the Ottoman empire, which came to dominate the Balkans and the eastern Mediterranean. Their tombs, rebuilt during the nineteenth century, can still be seen on the citadel overlooking Bursa.

The approximate distribution of the various Turkish emirates in Anatolia during the early 14th century. Within a century, the emirate nearest Constantinople—the Ottoman—had become the most dominant one and the precursor of an empire.

THE LOSS OF ASIA MINOR

George Pachymeres, a clergyman in the cathedral of Hagia Sophia in Constantinople in the early fourteenth century, wrote a graphic account of the upheavals of his time. He blamed Byzantium's loss of Asia Minor on the emperor Michael VIII Palaeologus, who had taxed the region too heavily: "Its inhabitants, unable to find the tax in currency, which they were required to do, gave up the hopeless task and went over to the Turks day by day, regarding them as better masters than the emperor. The trickle of defectors became a flood and the Turks employed them as guides and allies to lead them the other way and to ravage the lands of those who remained loyal to the emperor, at first by way of raiding parties, but soon as permanent settlers taking over the land."

THE MARITIME LEAGUE

HUMBERT'S CRUSADE

The expedition led by the French aristocrat Humbert II, dauphin (ruler) of Viennois, has been described by one historian as "one of the most pathetic crusading ventures of the period." A romantic and dreamy character, Humbert had already founded his own order of chivalry, the Order of St. Catherine. Roused to enthusiasm by the news of the capture of Smyrna (see main text), Humbert begged the pope to appoint him "Captain General of the Crusade against the Turks and those Unfaithful to the Holy Church of Rome." Having taken the cross, he sailed for Smyrna with a force of volunteers in the autumn of 1345. Once there, however, Humbert found the heat intolerable and complained that the dust was so thick that it came up to his men's knees. He mounted a few sorties but was unable to dislodge the Turks from the fortress that they still held overlooking the town. Although he had sworn to remain in the East for three years, Humbert returned to France in November 1346 and spent the rest of his days as a Dominican friar.

At first, western Europeans failed to react to the Turkish conquest of Asia Minor or to realize the inevitable dire consequences for the Christian position in the East. However, matters changed in the early fourteenth century, when the Turks captured ports such as Ephesus and Smyrna, and thus gained access to the Aegean. The new rulers of these towns used local Greek labor to build warships and launch piratical attacks against Christian ships. Venetian merchant galleys, lumbering to and from Constantinople, were particularly vulnerable. The most dangerous of the Turkish *amirs* was Umur of Aydin (see box), who by 1341 could muster a fleet of 350 vessels and an army of 15,000 men and whose base at Smyrna, tucked away on a wide bay at the base of a fortified hill, provided a perfect haven.

Alarmed by these developments, Pope Clement VI (1342–52) formed a maritime league with a fleet of twenty galleys from Venice, Cyprus, and the Hospitaller island of Rhodes, along with some vessels of his own, paid for by taxing the clergy. The fleet was placed under the command of Enrico d'Asti, the Latin patriarch of Constantinople, and assembled at Negroponte on the island of Euboea, Greece, in September 1343. At first the fleet's chances of success seemed slim, its leaders bickering over finance and objectives. But in October 1344 it arrived at Smyrna to find the port poorly defended and Umur absent with most of his army. This great stroke of luck enabled the Christians to sail in unopposed, burn most of the Turkish ships in the harbor, and occupy both the port and the town.

UMUR, "THE LION OF GOD"

The exploits of Umur, *amir* of Aydin (1336–44), against Christian shipping in the Aegean were later celebrated in a verse chronicle by the fifteenth-century Turkish poet Enveri, who lauded Umur as "the Lion of God." However, contemporary sources paint a less flattering picture. Two ambassadors from Venice, who visited Umur at Ephesus in 1345, reported that he was immensely fat, with a stomach "like a wine cask." They found him dressed in silk, drinking almond milk and eating eggs, spices, and rice with a golden spoon. Moreover, in spite of his reputation, Umur failed to dislodge the Christians from Smyrna and in 1348 was killed in the subsequent fighting.

The following January, Enrico d'Asti led a foray inland and was killed with many of his followers. In general, though, the league had enjoyed a great success. It had neutralized the main center of Turkish piracy in the Aegean and captured an important base for further operations on the coast of Asia Minor. Umur died in fighting in 1348, and in April that year a treaty was made with his brother, who promised to dismantle his fleet and to suppress Turkish piracy in the Aegean. The pope dissolved the league in 1350 and Smyrna was handed over to the Knights Hospitaller, who held the city until 1402.

The league's triumph was ephemeral. By concentrating solely on the threat to shipping, the allies failed to see the greater danger posed by Turks who might one day succeed in crossing into Europe. Thus they took no action against the Ottomans, who were penned into northwestern Asia Minor, with no access to the Aegean.

A Venetian Fleet at the Siege of Chioggia, 1379 (detail), an anonymous 16th-century painting. War galleys from Venice formed the core of the Maritime League, just as they had earlier played a crucial role in supporting the crusader states (see pages 48–49, 102–103), together with the ships of Venice's great rival, Genoa. This painting depicts an episode during a series of wars between the two Italian maritime states, who competed for centuries to control lucrative eastern trade routes and markets.

THE CONQUEST OF THE BALKANS

The Turkish conquest of Byzantium came to a halt in the early fourteenth century, when it reached the sea and could go no further. At two points in northwestern Asia Minor, the Bosporus and the Dardanelles, the sea was a narrow strait, but these two potential crossing points were guarded on the western side respectively by the Byzantine capital of Constantinople and by the fortified town of Gallipoli. The Ottomans, whose territory lay to the east, were thus prevented from extending their conquests northwestward. That is how the situation would have remained, had it not been for a natural calamity.

On the night of 2nd March 1354 a violent earthquake struck Byzantine Thrace, and Gallipoli was devastated. Suleyman, a son of the Ottoman *amir* Orhan, at once—apparently on the same day—crossed the Dardanelles with his army to occupy the ruins of Gallipoli. The Ottomans had their first foothold in Europe.

In 1366 Count Amedeo of Savoy recaptured Gallipoli and handed it back to the Byzantines, but it was already too late. During the previous twelve years, Turk settlers had flooded into Thrace, and in 1361 the Turks took the Byzantine city of Adrianople (Edirne), effectively

The Selimiye mosque, Edirne, built by the great Ottoman architect Sinan during the reign of the sultan Selim II (1566–74). Edirne (formerly Adrianople) is the largest Turkish city in Europe after Istanbul and served as the Ottoman capital from the 1360s until 1453.

cutting Constantinople off by land. The Turks could not take the Byzantine capital itself, largely because of its massive fortifications.

Christian resistance in the Balkans was led not by the enfeebled Byzantine empire but by the Serbs, until they suffered a disastrous defeat on the Marica river in September 1371. One by one, the Christian rulers of the Balkans were forced to come to terms. The Serbs became vassals of the Ottomans, and from ca. 1373 the Bulgarian *tsar* and the Byzantine emperor had to accept a similar status. Adrianople replaced Bursa (Prousa) as the Ottoman capital and Orhan's successor, Murad I (1362–89), adopted the more prestigious title of sultan. The Ottomans were the new masters of the Balkans.

But Christian resistance had not ended. In the 1380s the Serbian prince Lazar (1371–89) led a revolt and on 15th June 1389 met the armies of Murad I at Kosovo Polje, the Field of Blackbirds. At first the battle went well for the Serbs, who killed the sultan. But the Turks rallied under his son, Bayezid, and in the counterattack Lazar fell along with thousands of his followers. The victorious new sultan, Bayezid I (1389–1402), executed most of the Serbian prisoners, extended his direct control over Serbia, and in 1394 besieged Constantinople. The only hope for the Balkan Christians now was that help would come from the West in the form of a crusade.

TSAR DUSHAN OF SERBIA

Formerly a weak client state of the Byzantine empire, Serbia had expended rapidly in the early fourteenth century under Stephen Dushan (1331–55), who took advantage of a Byzantine civil war to seize much of the southern Balkans. Adopting the title of *tsar* (derived from Caesar, the ancient title of the Roman emperors), Dushan modeled his court on that of Constantinople, with its elaborate ritual and ceremonial. However, his new empire lacked any centralized structure and was incapable of surviving defeat at the hands of the Turks. Dushan's successors were reduced to the status of Ottoman vassals.

THE JANISSERIES

One reason for the phenomenal success of the Ottomans in conquering the Balkans so rapidly in the late fourteenth century was the abundant manpower that they had at their disposal. The most useful source of high-quality troops was the corps known as the Janisseries, or the "New Levies" (Turkish *yeni çeri*), created around the time of the capture of Adrianople in 1361 (see main text) as a standing army directly under the command of the sultan.

At first the soldiers who made up this élite regiment were recruited from Christian prisoners of war, but later the sultans took an annual tribute from the Christians living under their rule (the Devshirme) payable in young boys of about eight years old. These children were then encouraged to convert to Islam and trained to be soldiers. In the course of time, they were enrolled in the Janisseries, where their loyalty to the sultan and their bravery in battle became legendary. They fought in all the major Ottoman campaigns.

A Turkish Janissery, by a 16th-century French artist. Unlike other Muslims, Janisseries were forbidden to grow beards, but could wear a mustache.

THE CRUSADE OF NICOPOLIS

Manuel II, here shown on a silver coin of his reign, ruled a Byzantine empire that consisted of little more than Constantinople. Following the defeat at Nicopolis, he journeyed to the courts of western Europe to appeal in person for help. He received sympathy but little else.

In 1394 appeals for help had reached the West from the Byzantine emperor, Manuel II Palaeologus (1391–1425), and from the king of Hungary, Sigismund (1387–1437), along with ominous reports that the Ottoman sultan Bayezid I was boasting that he would soon lead his armies to France, stopping off at Rome to feed his horse on the altar of St. Peter's. Both the pope of Rome and his rival at Avignon (see page 141) issued crusading bulls and the response was enthusiastic, with more than 10,000 volunteers flocking to the standard of John, count of Nevers, the son of the duke of Burgundy. However, in spite of this auspicious beginning, the crusade of Nicopolis, as it became known, was to be the last of the great crusading expeditions.

The French knights traveled east in magnificent array, followed by twenty-four cartloads of expensive tents and pavilions alone, all made of green velvet and embroidered, with the arms of the count of Nevers picked out in gold thread. When they entered Buda, the Hungarian capital, in July 1396, King Sigismund was so impressed that he exclaimed that not only would he now be able to drive the Turks from Europe, but were the sky to fall, he would support it on his spears. Such optimism seemed justified when the combined French and Hungarian army moved south across the Danube. Two Turkish fortresses were taken with little trouble and when the crusaders laid siege to the fortress at Nicopolis (Nikopol, Bulgaria), few

SKANDERBEG OF ALBANIA

The most prolonged and successful resistance to the Turks in the Balkans was led by an Albanian chieftain who is known to history as Skanderbeg. Born Gjergj (George) Kastriotes ca. 1405, the son of a Christian Albanian client prince of the Ottomans, he was brought up as a Muslim at the Ottoman court at Edirne, where he was nicknamed Iskander Beg (Lord Alexander), after Alexander the Great, on account of his bravery. In 1444, after serving with distinction in the sultan's armies for several years, he escaped from Edirne and returned to his homeland, where he renounced Islam and led a revolt against his Turkish overlords. He held out for more than twenty years, helped by Albania's mountainous terrain

and by the knowledge of Turkish military techniques that he had acquired in the sultan's service.

Yet Skanderbeg's stand against the Turks received little help from western Christendom. When he visited Rome in 1466–67 to seek financial aid, the pope gave him so little money that he was scarcely able to pay his hotel bill. On Skanderbeg's death in January 1468, the rebellion he had started came to an end and in the years that followed many Albanians accepted Turkish rule and converted to Islam. Although today the majority of Albanians are (at least nominally) Muslims, as the champion of the country's independence Skanderbeg remains a national hero.

doubted that it would be swiftly taken and that the host would be able to move on to its ultimate goal, the relief of Constantinople.

But the crusaders had reckoned without the resourcefulness and military ability of Bayezid. As soon as he received news of the crusade, he broke off his siege of Constantinople and marched his entire army north to Nicopolis in less than three weeks, a feat that earned him the nickname of Yilderim (Thunderbolt). His arrival came as a devastating surprise to the crusade leaders, who were having dinner when a messenger burst in with the news.

When the two armies met on 25th September 1396, the French knights insisted on attacking immediately, without waiting for the Hungarians who were coming up more slowly behind. The initial French charge scattered the Turkish vanguard, but the knights then found themselves confronted with a steep slope, fortified with sharpened wooden stakes. While they were negotiating these obstacles, the knights were suddenly attacked by Bayezid's household cavalry, which emerged unexpectedly from some nearby woods. Outnumbered and tired, the French were easily overcome, and the Hungarians arrived to be confronted with the full weight of the advancing Ottoman army. In the ensuing rout, Sigismund escaped by ship down the Danube but John of Nevers and many other French nobles were taken prisoner. Crusaders drowned when they tried to swim out to the Christian ships anchored in the Danube: so overloaded did the vessels become that their crews pushed the fleeing soldiers back into the water.

When the news reached Paris, according to one chronicler, "bitter despair and affliction reigned in all hearts" and the defeat seems to have had a deep impact on enthusiasm for crusading in the East. Although projects for crusades would continue to be discussed, never again would an expedition against the Turks on this scale be mounted from a country such as France that was not in the front line of conflict with the Ottomans. Henceforward it would be left to those whose borders were directly threatened to defend Christendom against the expansion of Islam.

The armies of the sultan Bayezid I, the Thunderbolt, rout the European crusaders at the battle of Nicopolis, 1396. Bayezid is depicted at the center as the mounted swordsman wearing the large plumed turban. This illustration is from the Hunernama of Loqman, 1584, which is an account by Loqman, the Ottoman court historian, of the rule of Bayezid I.

DISASTER AT VARNA

Opposite: *The tomb of Timur Lang ("the Lame," 1336–1405) in Samarkand. One of the most successful and ruthless of Mongol conquerors, Timur led devastating expeditions from Samarkand that ranged from Asia Minor to India. His empire fragmented following his death.*

Below: *Timur's army in battle. His defeat of the Ottomans in 1402 delayed by half a century their conquest of Constantinople. Persian, 16th century.*

After the defeat at Nicopolis in 1396, the Christian position in the Balkans was redeemed by intervention from an unexpected quarter when the Ottoman sultan Bayezid I became embroiled in a war with the Mongols led by the fearsome Timur Lang, or Tamerlaine. Bayezid's army was defeated at Ankara on 28th July 1402 and Bayezid was captured. The once-proud sultan was reputedly kept in an iron cage until he died the following year. The siege of Constantinople was lifted because the Ottoman empire was plunged into civil war, with Bayezid's numerous sons fighting for his throne.

It was only a brief respite for Byzantium. Within twenty years the Ottoman empire was strong and united under one undisputed sultan, Murad II (1421–51), who soon made his intentions clear by mounting a brief siege of Constantinople in 1422 and by capturing the Byzantine city of Thessalonica in 1430. In view of the renewed threat, the Byzantine emperor John VIII Palaeologus (1425–48) once more appealed to the pope to send a crusade to save Constantinople from the Turks. To make his appeal more attractive, he affirmed his desire to end the schism which, despite attempts at reunion, continued to divide the Greek Orthodox and Roman Catholic churches. In 1438, accompanied by a large delegation, John attended a church council at Florence, where the schism was declared to be at an end and the churches reunited.

In return for his compliance, John was promised his crusade, and the pope dispatched Cardinal Giuliano Cesarini as legate to Hungary to coordinate the anti-Ottoman forces in the region. The resultant army was mainly composed of Hungarians and Poles under King Ladislas III of Poland and Hungary (1434–44), and Serbs under their ruler, George Brankovich (1427–56). No troops came from western Europe, although naval support was provided by the pope, the duke of Burgundy, and the Venetians.

By June 1443, preparations were complete and an army some 25,000 strong moved down through the Balkans to attack the Turks, capturing Nish and Sofia without much resistance. The crusaders then marched on Adrianople, but by that time winter was setting in and they were forced to retire beyond the Danube. In spite of these successes, Ladislas and Brankovich seem to have had doubts as to their ability to inflict a serious defeat on the Turks. Accordingly, in August the following year, an ambassador was sent to the court of Murad II and he concluded a ten-year truce, sealed by solemn oaths on both sides. Brankovich and the Serbs thereupon left the crusader

army but Ladislas was left to face the wrath of the papal legate. Cesarini denounced the truce as a betrayal of the cause of the crusade and urged Ladislas to break it, advising that oaths sworn to infidels were not, in any case, binding. Ladislas gave way and in September 1444 the army, now much smaller without the Serbian contingent, invaded Ottoman territory once more.

The sultan was shocked by the Christian volte-face and hurried back from Asia Minor to confront the invasion. He is said to have had the broken treaty fixed to his standard and to have exclaimed: "Christ, if you are God as your followers claim, punish them for their perfidy." When Murad caught up with the crusaders at Varna on the Black Sea, the Ottoman army outnumbered the Christians three to one, but the battle, fought in a driving wind, was fierce and long drawn out. Turkish casualties were so high that it took Murad three days to be sure that he had won. The Christian army, on the other hand, was almost completely annihilated, with Ladislas and Cesarini among the dead. In Hungary the legend persisted that Ladislas had survived the battle and spent the rest of his life as a wandering hermit, seeking to atone for his breach of faith, which had brought such disastrous consequences.

IBN KHALDUN'S "NEW WORLD"

The Christian reconquest of Spain, the rise of the Ottomans, and the even more dramatic successes of Timur influenced the great scholar Ibn Khaldun (1332–1406) of Tunis, whose family had fled Seville before it fell to Christian forces. In his famous *Prolegomenon (Muqaddima)*, he argues that a sedentary civilization will inevitably lose its dynamism, decay, and be replaced by a new, rising, dynamic force, one frequently inspired by faith. And so the cycle would continue. His theories were informed by observations about the fall of Muslim dynasties to more vigorous and motivated rivals. Ibn Khaldun, who served as an envoy to Castile and, later, to Timur, was especially aware that there were significant times of turbulence that heralded a new world order. This "new world" was being born in other lands (he does not say where), and he was painfully aware that his own civilization of al-Andalus was nearing its end.

THE FALL OF CONSTANTINOPLE

This 16th-century wall painting in the Orthodox monastery of Moldovita in Romania depicts the siege of Constantinople. The city's massive Roman land walls had stood for more than 1,000 years without being breached (the crusaders of 1204 had gained entry by assaulting the harbor walls on the Golden Horn). However, in 1453 they were subjected to bombardment by cannons, a recent addition to the weaponry of Muslim and Christian armies.

Although the Christians had been defeated at Varna, the whole episode was a sobering experience for the Ottomans. Fears of co-operation between Byzantium and the West were perhaps exaggerated, for there was intense opposition in Constantinople to the union of the churches agreed at the council of Florence in 1438 (see page 186), which many regarded as a betrayal of the Orthodox faith.

The new Ottoman sultan, Mehmed II (1451–81), decided as a priority to eliminate Constantinople and in April 1453 he laid siege to the city by land, as his predecessor Bayezid I had done. However, unlike Bayezid he possessed a number of cannon, with which he was able to bombard the ancient walls of Constantinople. The Byzantine emperor, Constantine XI Palaeologus (1449–53), sent last desperate appeals to Rome. In reply, Pope Nicholas V (1447–55) insisted that the union of Florence be implemented at once. As one Byzantine chronicler bitterly remarked: "We received as much help from Rome as we did from the [Mamluk] sultan [of Egypt]."

The Byzantines and their Venetian and Genoese allies had little chance against Mehmed's huge army. In the early hours of 29th May 1453 the Janisseries fought their way through a breach in the walls made by the bombardment, and by midday it was all over. Constantine XI was dead (see box) and the city founded by his namesake was in Turkish hands. Mehmed rode in triumph on a white horse into Hagia Sophia and declared the great cathedral to be a mosque.

News of the fall of Constantinople was greeted in western Europe with shock, and the pope at once called for a crusade to retake the city. One of the first to respond was Philip the Good, duke of Burgundy (1419–67), but he undertook to go only if the king of France or another powerful ruler were also to do so. In the event, no monarch felt secure enough to leave his own kingdom to take on the Turks and Philip's crusade was never launched.

It was not until the pontificate of Pius II (1458–64) that serious efforts were made to gather the means for a counterattack. After attempts to persuade secular rulers to lead the crusade proved fruitless, the elderly Pius mustered a fleet of his own at the Italian port of Ancona. In June 1464 he took the cross at a ceremony at St. Peter's in Rome and then set out for Ancona to lead the crusade in person. But by this time he was so frail that he had to be carried in a litter, and shortly after arriving at the port he fell ill and died. Few shared the late pope's enthusiasm for the venture and the ships that he had gathered quietly sailed for home. There was to be no crusade and Constantinople, once the greatest city of Christendom, remained in the hands of the Turks as the new capital of the Ottoman empire.

THE SIEGE OF BELGRADE

Christian encounters with the Ottoman Turks in the fifteenth century did not always end in catastrophic defeats like those of Nicopolis, Varna, and, above all, Constantinople. In July 1456 the Turks laid siege to Belgrade, which was then part of the kingdom of Hungary. The Hungarian king and his court fled to Vienna and it was left to a seventy-year-old Franciscan friar, John of Capistrano, to tour Hungary preaching the crusade and gathering an army of thousands of volunteers. Poorly armed and thoroughly disorganized as they were, Capistrano's force succeeded in driving the Turks from the walls of Belgrade, capturing 100 cannon, and inflicting more than 13,000 casualties.

THE LAST ROMAN EMPEROR

The contemporary Greek historian Doukas describes the last stand of Constantine IX as the Turks broke into Constantinople on the morning of 29th May 1453: "Despairing and hopeless, he stood [on the walls] with sword and shield in hand and poignantly cried out, 'Is there no one among the Christians who will take my head from me?' He was abandoned and alone. Then one of the Turks wounded him by striking him flush, and he, in turn, gave the Turk a blow. A second Turk delivered a mortal blow from behind and the emperor fell to the earth. They slew him as a common soldier, because they did not know he was emperor."

The last "Emperor of the Romans" was dead (though the Ottoman sultans adopted the title, in Turkish Kaisar-i-Rum). But his heroic resistance made him something of a folk hero for the Greeks in the following centuries of Turkish rule. The story grew up that Constantine had not died at all: at the last moment an angel had swooped down, turned him into a marble column, and hidden the column in a cave near the city walls. One day the angel would return, change the column back into the emperor, and place in his hand the sword that he had wielded in his last battle. The emperor would then drive out the Turks and reign once more in Constantinople.

KNIGHTS OF THE MEDITERRANEAN

The Knights Hospitaller suffered a very different fate from the other great crusading order, the Templars (see page 175). Ejected from the Holy Land, the Hospitallers at first took refuge on Cyprus, but in 1306 they gained a new base when they seized the island of Rhodes from the Byzantine empire. They fortified the main town and harbor, built castles across the island, and also maintained footholds on the coast of Asia Minor at Smyrna until 1402 and at Bodrum until 1523. From these bases, the knights once more became Christendom's frontline defenders against the remorseless Ottoman advance.

At first the Ottomans paid little attention to Rhodes, seeing it as a minor Christian outpost. However, by the 1470s it was clear that the Turks were planning an attack and the grand master of the Hospitallers, Fulk Villaret, began laying up supplies in preparation for a siege. In the spring of 1480, Sultan Mehmed II landed a force of about 15,000 on the island. The defenders numbered only 3,500, of whom only a few hundred were serving knights of the order, and the walls of Rhodes town were subjected to an intense bombardment. Nevertheless, the Turks were unable to take the port and were compelled to abandon the siege. The successful defense of Rhodes boosted the prestige of the Hospitallers in the West as never before.

However, it was only a matter of time before the Ottoman offensive was renewed, because Rhodes served as a base for piratical attacks on Turkish shipping as well as a safe haven for disaffected

JEAN DE LA VALLETTE

Much of the credit for the Hospitallers' successful defense of Malta in 1565 (see main text) belongs to the grand master at the time, Jean de la Vallette (1494–1568, above). Originally from Provence in the south of France, Vallette had joined the order at the age of twenty and was a veteran of the 1522 siege of Rhodes. He had prepared so well for the Ottoman attack on Malta that even on a barren island notoriously short of water, the garrison never suffered from hunger or thirst, while his inspiring leadership undoubtedly induced the defenders to stand firm in a situation that must have seemed hopeless. The city of Valetta, founded after the siege, was named in his honor, and his tomb still stands in the city's cathedral.

THE TURKS IN ITALY: OTRANTO

At the time of the first siege of Rhodes (see main text), the nightmare of an Ottoman invasion of western Europe seemed to be coming true. Provoked by raids on the coast of Asia Minor by a papal fleet, in August 1480 a Turkish force seized Otranto on the heel of Italy, and rounded up the inhabitants who were then sold into slavery. The elderly archbishop of Otranto, Stefano Pendinelli, was murdered along with most of his clergy. As the news spread, rumors grew thick and fast, greatly exaggerating the size of the Turkish force and prompting the pope to consider fleeing to France. However, the danger was soon contained. The army of the king of Naples and a fleet sent by the pope besieged the Turkish garrison in Otranto and it surrendered on 10th September 1481.

Ottoman royalty. In July 1522, when another Ottoman army landed on the island, the defenses were far stronger than they had been in 1480 and there were at least 7,000 troops to man them. But this time the Turks were going to stay for as long as it took to reduce the island, and with no prospect of help from the West, the grand master was forced to surrender. The sultan permitted the knights to withdraw honorably and on 1st January 1523 they sailed for Europe, ending their occupation of Rhodes after more than two centuries.

After some years in search of a new base, in 1530 the Hospitallers accepted Malta from the Holy Roman emperor—with some reluctance, since the island was barren and poor. The Hospitallers also complained that it would be difficult to defend, an assertion put to the test in the spring of 1565 when an Ottoman fleet began the third great siege fought by the order. Over the next five months, the grand master Jean de la Vallette (see sidebar) led a heroic defense. Against overwhelming odds, the Turks were held at bay for long enough to allow a Spanish relief force to arrive from Sicily.

The Hospitallers were once more left free to continue their attacks on Muslim shipping and Ottoman territories as far afield as Greece and Cyprus. Their presence on Malta came to an end at the hands not of the Turks but of Napoleon Bonaparte, who seized the island in 1798 as a base for his own operations in the Mediterranean.

In the following centuries the Most Venerable Order of the Hospital of St. John of Jerusalem reverted to its original role of caring for others. Perhaps its most visible offshoot today is the St. John Ambulance, the worldwide paramedic and first aid charity.

Above: *Much of the successful defense of Malta in 1565 centered on the fort of St. Elmo at the mouth of the Grand Harbor, Valetta. The present fortifications of the harbor (above) were constructed after the siege.*

Opposite: *Jean de la Vallette, grand master of the the Hospitallers. A later portrait by François-Xavier Dupré (1803–71).*

THE REFORMATION

While the battle to contain the expansion of the Ottoman empire continued unabated, in western Europe a development was taking place that was to have far-reaching implications for the crusading ethos. In 1517 the practice of selling indulgences—the principal inducement for Christians to participate in or finance crusades (see page 176)—came under vociferous attack from a German monk named Martin Luther (1483–1546). Luther argued that in promising remission of sin in return for money or military service, the pope was selling what was, in fact, a free gift, purchased by Christ's death and resurrection and available to all who sincerely repented.

The attack on indulgences soon became an assault on the institution of the papacy itself, which came to be seen by Luther and his followers as an instrument of the Devil to lead Christians astray. As the sixteenth century went on, new "Protestant" churches emerged

THE PAPAL ALUM MINES

The sale of indulgences was not the only source of revenue that the popes could draw on in order to finance crusading expeditions against the Turks. Alum, a naturally occurring sulfate of aluminum and potassium, was a vital ingredient in the dyeing process, helping the dye to adhere to the fabric. The only source was at Phocaea to the north of Smyrna (Izmir) in Asia Minor, in Turkish territory. However, in 1461 John of Castro discovered rich deposits of alum at Tolfa in the Papal States (central Italy).

Within a year 8,000 men had been set to work extracting the mineral, enabling the popes both to cut off the lucrative Turkish trade in alum and to provide a rich source of income for themselves, much of which went toward financing crusading expeditions.

in England, Scotland, Scandinavia, and northern Germany, which refused to acknowledge the authority of the pope.

Luther and his followers came to regard crusades as another of the false doctrines propagated by the pope. "How shamefully," wrote Luther, "the pope has this long time baited us with the war against the Turks, taken our money, destroyed so many Christians, and made so much mischief!" He claimed that to fight against the Ottomans was to oppose the judgment of God, who was using the Turks as an instrument to punish Christians for their sins: as proof Luther pointed to the disastrous outcome of the Varna expedition of 1444 (see pages 186–187) and other crusading enterprises.

Henceforth the defense of Christendom against the Turks, in which the popes had always taken a leading role, could never be seen in the same way in Protestant countries. The English divine John Foxe was uncertain whether the sultan or the pope "hath been the more bloody and pernicious adversary to Christ." Some extremists even saw the Turks as preferable, such as the English bishop who wrote in 1571 that if the Ottomans invaded Italy, they would at least "bridle the ferocity of Antichrist [the pope]." England and other Protestant powers saw no harm in supplying the Turks with war materiel—particularly tin, which was essential for bronze cannon—and thus assisting them in their attacks on Christian Europe.

By 1529, however, with the Turks approaching Vienna, even Luther was compelled to modify his views. In his *On the War with the Turks* (1529), he urged that the struggle against the "scourge of God" should be prosecuted vigorously, but by secular rulers, not the pope. Although not a follower of Luther, the Dutch humanist scholar Desiderius Erasmus (ca. 1469–1536) held views similar to Luther's later position. In Erasmus's view, war should be made on the Turks only as a last resort to defend Christian countries, and it would be infinitely preferable to convert them to the Christian faith.

Moreover, the old idea of a united Christendom facing the Muslim enemy was still a potent one. In 1571, when news arrived in Protestant England of the victory of the Catholic Don John of Austria over the Turkish fleet at Lepanto (see pages 194–195), there was general rejoicing in the streets of London, with bonfires, the ringing of church bells, and hearty banquets. In Calvinist Scotland, the young King James VI (later James I of England) celebrated Lepanto in an epic poem, drawing the moral that if God could give such a victory to false Christians, how much more merciful would he be to true believers. Thus, although the war with the Turks was largely left to the Catholic powers during the sixteenth century, the ideal of the crusade lived on, even in the Protestant world.

Opposite: *Demons crowning the Antipope, from a 14th-century manuscript. Luther's attack on the papacy echoed those of the reform movements of the period of the Great Schism, which had ended a century earlier (see pages 140–141).*

Below: *Desiderius Erasmus in his Study, by Hans Holbein the Younger (1497–1543). In his Consideration of the War that should be Waged against the Turks (1530), the great Dutch humanist scholar identified two mistaken views. The first was to portray the Turks as savage barbarians, since Christians were often responsible for far worse atrocities. The second was to do nothing while the Ottomans overran eastern Europe and "abandon our brothers to a servitude which they do not deserve."*

THE BATTLE OF LEPANTO

In the first half of the sixteenth century, the Holy Roman emperor Charles V (ruled 1519–56) became, by a series of genealogical accidents, the ruler of much of western and central Europe. From one grandfather he inherited the kingdoms of Spain and Naples and from another the Habsburg lands of Austria and central Europe. His enormous realm also benefited from the plentiful supply of gold then flowing in from the Spanish conquests in the Americas. It was only natural that such a powerful Catholic ruler should lead the war against the Turks, and all the more so because, after a period of passivity between 1481 and 1512, the Ottomans were once more on the move. The sultan Selim I (1512–20) conquered Syria and Egypt from the Mamluks, and added Jerusalem to the Ottoman empire. Selim's successor, Suleyman the Magnificent (1520–66), took Rhodes from the Hospitallers in 1522 (see page 189) and subdued the kingdom of Hungary with his victory at Mohács in 1526, thus bringing the Ottomans to the borders of the Habsburg domains.

However, the war that developed between the Habsburgs and Ottomans in the sixteenth century was largely fought in the Mediterranean where, following the conquest of Egypt and Syria, and their alliance with the Barbary corsairs of North Africa, the Turks

The Battle of Lepanto, 1571, by an anonymous Venetian artist of the 16th century. By the standards of the time, the battle was on a massive scale. The Ottoman fleet numbered 275 vessels as opposed to 209 Christian ships, and at least 100,000 men must have been involved in the fighting. Eighty Turkish vessels were sunk and 117 captured, with about 30,000 men dead or captive, compared with Christian casualties of 8,000 dead and less than a score of ships lost.

posed an even greater threat than they did in the Balkans. In 1569, when the Turks invaded the Venetian-ruled island of Cyprus, the fleets of Spain, Venice, and the papacy were combined in a maritime league under the command of Don John of Austria, the illegitimate son of Charles V. On 7th October 1571, the ships of the league engaged the Turkish fleet off Lepanto in southern Greece, at the entrance to the Gulf of Corinth. Although the Turks had the advantage in terms of numbers, the Christians had more guns and their combined firepower had a devastating effect on the Ottoman fleet. It was a Christian victory on an unprecedented scale and it ended the myth of Ottoman invincibility at sea.

Yet Lepanto was by no means a turning point. Although the sultan, Selim II (1566–74), was so enraged by the news that he did not sleep for three days and nights, he later commented that "the infidel has only singed my beard. It will grow again." The Ottoman fleet was rapidly reconstructed, with the shipyards of Constantinople at one point turning out a new vessel every day. In the same year as Lepanto, the Turks went on to complete their conquest of Cyprus, and the maritime league, far from capitalizing on its success, broke up shortly afterward. In 1574 the new Turkish fleet expelled the Spanish from the foothold they had gained on the coast of Tunisia. The Ottoman threat was as real at the end of the sixteenth century as it had been a century before.

A hat jewel made for Don John of Austria, who led the Christian fleet to a resounding victory over the Ottoman fleet at Lepanto.

THE BARBARY CORSAIRS

Ottoman naval power in the Mediterranean was greatly assisted by an alliance with the pirates who operated from bases on the coasts of Barbary (the name given by Europeans to North Africa west of Egypt). In 1518, one of them, Hizir Reis, also known as Khayr al-Din Barbarossa, came to an agreement with the sultan whereby he would win Algiers with Ottoman help and in 1532 he was appointed grand admiral of the Ottoman navy. After 1587, the corsairs reverted to independent action, preying mercilessly on Christian shipping and coastal towns, and seizing captives to be sold as slaves or held to ransom.

The corsairs were not all Muslims (they recruited many Christians, some of whom converted to Islam) and their activities were by no means confined to the

Mediterranean. In the seventeenth century the inhabitants of the southern coasts of England and Ireland lived in constant fear of corsair attacks. Even after the English and French navies had neutralized the threat to their countries, corsairs continued to harry shipping of other countries into the eighteenth and nineteenth centuries. Corsair attacks on United States vessels sparked the young republic's first foreign war (1801–05), which ended with a decisive American naval victory over the Barbary states that harbored the corsairs. The Barbary War led to important developments in the United States Navy and was directly responsible for the creation of the United States Marine Corps. A second, briefer, war in 1815 ended the Barbary threat to American vessels once and for all.

THE GLORIES OF THE OTTOMANS

The Ottoman empire was by no means dedicated solely to warfare or to self-indulgence, as its Christian critics liked to think. Even the most warlike of sultans were patrons of art and architecture, and every one sponsored the building of at least one *külliye*, a complex of religious, educational, and charitable buildings, of which a mosque was the central feature.

In their patronage, the sultans were extraordinarily eclectic, employing artists from among the peoples they had conquered. Two of the greatest Ottoman architects, Christodoulos and Mimar Sinan, were Greeks by birth. The sultans also imported luxury goods from outside the empire, particularly Chinese pottery, which was to be an important influence on Ottoman ceramics. Such outside influences ensured that the Ottoman empire developed a style of art and architecture that was a synthesis of the Islamic traditions of the Near East and those of the Classical world and Byzantium.

The most obvious and visible legacy of the Ottoman empire is its architecture, especially the *külliye*s built in

Constantinople (Istanbul) and other cities. Of these the most striking is the vast Suleymaniye, built by Sinan from 1550–57 for Suleyman the Magnificent. The central dome of the mosque is surrounded by no fewer than 400 smaller domes that cover a hospital, an orphanage, a soup kitchen, an asylum, a library, baths, a travelers' hospice, and Suleyman's tomb. Between the buildings are colonnaded courts with fountains. The complex projects Ottoman power and grandeur but also, in the purposes of the individual buildings, the humanity and philanthropy enjoined on Muslims in the *Quran*.

If Ottoman buildings are impressive when viewed from the outside, the interiors are often even more memorable owing to the use of glazed ceramic tiles in the decoration. The tiles produced from the later fifteenth century in the town of Nicaea (Iznik), achieved a richness and variety of pattern and color that has never been equaled. These tiles were used lavishly on the interior walls of Constantinople's mosques. The magnificent Blue Mosque of Sultan Ahmed I (1603–17) takes

its name from the hue of the Iznik tiles that decorate its walls and soaring arches. Some of the finest examples are found in the mosque of Rustem Pasha, built in 1561 by Sinan. Iznik tiles also feature prominently in the decoration of the Topkapi palace, the residence of Ottoman sultans for nearly three centuries.

There was another area in which Ottoman artists advanced beyond traditional Islamic art. The sultans employed painters to provide miniature illustrations for chronicles of the important events of their reigns and other official books. As in the case of tiles, these illustrations show a delight in vibrant color, particularly scarlet. The *Suriname* or *Book of Festivals*, commissioned by Sultan Murad III (1594–95), is a fine example of the work of these artists.

Above: *The Suleymaniye Mosque, Istanbul, built by Sinan in the 1550s for Suleyman the Magnificent (1520–66). The greatest of the Ottoman sultans, and regarded as such in his own lifetime, Suleyman presided over an empire whose power and reputation were at their height.*
Opposite: *A Turkish miniature painting of Dervishes, members of a Muslim sect, performing their characteristic "whirling" devotional dance.*
Left: *The tiled interior of the Baghdad Pavilion in the Fourth Court of the Topkapi palace, Istanbul.*

THE END OF THE CRUSADES

A DIPLOMAT'S VIEW OF THE OTTOMAN EMPIRE

Sir Paul Rycaut (1628–1700) was appointed private secretary to the English ambassador in Constantinople in 1660 and wrote of his experiences in *The Present State of the Ottoman Empire* (1668). He portrayed the Turks in very negative terms, not because they were not Christians, but because their system of government was a "fabric of slavery," characterized by "severity, violence, and cruelty," an absolute monarchy where the individual had no protection against the arbitrary whims of the sultan. But he regarded this system as a natural one for an oriental people like the Turks to live under, just as it was natural for Englishmen to enjoy the protection of the law, even against the king. Rycaut's view was typical of how the Ottoman empire was then being seen in western Europe, and indeed of how westerners have tended to perceive the "oriental" world ever since—as exotic and fascinating, but at the same time intrinsically corrupt and cruel.

The reality of the Turkish threat in the mid-seventeenth century was brought home when the Ottomans invaded the Venetian-ruled island of Crete in 1645, finally conquering it in 1669, after twenty-four years of fighting. In July 1683 the Ottoman grand vizier, Kara Mustafa Pasha, penetrated Habsburg lands with a huge army and laid siege to Vienna. The city was poorly prepared for a siege since a peace treaty with the Ottomans was still in force, but it managed to hold out until 11th September, when a relieving force under King John III Sobieski of Poland came to the rescue.

Given the continuing danger, Catholic Europe maintained the rhetoric and institutions of the crusade. Papal indulgences were issued for those who took part in the defense of Crete and Vienna, and in 1684 a Holy League was formed by Pope Innocent IX, the Holy Roman empire, Poland, and Venice. Special preaching attracted thousands of volunteers to the league. These last crusaders even included Protestants such as the fiery Scottish republican Andrew Fletcher (1655–1716).

It was also in the later seventeenth century that attitudes began to change. There were two reasons behind this. The first was the slow evaporation of the Ottoman threat: between 1684 and 1697 the Holy League operated with unprecedented success, largely thanks to western technical superiority, which made itself felt for the first time. While western armies now had the advantage of professional well-trained infantry supported by mobile field artillery, the Ottoman Janisseries, who had once been key to Turkish success, had become a powerful force for conservatism, vigorously opposing the introduction of new military techniques. Consequently, in the 1690s the Austrians were able to drive the Turks back south of the Danube. By the treaty of Karlowitz of January 1699, the sultan was compelled for the first time to yield large tracts of territory, ceding most of Hungary to Austria and giving up other areas to Poland, Venice, and Russia. As the eighteenth century progressed, it became clear that there was no longer any likelihood of the sultan marching into Rome at the head of his troops. The Ottoman empire now entered on its long period of decline which was to end in its formal dissolution in 1923.

The second factor was a new attitude to the place of religious belief in society. Philosophers such as John Locke (1632–1704), David Hume (1711–76), and Voltaire (1694–1778) argued that religion was a matter of private conscience alone and had nothing to do with government policy or the state. It certainly did not provide the grounds for going to war with a foreign power. Crusades were no longer seen as the heroic defense of a beleaguered Christendom but as the savagery of a barbarous and superstitious past. For Hume, the crusades were "the most signal and durable monument of human folly that has yet appeared in any age or nation." Not that these intellectuals were admirers of the Ottomans, whose government they regarded as arbitrary and cruel. Rather, they regarded the superiority of Christendom as resting not on a set of "correct" religious beliefs, but on a set of cultural, political, and social values, particularly the rule of law, limits on the powers of government, and freedom of the individual.

In future, western European relations with the Ottoman empire would be based solely on commercial and strategic considerations, with Britain and France often supporting the Turks against Christian Russia, most notably during the Crimean War of 1854–56.

The Siege of Vienna, 1683, by an anonymous 17th-century artist. The city was saved from Kara Mustafa's forces by the timely intervention of King John III Sobieski of Poland. Although the rapid Turkish retreat offered a good opportunity to inflict a significant defeat, the Austrians were uneasy about being beholden to a foreign prince and declined to join the Polish king in pursuit, causing him to lament "the ingratitude of those whom we have saved." Kara Mustafa drew little benefit from his escape: he was strangled soon afterward by some Janisseries at Belgrade on the orders of the sultan.

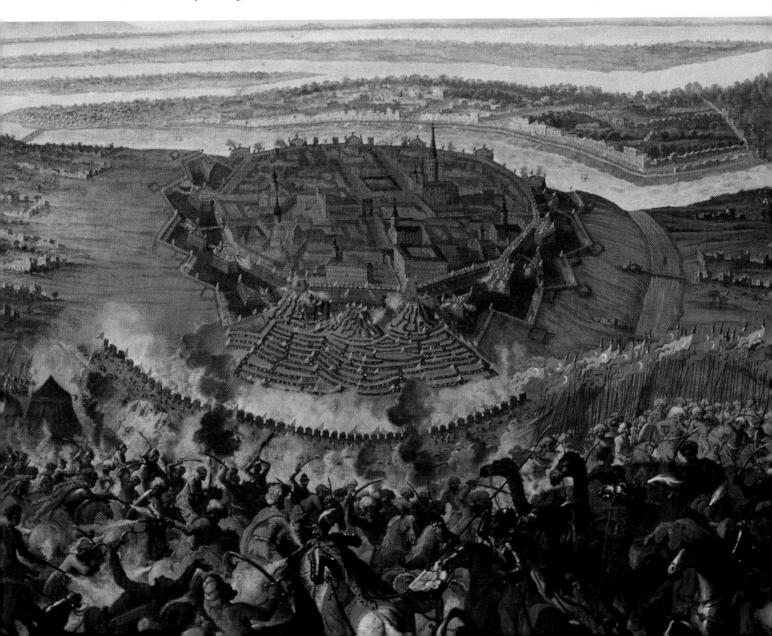

THE LEGACY
OF THE
CRUSADES

CAROLE HILLENBRAND

CRUSADING IN THE WESTERN IMAGINATION

Despite having lost the Holy Land, Europeans did not forget the crusades; and memories of this momentous interlude in their history remained, even after the Ottoman empire had ceased to pose a real threat to Europe. Many European perceptions of Muslims and the Muslim world were rooted in the crusading experience and Europe created myths and ideals based on it.

Napoleon's Egyptian campaign of 1798 may be taken as a key moment in the growth of orientalism in Europe and of scholarly interest in the crusades. Thereafter, the academic study of the crusades began in earnest, and the sixteen volumes of the *Recueil des historiens des Croisades* produced (1841–1906) in France by the august Académie des Inscriptions et Belles Lettres, were a monument to nineteenth-century scholarship. Unlike earlier luminaries of the Enlightenment, such as Voltaire, Gibbon, and Hume, who had criticized crusading as irrational fanaticism, nineteenth-century scholars had a more positive attitude.

But imaginative fiction was more influential than historiography in molding public perceptions of the crusades. Torquato Tasso's epic poem of the First Crusade, *Gerusalemme Liberata* (1581), was a particularly rich resource for nineteenth-century creative artists. The romantic lure of the crusades became a potent source of inspiration for many novelists, playwrights, poets, musicians, and artists, who portrayed the crusaders as the flower of medieval European chivalry in conflict with an exotic Muslim enemy. The crusades could also be seen to epitomize, and indeed to intensify, the epic struggle between Christianity and Islam that had begun in the seventh century.

Benjamin Disraeli (1804–81), the British prime minister and novelist, visited the tombs of the crusader kings in 1831, and the Near East was a setting for several of his novels. Artists such as David Roberts (see illustration, opposite), Edward Lear, and Jean-Léon Gérome painted the Holy Land; other painters depicted crusader subjects. Rossini and Verdi, among others, composed operas in crusader settings. Poets such as Lamartine and Nerval evoked the Orient. William Wordsworth wrote four sonnets about the crusades.

Sir Walter Scott (1771–1832) deserves special attention in this context. Although he criticized the crusades in his *Essay on Chivalry* published in 1818, his attitude toward them was generally romantic. Of his four popular novels with crusader backgrounds, *The Talisman*

(1825) was especially famous. Scott's depiction of Saladin drew on a literary tradition stretching back to medieval times, idealizing him with a blend of Orientalist fantasy and chivalric legend. Scott contrasts, albeit with Eurocentric condescension, "the Christian and English monarch" Richard the Lionheart, who showed "all the cruelty of an Eastern [sovereign]," and Saladin, "who displayed the deep policy and prudence of a European sovereign."

Notwithstanding Scott, it was probably paintings that most influenced the Victorian public's imagination. Paintings worked on multiple levels, some obvious, some perhaps only subliminal. They treat much more than the crusades as a historical phenomenon. They are about pride in national heritage; bringing the cross to the heathen; imperial claims to distant lands; the lure of the exotic; romanticism; and the mystique of the Middle Ages. All these themes resonated in nineteenth-century British society—and their echoes reverberate to this day. In Victorian England and elsewhere, pictures reached a wider public than did any scholarly account of the crusades.

In the nineteenth century the foremost ruler of the world's Muslims was Queen Victoria. Imperial expansion by Britain, France, Germany, and other European states in non-Christian regions was inevitably accompanied by Christian missions undertaking, as the title of a popular British series of books proclaimed, the *Conquests of the Cross*. European nationalism also brought to the fore crusading heroes such as Louis IX (St. Louis) in France, Richard the Lionheart in England, and Frederick Barbarossa in Germany. Belgium, established only in 1830, proudly commemorated Godfrey of Bouillon.

The Damascus Gate, Jerusalem, *by David Roberts (1839). The crusades fitted well into the 19th-century European view of the Orient as, in the words of the Palestinian writer and academic Edward Said (1935–2003), "a place of romance, exotic beings, haunting memories and landscapes, remarkable experiences."*

ISLAM, "ENEMY OF CIVILIZATION"

The French writer François-René de Chateaubriand (1768–1848) visited the Holy Land in 1806 and was made a papal knight of the Holy Sepulcher, vowing to recover it from the "infidel." His *Itinéraire de Paris à Jérusalem et de Jérusalem à Paris* **(1811) describes the crusades as a confrontation between Islam and "civilization":**

"The crusades were not only about the deliverance of the Holy Sepulcher, but more about knowing which would win on earth: a religion [Islam] that was the enemy of civilization, systematically favorable to ignorance, to despotism, to slavery; or a religion that had caused to reawaken in modern people the genius of a sage antiquity, and had abolished base servitude."

MARK TWAIN IN THE HOLY LAND

The crusades inspired some American art, such as *The March of the Crusaders* by George Innes (1825–94), but otherwise the romantic idealization of crusading did not make great headway in the United States, which tended to shy away from anything that glorified the Old World. The crusades were also deeply linked with Catholicism, which was widely criticized at the time as un-American, and there was a wide antipathy toward such ideas as nobility, feudalism, and wars of religion.

The novelist Mark Twain visited Europe and the Holy Land in 1867, and describes his travels in *The Innocents Abroad* (1869), his most popular work in his lifetime. With quiet irony and a skepticism typical of contemporary Americans he describes the purported sacred relics displayed by the Catholic monks in the church of the Holy Sepulcher. Most impressive of all the church's "relics," however, is the sword of Godfrey of Bouillon:

"No blade in Christendom wields such enchantment as this—no blade of all that rust in the ancestral halls of Europe is able to invoke such visions of romance in the brain of him who looks upon it—none that can prate of such chivalric deeds or tell such brave tales of the warrior days of old. ... It speaks to him of Baldwin, and Tancred, the princely Saladin, and great Richard of the Lion Heart. It was with just such blades as these that these splendid heroes of romance used to segregate a man, so to speak, and leave the half of him to fall one way and the other half the other."

THE FIRST WORLD WAR: "A GREAT CRUSADE"

Some commentators used crusading imagery in connection with the First World War, seeing it as a "war to end all wars" and depicting it as a conflict between cultures, fought to contain German militarism. Despite the loss of life, some clergy saw it as a crusade to defend freedom and to liberate the Holy Places from the control of Germany's Muslim ally, the Ottoman empire. Basil Bourchier, a British clergyman, wrote: "Not only is this a holy war. It is the holiest war that has ever been waged.... [The pagan god] Odin is ranged against Christ. Berlin is seeking to prove its supremacy over Bethlehem." In 1916 the British premier, David Lloyd George, declared: "Young men from every quarter of the country flocked to the standard of international right, as to a great crusade." When Britain's General Allenby took Jerusalem from the Turks in December 1917, *Punch* magazine published *The Last Crusade*, a cartoon depicting Richard the Lionheart looking down on Jerusalem and saying "At last my dream come true."

Crusading ancestry was a source of pride and was echoed in family heraldic devices in Britain, France, and elsewhere. Attempts were made in the nineteenth century to revive the Knights Templar, but calls for the Order of St. John (the Knights Hospitaller) to return to its military role and help free the Holy Land from the Muslim Ottoman empire had little impact. Instead, the order successfully reverted to its original role of caring for the sick and needy.

Crusading imagery was applied to contemporary political situations, despite a lack of historical verisimilitude; thus the Crimean War (1854–56) was seen as a kind of crusade for the custodianship of the Holy Places, although France and Britain fought on the side of the ailing Ottoman empire against Christian Russia.

Kaiser Wilhelm II of Germany (1888–1918) visited the Near East in 1898 and in Jerusalem saw a recently established German Templar colony. In Damascus, in a carefully orchestrated act, he placed a bronze wreath on Saladin's tomb. The wreath (seized as a trophy during the First World War by T.E. Lawrence, "Lawrence of Arabia," and now in London) is ornately decorated with Arabic inscriptions, some from of the *Quran* and one that mentions Saladin by name.

Crusade imagery was also exploited by both sides in the Spanish Civil War, and by General Dwight D. Eisenhower in the Second World War. On 6th June 1944, at the beginning of Operation Crusader, the Allied invasion of Europe, he declared: "Soldiers, sailors, and airmen of the Allied Expeditionary Forces, you are about to embark on a great crusade." In the nineteenth century, the metaphorical use of crusade to mean the pursuit of a worthy cause had become widespread, building on Thomas Jefferson's phrase "crusade against ignorance." But Eisenhower claimed to use the term literally: "Only by the destruction of the Axis was a decent world possible; the war became for me a crusade in the traditional sense of that often misused word" (*Crusade in Europe*, 1948).

The symbolism of the crusades was, therefore, versatile. For the artists of romanticism the crusades provided a rich vein of inspiration—acts of courage in a "just war" in the exotic East, the emotional homecoming of the crusader, and so on. Nationalists could adopt and celebrate individual crusading heroes, while contemporary political and military situations called forth crusading analogies.

Yet the crusades have not always been a source of inspiration, as the attitudes of Voltaire, Hume, and other eighteenth-century luminaries demonstrate. Some Christians have been assailed by a sense of guilt; for example, Sir Steven Runciman described the Crusades as "a tragic and destructive episode." More recently, the "Reconciliation Walk," led in 1999 by an American child in the build-up to the 900th anniversary of the fall of Jerusalem in 1099, distributed a written statement: "We deeply regret the atrocities committed in the name of Christ by our predecessors."

The Taking of Jerusalem by the Crusaders, 15th July 1099, by Emile Signol (1804–92). The French were very aware of the leading role played by their kinsmen in the crusades. In the 1830s French noble families competed to place their coats of arms in the Salles des Croisades at Versailles, which the king set aside for French families who, like himself, had distinguished crusading ancestors.

ISLAMIC RESPONSES TO THE WEST

PAN-ARABISM AND THE POWER OF THE CRUSADER METAPHOR

The year after the Suez crisis of 1956, when an attempt by British, French, and Israeli forces to seize the Suez Canal was successfully rebuffed, the Egyptian historian Muhammad Kamal Husayn declared: "The struggle conducted today by the leaders of the Arab liberation movement is the same as that conducted in the past by the Ayyubids and Mamluks to oust the crusaders. And, as the Arabs were victorious in the past, they will be in the present."

In such statements it matters little that the Ayyubids (including Saladin) were Kurds or that the Mamluks were Turks. The rhetoric allows modern Arabs to claim these victories as their own. In Arab nationalist discourse, Islam is not necessarily in the foreground; crusading metaphors are flexible enough to fit secular contexts and nationalist ideals.

The Islamic world reacted to western imperialism and colonization in a variety of ways. The Egyptian scholar Abd al-Rahman al-Jabarti (1754–1825), considered by many as the first voice of the modern Arab renaissance, wrote two contemporary accounts of Napoleon's occupation of Egypt in 1798. He attacked the French for the materialist ethos of their revolution, but following the expulsion of the French and the return of the Ottomans, he criticized Muslim society and expressed admiration for European science.

Nineteenth-century Muslim intellectuals fell broadly into two groups. Those who embraced the challenge of modernization and western scientific ideas, the "modernists" as they came to be called, such as Indian educationalist and jurist Sayyid Ahmad Khan (1817–98), who tried to integrate the advances of western science and technology into Islam. Others, the "traditionalists," epitomized by the Wahhabi movement in what is now Saudi Arabia, turned inward and sought a return to the pristine values of early Islam, a society uncontaminated by external, above all European, influences and based only on the principles of the *Quran* and *hadith* (see page 19).

In the twentieth century, as European imperialism gave way to United States hegemony, the response of traditionalists was the same. Extremist groups with an Islamic platform, such as the Muslim Brotherhood in Egypt, struggled against all corrupt rulers in order to establish a unified Muslim state on Earth. Their leading ideologue, Sayyid Qutb (1906–66), who was executed for treason by President Nasser, spoke of the age-old confrontation between Islam and "polytheists"—including Christians, Hindus, and Communists.

Qutb was influenced by the prolific Indian writer Sayyid Abu'l A'la Mawdudi (1903–79), whose work has been seminal among radicals trained in the religious colleges (*madrasa*s) of Pakistan, and notably among the Taliban in Afghanistan. The concept of *jihad* plays a paramount role in Mawdudi's thinking. His book *Jihad in Islam* has gone through many editions; the fifth has on its cover the word *jihad* written as a calligraphic blood-red sword. For Mawdudi, Islam is not concerned with one nation to the exclusion of others; he stresses the universality of Islam, since "Islam wants the whole Earth."

Nowadays *jihad* is an overused word; but it can serve as a powerful rallying cry against perceived forces of aggression and interference. For some, the call for *jihad* has a specific political focus, such as Palestine. Other Muslim pressure groups take a strongly ethical stance against America's global economic as well as political

domination; hence the recently instituted "*jihad* against Coca Cola," an attempt to undermine the product which symbolizes the United States around the world. Two rival Muslim companies, Mecca Cola and Qibla Cola, declare that they give the statutory ten percent of their income, as decreed by Islam, to Muslim good causes.

But not all the rhetoric has an exclusively religious basis. Saddam Husayn's absolutist secular regime in Iraq fabricated an eclectic array of myths to bolster its fragile ideological base, and it spoke of the necessity for a great battle against the "American-Israeli conspiracy." Despite his clear lack of religious credentials, Saddam called on occasion for *jihad* against the West.

Modern Muslims have rediscovered and reinterpreted the crusades, which retrospectively provide powerful symbols for their

Napoleon Bonaparte in the Grand Mosque at Cairo, by Henri Lévy (1841–1904). The contemporary Egyptian scholar Abd al-Rahman al-Jabarti criticized Napoleon's occupation of 1798, calling the French "materialists who deny all God's attributes, the Hereafter and Resurrection, and who reject Prophethood." On the other hand, he was impressed with the army of scholars and scientists brought by Napoleon to conduct a comprehensive survey of Egypt's flora, fauna, and monuments.

Opposite, above: *Jerusalem Day 1988 was commemorated by this Iraqi stamp bearing the image of Saladin and his fellow Tikriti, President Saddam Husayn, the self-styled "Second Saladin" (see sidebar on opposite page).*

Opposite, below: *A Saudi Arabian stamp issued to mark the 800th anniversary of Saladin's victory over the crusaders at Hattin in 1187. Both this and the Iraqi stamp above feature the Dome of the Rock, the quintessential icon of the Holy City.*

Below: *A monumental statue of Saladin, flanked by warriors and a sufi (on the far side and not visible here) stands majestically in front of the medieval citadel of Damascus, capital of the republic of Syria and site of Saladin's tomb. At the base of the statue, visible at bottom right, are two slumped Franks, symbolizing defeated men. The two are King Guy, who holds a bag of ransom money, and Reynald of Chatillon, who wears the haunted look of a man not expecting to survive.*

politicians. According to such thinking, the crusader states were "proto-colonies," prefiguring Napoleon's Egyptian expedition, the mandate period after 1918 (when Britain and France occupied Arab territories of the former Ottoman empire under League of Nations mandates), and, above all, the creation of the state of Israel in 1948. Arab nationalists and nationalist movements have evoked the victorious struggle of Muslim rulers against the Franks in the twelfth and thirteenth centuries (see sidebar on page 206).

For figures such as Sayyid Qutb, who spoke of "international crusaderism," the crusades never ended; the struggle between Christianity and Islam is ongoing. Others interpret the crusades as the first acts of western imperialism (called in Arabic "premature imperialism"), and it is a sober fact that most traditionally Muslim countries have at one time been colonized by Europeans. The rhetoric of such political discourse is strongly anti-imperialist, anti-western, and anti-Christian, its imagery evoking stereotypes from the crusading period. Christian westerners have "polluted" Islamic territory and its most sacred places. Mehmet Ali Agca, the Turk who attempted to kill the pope in 1981, wrote in a letter: "I have decided to kill Pope John Paul II, supreme commander of the crusades."

Just as in Saladin's day, the recapture of Jerusalem, the third holiest city in Islam, is still the principal aim of certain Arab and Muslim activists. And all Palestinians outside Jerusalem yearn to have access to the Muslim religious places in the Holy City.

Some Muslims draw analogies between the Latin kingdom of Jerusalem and the state of Israel. The fact that one was Christian and the other is Jewish does not, in their view, undermine the basic truth of infidel violation of Muslim space. Groups such as Hamas (Movements of Islamic Resistance) and Hizballah (Party of God) were set up under a religious banner to fight for the liberation of Palestine and against western "crusader" intervention and support for Israel.

The vast majority of Muslims do not share such extreme views, but it is undeniable that for many Muslims Jerusalem is as focal today as it was after 1099, when the Holy City fell to the Franks, who occupied it until Saladin retook it in 1187. As in 1099, the loss of Jerusalem in the Six Day War of 1967 was a terrible blow to the Muslim world. The poignancy of the loss was made more acute that same year by an arson attack on the Aqsa mosque by an Australian Christian zealot. The attack destroyed the beautiful pulpit commissioned by Nur ad-Din and placed in the mosque by Saladin in 1187.

The founder of the Islamic Republic of Iran, Ayatollah Khomeini, was fully behind the Muslim, anti-Zionist struggle to liberate Jerusalem. In the Iran-Iraq war of the 1980s, Iranian soldiers were issued maps of their route via Iraq to Jerusalem. Khomeini made the last Friday of Ramadan into "Jerusalem Day" and a famous Iranian stamp of 1980 commemorating "Universal Jerusalem Day" bears the words "Let us liberate Jerusalem" in Arabic, Persian, and English. Jerusalem Day is now marked throughout the Muslim world by stamps that also depict the Dome of the Rock or Saladin on horseback, returning to recapture Jerusalem.

The obsession with the crusades for some Muslim thinkers is a modern phenomenon, as is the Muslim "rediscovery" of Saladin. Although, ironically, this was largely due to his iconic status in western Europe (see page 93), Saladin's historical role as a key figure in the struggle against the Franks has been eagerly seized upon by modern Arab and Islamic thinkers. Arab political leaders, such as Nasser and Sadat in Egypt and Saddam Husayn in Iraq (see sidebar), aspired to become the "Second Saladin." Despite Saladin's Kurdish origins, his mantle has been donned by Arab and wider Islamic militant groups eager to fight the "crusaders," the *salibiyyun* (cross bearers)—the West and specifically the United States. To some, Saladin embodies the heroic spirit of the Arab nation; others espouse the Islamist viewpoint, that he unites the Middle East under the banner of Islam.

SADDAM, THE "SECOND SALADIN"

The self-styled *jihad* fighter Saddam Husayn modeled himself on Saladin, exploiting the fact that they both came from Tikrit—Saddam even tweaked his birth date to coincide with Saladin's. In July 1987, the 800th anniversary of Saladin's great victory over the crusaders at Hattin (see pages 74–75), a celebratory conference entitled "The Battle of Liberation: from Saladin to Saddam Husayn" was held in Tikrit. The same year a children's book called *Saladin the Hero* was published, with a picture of Saddam on its cover. Its pages recorded the "heroic" deeds of Saddam, the "Second Saladin." The irony of such manipulation of the truth was not lost on Saddam's critics: He massacred thousands of Saladin's Kurdish countrymen and was not, unlike Saladin, renowned for his clemency. Perhaps most glaringly, Saddam's military exploits ended in failure.

A CLASH OF CIVILIZATIONS?

REMEMBERING THE CRUSADES

The Palestinian writer Mahmud Darwish (born 1941) writes movingly of the Israeli invasion of Lebanon in 1982 in his book *Memory for Forgetfulness*. The work is infused with the memory of the crusades and shifts effortlessly between bombed Beirut and the crusader occupation of the Holy Land. The word "Frank" in Arabic primarily means "western European," but is also popularly used to mean "foreigner" in general. Darwish sees the term as an extended metaphor for the foreign invaders who have occupied Arab lands. Despite his melancholy reflections about the Lebanon and the Levant, he remains optimistic about the future of the region.

The historian Bernard Lewis was the first to coin the phrase "clash of civilizations" when he wrote in 1990 of "the perhaps irrational but surely historic reaction of an ancient rival [Islam] against our Judeo-Christian heritage, our secular present, and the worldwide expansion of both." Lewis's idea was elaborated by Samuel Huntington, and although Huntington has modified his views since 11th September 2001, his hypothesis remains very influential because of the polarization he sees between the West and the Islamic world.

Huntington speaks of a new era of world politics in which countries group themselves according to "civilization." As the world becomes a smaller place, with increased immigration and interactions among peoples, their consciousness of the deep-rooted civilization to which they belong intensifies. The revival of religion (and here he singles out Islam) provides an identity above national boundaries. Nowadays, with the West at the peak of its power, other civilizations turn inward, but are faced with America's global influence on lifestyle and material goods. Huntington identifies global fault lines, flashpoints for crisis and bloodshed (such as the Balkans), and highlights the ancient "bloody borders" between Islam and the West,

where their troubled interaction could become more virulent: "The fault lines between civilizations will be the battle lines of the future."

For many, Huntington's paradigm is too adversarial and simplistic. In 2001 the Palestinian commentator Edward W. Said (1935–2003) accused Lewis and Huntington of conjuring up "a cartoon-like world where Popeye and Bluto bash each other mercilessly," ignoring "the internal dynamics and plurality of every civilization." Like other world faiths, Islam is not monolithic, and it is by no means a given that a Persian-speaking Iranian Shiite will make common cause with an Arabic-speaking Saudi Sunni, though both rightly call themselves Muslims. Nor will an Indonesian, Turkish, or Balkan Muslim necessarily feel a great affinity with either. And where do Arab Christians fit into Huntington's model? They feel allegiance at once to their Arabness, their nation state, and their faith.

The prominence given to the speeches of Usama bin Laden in the world's media since the 11th September outrage does not help the majority of Muslims who stress that Islam and terrorism are incompatible and condemn the Western demonization of Islam. Nor does Usama's uncompromisingly hostile message against "global crusaders" (the United States and its allies) help to allay Western fears.

What of the Western "side" of the "clash"? In the wake of 11th September, President George W. Bush declared: "This crusade, this war on terrorism, is going to take a while." His aides rapidly denied that he had used the term literally, but it still provoked a storm in the Muslim world. It is doubtful whether the West's leaders or its media are conscious that the historic root of "crusade" is the Latin *crux* (cross). But this root is not lost in Arabic, which has no single word for "crusade," and translates it, for example, as *harb al-salib* (war of the cross), *harb salibiyya* (cross war), or *hamla salibiyya* (cross attack). It is hardly surprising that Muslims are sensitive to the term.

Certainly, to some Muslim propagandists at least, the rhetoric of conflict is expressed in religious terms, as being against "Christians" and "crusaders," even if it is in reality against American globalization and secularization. At the same time, "crusader" can simply be used in the Muslim world as a pejorative word for a western European.

But more importantly, both sides in the propaganda war bandy the terms crusade and *jihad* very loosely and invoke history in a cavalierly simplistic manner. Those who speak of "crusade" conveniently forget the Fourth Crusade (and others) where Christian fought Christian, not to mention times when Muslims allied with crusaders against other Muslims. And those who trumpet Saladin's conquest of Jerusalem conveniently forget that his descendants handed back the Holy City to the Franks thirty-nine years later.

Above: *The historic hostilities and suspicion between Christianity and Islam have prompted efforts by leaders of the two faiths to promote mutual understanding. To this end, on 6th May 2001 Pope John Paul II became the first pope to enter a mosque when Sheikh Ahmad Kuftaro, the Grand Mufti (most senior Muslim cleric) of Syria, welcomed him in the 8th-century Umayyad mosque in Damascus.*

Opposite: *The ruins of Mostar in Bosnia-Herzegovina during the civil war in the largely Muslim former Yugoslav republic, 30th September 1993. Although Bosnia was a secular state from its formation, the Bosnian armed forces included a battalion of mujahidin (jihad fighters) who had flocked from all over the Muslim world to aid the new state against "Christian and Serbian" enemies.*

FURTHER READING

General Readings

Andrea, Alfred J. *Encyclopedia of the Crusades.* Greenwood Press: Westport, 2003.

Brundage, James A. *Medieval Canon Law and the Crusader.* University of Wisconsin Press: Madison, 1969.

Cole, Penny J. *The Preaching of the Crusades to the Holy Land, 1095–1270.* Medieval Academy of America: Cambridge, Massachusetts, 1991.

Ellenblum, Ronnie. *Frankish Rural Settlement in the Latin Kingdom of Jerusalem.* Cambridge University Press (CUP): Cambridge and New York, 1998.

Folda, Jaroslav. *The Art of the Crusaders in the Holy Land, 1098–1187.* CUP: Cambridge and New York, 1995.

France, John. *Western Warfare in the Age of the Crusades, 1000–1300.* Cornell University Press: Ithaca, 1999.

Harris, Jonathan. *Byzantium and the Crusades.* Hambledon Press: London and New York, 2003.

Hillenbrand, Carole. *The Crusades: Islamic Perspectives.* Edinburgh University Press: Edinburgh, 1999.

Kedar, Benjamin Z. *Crusade and Mission: European Approaches toward the Muslims.* Princeton University Press (PUP): Princeton, 1984.

Kennedy, Hugh. *Crusader Castles.* CUP: Cambridge and New York, 1994.

Lilie, Ralph-Johannes. *Byzantium and the Crusader States, 1096–1204.* (Trans. J.C. Morris and Jean E. Ridings.) Clarendon Press: Oxford and New York, 1993.

Madden, Thomas F. *A Concise History of the Crusades.* Rowman and Littlefield: New Lanham, 1999.

Marshall, Christopher. *Warfare in the Latin East, 1192–1291.* CUP: Cambridge and New York, 1992.

Mayer, Hans E. *The Crusades.* 2nd edition. (Trans. John Gillingham.) Oxford University Press (OUP): Oxford and New York, 1988.

Phillips, Jonathan. *Defenders of the Holy Land: Relations between the Latin East and the West, 1119–1187.* Clarendon Press: Oxford and New York, 1996.

Prawer, Joshua. *The Latin Kingdom of Jerusalem.* Weidenfeld and Nicolson: London, 1972.

Richard, Jean. *The Latin Kingdom of Jerusalem.* (Trans. Janet Shirley.) North Holland: New York, 1979.

Richard, Jean. *The Crusades, c.1071–c.1291.* (Trans. Jean Birrell.) CUP: Cambridge and New York, 1999.

Riley-Smith, Jonathan. *The Crusades: A Short History.* Yale University Press: New Haven and London, 1987.

Riley-Smith, Jonathan. (Editor.) *The Oxford Illustrated History of the Crusades.* OUP: Oxford and New York, 1995.

Riley-Smith, Jonathan. *What Were the Crusades?* 3rd edition. Ignatius Press: San Francisco, 2002.

Runciman, Steven R. *A History of the Crusades.* 3 vols. CUP: Cambridge and New York, 1951–1954.

Setton, Kenneth M. (General editor.) *A History of the Crusades.* 6 vols. University of Wisconsin Press and University of Pennsylvania Press (UPP): Madison and Philadelphia, 1958–1989.

Siberry, Elizabeth. *Criticism of Crusading, 1095–1274.* Clarendon Press: Oxford and New York, 1985.

Smail, R.C. *Crusading Warfare, 1097–1193.* 2nd edition. CUP: Cambridge and New York, 1995.

Chapter 1

Berkey, Jonathan P. *The Formation of Islam: Religion and Society in the Near East, 600–1800.* CUP: Cambridge, 2002.

Brown, Peter. *The Rise of Western Christendom.* 2nd edition. Blackwell: Oxford and Cambridge, Massachusetts, 2003.

Cowdrey, H.E.J. *Pope Gregory VII: 1073–1085.* OUP: Oxford, 1998.

Elad, Amikan. *Medieval Jerusalem and Islamic Worship: Holy Places, Ceremony, Pilgrimage.* E.J. Brill: Leiden, 1995.

Esposito, John. (Editor.) *The Oxford History of Islam.* OUP: Oxford, 1999.

Luscombe, David and Riley-Smith, Jonathan. (Editors.) *The New Cambridge Medieval History, Vol. 4: c.1024–c.1198, Parts 1 and 2.* CUP: Cambridge, 2004.

Mango, Cryil. (Editor.) *The Oxford History of Byzantium.* OUP: Oxford and New York, 2002.

Perowne, Stuart. *The Holy Places of Christendom.* OUP: New York, 1976.

Prawer, Joshua and Ben-Shammai, Haggai. (Editors.) *The History of Jerusalem 638–1099.* NYU Press: New York, 1996.

Peters, F.E. *Muhammad and the Origins of Islam.* SUNY Press: Albany, New York, 1994.

Robinson, Francis. (Editor.) *The Cambridge Illustrated History of the Islamic World.* CUP: Cambridge, 1996.

Whittow, M. *The Making of Orthodox Byzantium, 600–1025.* Macmillan: Basingstoke, England, 1996.

Chapter 2

Angold, M. *The Byzantine Empire 1025–1204.* Longman: London, 1984.

Anonymous. *Gesta Francorum et aliorum Hierosolimitanorum.* (Edited by R.Hill.) Nelson: Edinburgh, 1962.

Asbridge, T.S. *The First Crusade.* Free Press: London, 2004

France, John. *Victory in the East: A Military History of the First Crusade.* CUP: Cambridge, 1994.

Holt, P.M. *The Age of the Crusades: The Near East from the Eleventh Century to 1517.* Longman: London, 1986.

Riley-Smith, Jonathan. *The First Crusade and the Idea of Crusading.* Athlone: London, 1986.

Chapter 3

Gabrieli, F. *Arab Historians of the Crusades.* Dorset Press: New York, 1969.

Hamilton, B. *The Leper King and his Heirs: Baldwin IV and the Crusader Kingdom of Jerusalem.* CUP: Cambridge, 2000.

Kedar, Benjamin K. "The Battle of Hattin Revisited" in B.K. Kedar. (Editor.) *The Horns of Hattin.* Ashgate: Aldershot, 1992, pp.190–207.

Kennedy, Hugh. *Crusader Castles.* CUP: Cambridge, 1994.

Lyons, M.C. and Jackson, D.E.P. *Saladin: The Politics of Holy War.* CUP: Cambridge, 1982.

Nicholson, H. *Templars, Hospitallers and Teutonic Knights. Images of the Military Orders 1128–1291.* Leicester University Press: Leicester, 1993.

Phillips, J.P. *Defenders of the Holy Land: Relations between the Latin East and the West 1119–1187.* OUP: Oxford, 1996.

Pryor, J. *Geography, Technology and War.* CUP: Cambridge, 1992.

Chapter 4

Edbury, Peter W. *The Conquest of Jerusalem and the Third Crusade: Sources in Translation.* Scolar: Aldershot, Hampshire, and Brookfield, Vermont, 1996.

Edbury, Peter W. "*The Templars in Cyprus*" in *The Military Orders: Fighting for the Faith and Caring for the Sick* by Malcolm Barber (Editor.). Variorum: Aldershot, 1994, pp.189–195.

Gillingham, John. *Richard I.* Yale University Press: New Haven, 1999.

Lyons, Malcolm Cameron and Jackson, D.E.P. *Saladin: The Politics of the Holy War.* CUP: Cambridge and New York, 1982.

Nicholson, Helen J. *Chronicle of the Third Crusade: a Translation of the* Itinerarium peregrinorum et gesta Regis Ricardi. Ashgate: Aldershot, Hampshire, and Brookfield, Vermont, 1997.

Pringle, R. Denys. "King Richard I and the walls of Ascalon" in *Palestine Exploration Quarterly* 116, 1984, pp.133–147; reprinted in D. Pringle (Editor.) *Fortification and Settlement in Crusader Palestine.* Variorum: Aldershot, 2000.

Rogers, Randall. *Latin Siege Warfare in the Twelfth Century.* Clarendon Press: Oxford, 1992.

Chapter 5

Andrea, Alfred J. *Contemporary Sources for the Fourth Crusade.* E.J. Brill: Leiden, 2000.

Angold, Michael. *The Fourth Crusade: Event and Context.* Longman: London and New York, 2003.

Brand, Charles M. *Byzantium Confronts the West, 1180–1204.* Harvard University Press: Cambridge, Massachusetts, 1968.

Lock, Peter. *The Franks in the Aegean, 1204–1500.* Longman: London and New York, 1995.

Madden, Thomas F. *Enrico Dandolo and the Rise of Venice.* Johns Hopkins University Press: Baltimore, 2003.

Queller, Donald E. and Madden, Thomas F. *The Fourth Crusade: The Conquest of Constantinople.* 2nd edition. UPP: Philadelphia: 1997.

Chapter 6

Christiansen, Eric. *The Northern Crusades: The Baltic and the Catholic Frontier, 1100–1525.* 2nd edition. Penguin: London, 1997.

Lambert, Malcolm. *Medieval Heresy: Popular Movements from the Gregorian Reform to the Reformation.* 2nd edition. Blackwell: Oxford, 1992.

Housley, Norman. *The Italian Crusades: the Papal-Angevin alliance and the Crusades against Christian Lay Powers, 1254–1343.* Clarendon Press: Oxford, 1982.

Kejr, Jiri. *The Hussite Revolution.* Orbis: Prague, 1988.

Nicolle, David. *Lake Peipus 1242: Battle on the Ice.* Reed International: London, 1996.

Partner, Peter. *The Knights Templar and Their Myth.* Destiny Books: Rochester, Vermont, 1990.

Chapter 7

Abulafia, David. *Frederick II: A Medieval Emperor.* Allen Lane: London, 1988.

Amitai-Preiss, Reuven. *Mongols and Mamluks: The Mamluk-Ilkhanid War, 1260–1281.* CUP: Cambridge, 1995.

Jordan, William Chester. *Louis IX and the Challenge of the Crusade.* PUP: Princeton, 1979.

Kedar, Benjamin Z. *Crusade and Mission: European Approaches toward the Muslims.* PUP: Princeton, 1984.

Lilie, Ralph-Johannes. *Byzantium and the Crusader States.* (Trans. J. Morris and J. Ridings.) Clarendon Press: Oxford, 1993.

Maier, Christoph. *Preaching the Crusades: Mendicant Friars and the Cross in the Thirteenth Century.* CUP: Cambridge, 1994.

Powell, James M. *Anatomy of a Crusade.* UPP: Philadelphia, 1986.

Richard, Jean. *Saint Louis: Crusader: King of France.* (Trans. Jean Birrell.) CUP: Cambridge, 1992.

Chapter 8

Bicheno, Hugh. *The Cross and the Crescent: The Battle of Lepanto 1571.* Weidenfeld and Nicolson: London, 2003.

Bradford, Ernle. *The Great Siege: Malta 1565.* Hodder and Stoughton: London, 1961.

Brockman, Eric. *The Two Sieges of Rhodes, 1480–1522.* John Murray: London, 1969 (reprinted New York: Barnes and Noble, 1995).

Edbury, Peter W. *The Kingdom of Cyprus and the Crusades, 1191–1374.* CUP: Cambridge, 1991.

Goodwin, Jason. *Lords of the Horizons: A History of the Ottoman Empire.* Henry Holt: New York, 1998.

Housley, Norman. *Documents on the Later Crusades, 1274–1580.* Palgrave Macmillan: London and New York, 1996.

Housley, Norman. *The Later Crusades, 1274–1580.* OUP: Oxford, 1992.

Imber, Colin. *The Ottoman Empire.* Palgrave Macmillan: London and New York, 2002.

Levey, Michael. *The World of Ottoman Art.* Thames and Hudson: London, 1975.

Nicol, D.M. *The Last Centuries of Byzantium, 1261–1453.* 2nd edition. CUP: Cambridge, 1993.

Nicolle, David. *Constantinople 1453: The End of Byzantium.* Osprey: Oxford, 2000.

Nicolle, David. *Nicopolis 1396: The Last Crusade.* Osprey: Oxford, 1999.

Runciman, Steven R. *The Fall of Constantinople, 1453.* CUP: Cambridge, 1965.

Stoye, John W. *The Siege of Vienna.* London: Collins: London, 1964.

Vaughan, Dorothy M. *Europe and the Turk: A Pattern of Alliances, 1350–1700.* Liverpool University Press: Liverpool, 1954.

Chapter 9

Elizabeth Siberry. *The New Crusaders. Images of the Crusades in the 19th and early 20th centuries.* Ashgate: Aldershot, 2000.

Hillenbrand, Carole. *The Crusades: Islamic Perspectives.* Edinburgh University Press: Edinburgh, 1999, pp.589–616.

Riley-Smith, Jonathan. (Editor.) *The Oxford Illustrated History of the Crusades.* OUP: Oxford and New York, 1995, pp.365–391.

Mahmud Darwish. *Memory for Forgetfulness.* (Trans. Ibrahim Muhawi.) University of California Press: Berkeley, 1995.

CHRONOLOGY

634 – 644 Muslim armies of Caliph Umar capture Egypt, Syria, and the Holy Land from the Byzantine empire.

711 – 716 Muslims occupy most of Iberia.

756   Caliphate of Córdoba established.

844   Ramiro I of Asturias defeats Muslims at battle of Clavijo.

969   Antioch recaptured by Byzantium; Fatimids capture Cairo.

1009   Fatimids destroy Holy Sepulcher.

1051   Caliphate of Córdoba fragments.

1055   Seljuk Turks seize Baghdad.

1071   Seljuks defeat Byzantines at Manzikert.

1092   Death of Seljuk sultan Malik Shah; Seljuk empire fragments.

1095   Byzantine emperor Alexius appeals for aid; Pope Urban II calls at the council at Clermont for holy war in the East backed by papal indulgence.

1096 – 99 The First Crusade

1096   Crusaders depart; People's Crusade.

1097   Crusader victory at Dorylaeum.

1098   *March* Baldwin of Boulogne founds first crusader state at Edessa.
November Crusaders take Antioch.

1099   Crusaders take Jerusalem; Godfrey of Bouillon becomes first ruler of Latin kingdom of Jerusalem.

1100 – 1101 Follow-up crusade defeated in Asia Minor by Turks.

1107 – 1110 King Sigurd of Norway brings army to Holy Land.

1112   The Hospital of St John receives papal approval and protection.

1120   Foundation of the military order of the Knights Templar.

1123 – 24 Venetian expedition to Holy Land.

1139   Order of the Hospital of St. John (Hospitallers) begins military activities, taking over the fortress of Bethgibelin near Ascalon.

1144   Zengi, ruler of Mosul and Aleppo, captures Edessa.

1146   Death of Zengi.

1147   Preaching of Second Crusade; Wendish Crusade launched.

1148 – 49 The Second Crusade

1149   Siege of Damascus fails; end of Second Crusade.

1153   Capture of Ascalon by forces of King Baldwin III of Jerusalem.

1154   Nur ad-Din, son of Zengi, captures Damascus.

1166 – 69 Campaigns of King Amalric I of Jerusalem against Egypt.

1169   Saladin becomes vizier of Egypt.

1174   Death of Nur ad-Din; Saladin seizes Damascus.

1187   *July* Saladin defeats King Guy of Jerusalem at Hattin.
2nd October Saladin takes Jerusalem.
29th October Papal bull *Audita tremendi* proclaims Third Crusade.

1189 – 92 The Third Crusade

1190   Emperor Frederick I drowns in Asia Minor en route to the Holy Land.

1191   *June* Richard I captures Cyprus.
July Acre falls to Richard I and Philip II.

1192   Treaty of Jaffa; end of Third Crusade

1197 – 98 German crusade recovers some territory; German hospital at Acre becomes a military order (the Teutonic Order).

1201 – 05 The Fourth Crusade

1204   Crusaders sack Constantinople and found Latin empire.

1209 – 29 Albigensian Crusade in France.

1215   Fourth Lateran council.

1216   Honorius III succeeds Innocent III.

1217 – 29 The Fifth Crusade

1218   Fifth Crusade lands near Damietta in Egypt.

1219   *August* Francis of Assisi preaches to crusaders and the sultan.
November Crusaders take Damietta.

1221   Crusaders surrender to Ayyubid sultan al-Kamil.

1225 – 30 Teutonic Order begins military operations in Prussia.

1225   Emperor Frederick II vows to leave on crusade by 31st August 1227 and is betrothed to the heiress of the kingdom of Jerusalem.

1227   *September* Frederick sails for the East but illness forces him back; Pope Gregory IX excommunicates him.

1228   Frederick sets out on crusade again.

1229   Christians regain Jerusalem by treaty of Jaffa between Frederick and al-Kamil; end of Fifth Crusade.

1230   Frederick's excommunication lifted.

1236   Ferdinand III of Castile takes Córdoba.

1239 – 41 Crusades of Theobald IV of Champagne and Richard of Cornwall.

1239   Crusade against Frederick II; Swedish crusade against Finns.

1241   Gregory IX dies; papal vacancy.

1243   Innocent IV elected pope.

1244   Kwarizmians take Jerusalem; city lost to Christians for the last time.

1244   Egyptians defeat Franks and Syrians at Gaza.

1248 – 49 First crusade of King Louis IX of France captures Damietta.

1250   Surrender of Louis near al-Mansurah.

1250   Mamluks seize power in Egypt.

1254   Louis IX returns from Acre to France.

1258   Mongols sack Baghdad and kill last Abbasid caliph.

1260   Baibars defeats Mongols at Ain Jalud.

1261   Michael Palaeologus expels Latins from Constantinople and becomes Byzantine emperor as Michael VIII.

1268   Baibars conquers Antioch.

1270   Louis IX dies on crusade near Tunis.

1270 – 72 Crusade of the Lord Edward.

1277   Charles of Anjou purchases claim to throne of Jerusalem.

1277   Sultan Baibars dies.

1282   Sicilian Vespers; Charles of Anjou loses Sicily to Aragon.

1289   Mamluks capture Tripoli.

1291   Mamluks capture Acre; last Frankish base on mainland lost.

1306   Knights Hospitaller move to Rhodes.

1307   Knights Templar suppressed.

1309   Teutonic Order moves headquarters to West Prussia.

1312   Knights Templar abolished.

1344   Maritime League captures Smyrna.

1354   Ottoman Turks establish their first base in Europe at Gallipoli.

1365   Cyprus captures, then abandons, Alexandria.

1389   Ottomans crush Serbs at Kosovo Polje.

1396   Failed crusade of Nicopolis.

1410   Teutonic Order defeated at Tannenberg.

1420 – 31 Crusades against the Hussites.

1426   Mamluks defeat Cyprus.

1444   Ottomans crush Polish and Hungarian crusaders at Varna.

1478   Cyprus ceded to Venice.

1453   Ottomans capture Constantinople.

1523   Ottomans expel Hospitallers from Rhodes.

1529   Ottomans besiege Vienna.

1530   Hospitallers resettle on Malta.

1571   *August* Ottomans capture Cyprus from Venice.
September Don John of Austria defeats Ottoman fleet at Lepanto.

1683   Ottomans driven from Vienna.

1699   Treaty of Karlowitz: Ottomans concede territory for the first time.

1798   Napoleon expels the Hospitallers from Malta.

INDEX

TEXT ACKNOWLEDGMENTS

Translated extracts from primary sources not acknowledged below are the work of the author. Every care has been taken to acknowledge sources and/or copyright holders. However, if we have omitted anyone we apologize, and will, if informed, make corrections in any further edition.

Chapter 1

Page 16: Extract from Pope Gelasius's letter to Emperor Anastasius I from Brian Tierney (ed. and trans.), *The Crisis of Church and State, 1050–1300*. Englewood Cliffs, New Jersey: Prentice Hall, 1964.

Page 22: Extract from *surah* 22, "Pilgrimage," from *Al-Qur'an* (trans. Ahmed Ali). Princeton: Princeton University Press, 1988.

Page 26: Extract from Ibn Abi Zayd al-Kayrawani, *The Treatise on Law*, edited and ranslated by Leon Bercher as *La Risâla ou Epître sur les éléments du dogme et de la loi l'Islam selon le rite mâlikite*. Algiers: J. Carbonel, 1960, 5th ed., p.163. Extract translated into English by A.J. Andrea.

Chapter 2

Note on title: The phrase "impelled by the love of God" is taken from the description of Peter the Hermit (see page 37) by his contemporary, the chronicler Fulcher of Chartres.

Page 34: Extract from al-Jahiz in J.D. Latham and W. Paterson, *Saracen Archery*. London: Holland Press, 1970, xxiii.

Page 35: Extract from Matthew of Edessa's *Chronicle* in S.Vryonis, *The Decline of Medieval Hellenism in Asia Minor*. Berkeley: University of California Press, 1971, pp.80–81.

Page 36: Extract from Robert the Monk's *Historia Iherosolimitana* in A.C. Krey (ed. and trans.), *The First Crusade*. Gloucester, Mass.: Peter Smith, 1958, p.31.

Page 39: Extract from Albert of Aachen's *Historia Hierosolymitana*, Book 1, Chapter 30, S.B. Edgington (ed. and trans.). (Edition in preparation for Oxford Medieval Texts; reproduced with author's permission.)

Pages 40, 41 (main text): Extracts from Fulcher of Chartres's *A History of the Expedition to Jerusalem*, H.S. Fink (ed. and trans.). Knoxville: University of Tennessee Press, 1969, p.85.

Page 45: Extracts from Raymond of Aguilers' *History of the Franks who Captured Jerusalem*, in A.C. Krey (ed. and trans.), *The*

First Crusade. Gloucester Mass: Peter Smith, 1958, pp.213, 225.

Page 47: Extract from Raymond of Aguilers' *History of the Frankish Conquerors of Jerusalem*, J.H. Hill and L.L. Hill (ed. and trans.). Philadelphia: Philosophical Society of America, 1969, pp.127–8.

Page 48: Extract from Walter the Chancellor's *The Antiochene Wars*, T.S. Asbridge and S.B. Edgington (ed. and trans.). Aldershot, England: Ashgate, 1999, p.163.

Page 51: Extract from Pope Urban II's *Letter to the Counts of Catalonia* in J. Riley-Smith, *The First Crusade and the Idea of Crusading*. London: Athlone, 1986, p.19.

Page 55: Extract from William of Tyre's *A History of Deeds done Beyond the Sea*, E.A. Babcock and A.C. Krey (ed. and trans.). New York: Columbia University Press, 1943, p.143.

Chapter 3

Page 60: Extract from St. Bernard's letter to Archbishop Henry of Mainz, 1146, in B.S. James (ed. and trans.), *The Letters of St. Bernard of Clairvaux*. London: Burns Oates, 1953, p.466.

Page 61: Extract from Odo of Deuil's *The Journey of Louis VII to the East*, V.G. Berry (ed.). New York: Columbia University Press, 1948, p.9; extract from St Bernard's letter to his uncle in B.S. James (ed. and trans.), *The Letters of St. Bernard of Clairvaux*. London: Burns Oates, 1953, p.479.

Page 62: Extract from William of Tyre's *A History of Deeds done Beyond the Sea*, E.A. Babcock and A.C. Krey (ed. and trans.). New York: Columbia University Press, 1943, p.196

Page 65: Extract from Ibn al-Qalinisi from A.R. Gibb (ed. and trans.), *The Damascus Chronicle of the Crusades*. London: Luzac, 1932, p.128.

Page 67: Extract from Usama's *Memoirs* in F. Gabrieli (ed. and trans.), *Arab Historians of the Crusades*. New York: Dorset Press, 1969, p.73.

Page 70: Extract from William of Tyre's *A History of Deeds done Beyond the Sea*, E.A. Babcock and A.C. Krey (Editors and translators). New York: Columbia University Press, 1943, book 22, chs. 29–30.

Page 71: Extract from Baha ad-Din's *Life of Saladin* in F. Gabrieli (ed. and trans.), *Arab Historians of the Crusades*. New York: Dorset Press, 1969, pp.99–100.

Page 77: Extract from the *Estoire d'Eracles* in P. Edbury (ed. and trans.), "The Old French Continuation of William of Tyre," in *The Conquest of Jerusalem and the Third Crusade*. Aldershot, England: Scholar Press, 1996, p.69.

Chapter 4

Page 80: Extract from *Audita tremendi* in William Stubbs (ed. and trans.), *Gesta Regis Henrici Secundi: The Chronicle of the Reigns of Henry II and Richard I*. Two vols., RS 49 (London, 1867); vol. 2, pp.15–19;

Page 84: Extract from "*Historia de expeditione Friderici, der sogenannte Ansbert*," in A. Chroust (ed.), *Quellen zur Geschichte des Kreuzzuges Kaiser Friedrichs I*, in *Monumenta Germaniae Historica: Scriptores rerum Germanicarum nova series 5* (Berlin, 1928), pp. 91–2; translated into English by Helen Nicholson.

Page 86: Extract from the *Itinerarium Peregrinorum et Gesta Regis Ricardi (The Journey of the Pilgrims and Deeds of King Richard)* in Helen Nicholson, *Chronicle of the Third Crusade*. Aldershot, England: Ashgate, 1997.

Page 87: Extract from *Ibn al-Athir's al-Kamil fi'l-tarikh (The Complete History)*, translated into French as *le Kamel Altevarykh*, in *Recueil des Historiens des Croisades: Historiens Orientaux* (Paris, 1887); vol. 2, p.24; translated into English by Helen Nicholson.

Chapter 5

Page 101: Extract from a sermon by Abbot Martin of Pairis in Alfred J. Andrea (ed. and trans.), *The Capture of Constantinople: The Hystoria Constantinopolitana of Gunther of Pairis*. Philadelphia: University of Pennsylvania Press, 1997, pp.69–70; extract from Gaucelm Faidit's *planh* (lament) *Fortz chausa es que tot lo major dan* from Samuel N. Rosenberg, Margaret Switten, and Gérard Le Vot (eds. and trans.), *Songs of the Troubadours and Trouvères*. New York and London: Garland Publishing, 1998, p.129.

Page 102: Extract from the treaty between Venice and the crusader barons in G.L.Fr. Tafel and G.M. Thomas (eds.) *Urkunden zur älteren Handels- und Staatsgeschichte der Republik Venedig*. Three vols. Vienna: Kaiserlich-Königliche Hof- und Staatsdruckerei, 1856–57, no. 92, 1: 365; translated into English by T.F. Madden.

Page 109: Extract from Geoffrey of Villehardouin's *Memoirs of the Crusades*, trans. Frank Marzials. London: J.M. Dent and Sons, 1908, p.31; extract from Robert of Clari's *The Conquest of Constantinople*, trans. Edgar Holmes McNeal. New York: Columbia University Press, 1964, p.112.

Page 110: Extract from Robert of Clari's *The Conquest of Constantinople*, trans. Edgar Holmes McNeal. New York: Columbia University Press, 1964, pp.108–110;

Page 111: Extract from *O City of Byzantium: Annals of Niketas Choniates*, trans. Harry J. Magoulias. Detroit: Wayne State University Press, 1984, p.303.

Page 112: Extract from Gunther of Pairis in Alfred J. Andrea (ed. and trans.), *The Capture of Constantinople: The* Hystoria Constantino-politana *of Gunther of Pairis*. Philadelphia: University of Pennsylvania Press, 1997, pp.109–111.

Page 113: Extract from *O City of Byzantium: Annals of Niketas Choniates,* trans. Harry J. Magoulias. Detroit: Wayne State University Press, 1984, pp.317, 357, 359.

Page 114: Extract from Robert of Clari's *The Conquest of Constantinople*, trans. Edgar Holmes McNeal. New York: Columbia University Press, 1964, p.112.

Chapter 6

The author gratefully acknowledges the advice and assistance of Alfred J. Andrea and Thomas F. Madden in the preparation of this chapter. In particular he would like to thank Alfred J. Andrea for the sidebar on page 123 ("The Iberian Military Orders") and Thomas F. Madden for the feature on pages 124–125 ("The Fruits of Three Faiths").

Chapter 7

Page 148: Extract from Ibn al-Athir in F. Gabrieli (ed. and trans.), *Arab Historians of the Crusades* (Ibn al-Athir, XII, 209). (Reprint edition.) Berkeley: University of California Press, 1984, p.259.

Page 158: Extract from Ibn al-Furat's *Tarikh al-Duwal wa'l-Muluk* in U. and M.C. Lyons, *Ayyubids, Mamlukes and Crusaders* (with notes and introduction by J. Riley-Smith). Cambridge: Heffer, 1971, pp.28–9.

Page 160: Extract from Ibn al-Furat's *Tarikh al-Duwal wa'l-Muluk* in U. and M.C. Lyons, *Ayyubids, Mamlukes and Crusaders* (with notes and introduction by J. Riley-Smith). Cambridge: Heffer, 1971, pp.32–3.

Page 165: Extract from Ibn al-Furat's *Tarikh al-Duwal wa'l-Muluk* in U. and M. C. Lyons, *Ayyubids, Mamlukes and Crusaders* (with notes and introduction by J. Riley-Smith). Cambridge: Heffer, 1971, p.121.

Page 171: Extract from the Templar of Tyre in *Chronicles of the Crusades*, ed. by Elizabeth Hallam. New York: Welcome Rain, 2000, p.281; retranslated by James M. Powell.

Chapter 8

Page 175: Extract from *The Book of Margery Kempe*, ed. W. Butler-Bowden. London: Jonathan Cape, 1936, p.107.

Page 179: Extract from George Pachymeres in Donald M. Nicol, *The Last Centuries of Byzantium, 1261–1453*. Cambridge: Cambridge University. Press, 1993, 2nd ed., p.83.

Page 187: The publishers acknowledge the assistance of Carole Hillenbrand for the sidebar on Ibn Khaldun.

Page 189: Extract from Doukas in Harry J. Magoulias (ed. and trans.) *The Decline and Fall of Byzantium to the Ottoman Turks.* Detroit: Wayne State University Press, 1975, pp.224–7.

Page 193: Quotation (in main text) from Martin Luther is from K.M. Setton, "Lutheranism and the Turkish peril," in *Balkan Studies* vol. 3 (1962), pp.133–68, at p.142; quotation (in caption) from Erasmus is from Norman Housley (ed.), *Documents on the Later Crusades, 1274–1580*. London and New York: Macmillan, 1996, p.178.

Chapter 9

Page 203: Extract from François-René de Chateaubriand's *Itinéraire de Paris à Jérusalem et de Jérusalem à Paris*. Paris: Le Normant, 1811.

Page 204: Extract from Mark Twain's *The Innocents Abroad*. Hartford, Connecticut: American Publishing Company, 1869, chapter 53.

Captions for Chapter Opener Illustrations

Chapter 1: *A colored woodcut of Jerusalem from the* World Chronicle *by Hartmann Schedel, ca. 1493. The church of the Holy Sepulcher, dominating the center, is erroneously labeled "Templum Salomonis" (Temple of Solomon), the crusader name for al-Aqsa mosque. The mosque, which was converted to a church during the Christian occupation of 1099–1187, was the "Temple" that served as the first headquarters of the Knights Templar.*

Chapter 2: *The crusader attack on Antioch in June 1098, during the First Crusade; from a French manuscript (ca. 1280) of Bishop William of Tyre's History of Deeds done Beyond the Sea, a chronicle of the crusades to ca. 1185.*

Chapter 3: *The siege of Damascus in 1148, during the Second Crusade, from a 15th-century French manuscript of Sebastien Mamerot's Passages Faitz Outre Mer par les Français.*

Chapter 4: *St. Hilarion castle, Cyprus. Built on the site of a Byzantine monastery, it was captured by Richard I in 1191 during his conquest of Cyprus en route to the Third Crusade, and was a stronghold of the Lusignan kings of Cyprus.*

Chapter 5: *Christ in Majesty, a 14th-century mosaic in the dome of Kariye Camii mosque, Istanbul, the former church of Chora monastery. The church was founded in the 6th century and rebuilt by the Comnenus emperors in the 11th and 12th centuries. Second in splendor only to Hagia Sophia, the church was apparently looted and damaged during the Fourth Crusade and Latin occupation (1204–61). The mosaic and dome were added during restoration work in the 14th century. Following the Turkish conquest the church became a mosque; today it is a museum.*

Chapter 6: *Córdoba cathedral, formerly the Great Mosque (Mesquita), built from the 8th century by the caliphs of Córdoba and one of the world's largest Islamic buildings. As the seat of an independent state (756–1031) embracing most of Muslim Iberia, Córdoba attained a magnificence and cultural sophistication exceeded in Europe and the Islamic world only by Constantinople and Baghdad.*

Chapter 7: *Crusaders and Saracens fighting at Damietta during the Fifth Crusade, from the world history written and illustrated by the English monk Matthew Paris (ca. 1200–59).*

Chapter 8: *The Hungarians surrender Belgrade to the Ottomans in 1521. From The Book of Accomplishments (1588) by the Turkish author Loqman, a work devoted to the military campaigns of the sultan Suleyman the Magnificent (1520–66).*

Chapter 9: The Battle Between King Richard I and Saladin, *by Philip James (Jacques) de Loutherbourg (1740–1812), an English painter of French birth. This painting is based on the popular legend, dating back to medieval times, of Richard the Lionheart's single combat with Saladin. In fact, the two rulers never faced each other in combat, and indeed never met.*

PICTURE CREDITS

The publisher would like to thank the following individuals, museums, and photographic libraries for permission to reproduce their material. Every care has been taken to trace copyright holders. However, if we have omitted anyone we apologize and will, if informed, make corrections to any future edition.

Key

AA   The Art Archive, London
AKG   A.K.G.-images, London
BAL   Bridgeman Art Library, London
BL   British Library, London
BM   British Museum, London
Corbis Corbis, London
RHPL Robert Harding Picture Library, London
SHP   Sonia Halliday Photographs, Buckinghamshire, England

a above; **b** below; **l** left; **r** right

Page 1 Werner Forman Archive, London; **2** Basilica di San Marco, Venice/BAL; **6** Sonia Halliday and Laura Lushington/SHP; **9a** Denys Pringle, Cardiff; **9b** Trinity College, Cambridge/AA; **10** F.H.C. Birch/SHP; **11** Archives of the town of Ravenna; **12–13** AKG; **15** Dagli Orti/AA; **16** Louvre, Paris/BAL; **17** Erich Lessing/AA; **18** Turkish and Islamic Art Museum, Istanbul/HarperCollins Publishers/AA; **19** Turkish and Islamic Art Museum, Istanbul/Dagli Orti/AA; **21** Dagli Orti/AA; **23a** Anxo Iglesias/Turismo de Santiago, Santiago de Compostela Tourist Office; **23b** Turkish and Islamic Art Museum, Istanbul/Dagli Orti/AA; **24** BM; **25a** Erich Lessing/AKG; **25b** Erich Lessing/AKG; **27** Louvre, Paris/Réunion des Musées Nationaux; **28** Scala, Florence; **29** Ancient Art & Architecture, Middlesex, England; **31** Bayerische Staatsbibliothek, Munich (Lat. 4456, fol. 11r); **32–33** Bibliothèque Nationale, Paris/SHP; **35** A.F. Kersting, London; **36** Bibliothèque Nationale, Paris/BAL; **37** Castello della Manta, Saluzzo/BAL; **38** BL/AKG; **40** Bibliothèque Nationale, Paris/SHP; **41** BM; **43** Erich Lessing/AKG; **44** Nik Wheeler/Corbis; **45** Bibliothèque Nationale, Paris/AKG; **46** Koninklijke Bibliotheek, The Hague (Ms 76 F5 fol.1r); **49a** A.F. Kersting, London; **49b** Bibliothèque Nationale, Paris/BAL; **50** BL/AKG; **51** Bryan Knox/SHP; **52** Bodleian Library, Oxford (Ms Ashmole 813, fols.3c–4r); **53** Cathedral Museum, Cuenca/Album/Joseph Martin/AA; **54** BL/BAL; **56** Christopher Rennie/RHPL; **57a** A.F. Kersting, London; **57b** Christopher Rennie/RHPL; **58–59** Bibliothèque Nationale, Paris/AKG; **60** Bodleian Library, Oxford (MS Laud Misc. 385 fol.41v)/AA; **62** Micheline Pelletier/Corbis Sygma; **63** Museum für Angewandte Kunst, Vienna/Erich Lessing/AKG; **65** A.F. Kersting, London; **66** Eitan Simanor/RHPL; **67a** Richard T. Nowitz/Corbis; **67b** A.F. Kersting, London; **69** Bibliothèque Nationale, Paris/SHP; **70** and **71** BM; **72** Erich Lessing/AKG; **73** BM; **74** Master and Fellows of Corpus Christi College, Cambridge (CCC Ms 26. fol.140r); **75** Erich Lessing/AKG; **76** BL (Yates Thompson 12 fol.161); **77** BL (Royal 10 E. IV, fol.19); **78–79** Christopher Rennie/RHPL; **80** Jean-François Amelot/AKG; **81** Landesbibliothek, Fulda/Alinari/BAL; **82** Biblioteca Monasterio del Escorial, Madrid/BAL; **84** AKG; **85** Roman Catholic parish church, Cappenburg, Germany/AKG; **86** BL/Scala, Florence; **87** SHP; **88a** Fitzwilliam Museum, University of Cambridge/BAL; **88b** Biblioteca Nazionale Marciana, Venice/Erich Lessing/AKG; **89** Victoria and Albert Museum, London; **91** Richard T. Nowitz/

Corbis; **92** Pierpont Morgan Library, New York/BAL; **93** BL/BAL; **95** BL/AKG; **96** Bürgerbibliothek, Bern/AKG; **97** BM; **98–99** Dagli Orti/AA; **100** Sacro Speco monastery, Subiaco, Italy/HarperCollins Publishers/AA; **102** Bodleian Library, Oxford (MS Bodley 264 fol. 218r)/AA; **103** Palazzo Ducale, Venice/Cameraphoto/AKG; **105** Private Collection/Dagli Orti/AA; **106** Palazzo Ducale, Venice/Cameraphoto/AKG; **107l** Archives of the town of Ravenna; **107r** Archives of the town of Ravenna; **108** Bodleian Library, Oxford (MS Laud Misc 587, fol.1)/AA; **111a** University Library, Istanbul/SHP; **110–111b** BL/AKG; **112** and **113** Archives of the town of Ravenna; **114** Bibliothèque Nationale, Paris/BAL; **115** Erich Lessing/AKG; **116a** Treasury of San Marco, Venice/BAL; **116b** Museo Marciano, Basilica di San Marco, Venice/Cameraphoto Arte Venice/BAL; **117** Treasury of San Marco, Venice/BAL; **118–119** A.F. Kersting, London; **120–121** Institut Amatller d'Art Hispanic, Barcelona; **122a** Paul Almasy/Corbis; **122b** Sheldan Collins/Corbis; **124** Hans Georg Roth/Corbis; **125a** Science Museum, London/Science and Society Picture Library, London; **125b** Bodleian Library, Oxford (MS Laud Or. 234 fol. 83V); **126** Paul Almasy/Corbis; **127** ZEFA visual media, London; **129** Universitätsbibliothek, Heidelberg/AKG; **130** Stefan Arczynski/AKG; **131** Secret State Archive, Berlin/AKG; **133** Dagli Orti/AA; **134** Louvre, Paris/Dagli Orti/AA; **135** and **136** BL/AKG; **137** Ruggero Vanni/Corbis; **138** Palatine Chapel, Palermo, Sicily/Dagli Orti/AA; **140** Národní Muzeum, Prague/AKG; **141** Erich Lessing/AKG; **142–143** Master and Fellows of Corpus Christi College, Cambridge (CCC Ms 16, fol.54v); **144** Scala, Florence; **145** Bargello, Florence/Alinari/BAL; **146** Hanan Isachar/Corbis; **149** Corpus Christi College, Cambridge/BAL; **150** Bibliothèque de la Sorbonne, Paris/Archives Charmet/BAL; **151** Louvre, Paris/Peter Willi/BAL; **152** Santa Croce, Florence/AKG; **153a** Bodleian Library, Oxford (MS Douce 180 fol.38r)/AA; **153b** BL/BAL; **154** AKG; **155** BL (MS Add. 24189, fol. 8); **156** BL (MS Royal 2A XXII fol.220)/AKG; **157** BL (Seal. XXXVI. 215); **158** Cabinet des Dessins, Louvre, Paris/Erich Lessing/AKG; **159** Bibliothèque Nationale, Paris/AKG; **161** BL/AKG; **163** and **164** A.F. Kersting, London; **165** Eitan Simanor/RHPL; **166** BL (Royal 16 G.VI, fol.440v); **169l** A.F. Kersting, London; **169r** Château–Musée de Cagnes-sur-Mer/BAL; **170** BL (Royal 14.cVII fol.4v2–5); **172–173** Topkapi Museum, Istanbul/Dagli Orti/AA; **174** BL/BAL; **176** Rolf Richardson/RHPL; **177** Rolf Richardson/RHPL; **179** SHP; **181** Museo Correr, Venice/Dagli Orti/AA; **182** Gian Berto Vanni/Corbis; **183** Bibliothèque Nationale, Paris/BAL; **184** Barber Institute of Fine Arts, Birmingham, England/Werner Forman Archive, London; **185** Jerome Wheelock Fund/Worcester Art Museum, Massachusetts/BAL; **186** BL/BAL; **187** Nevada Wier/Corbis; **188** Moldovita Monastery, Romania/Dagli Orti/AA; **190** Château de Versailles/BAL; **191** Charles & Josette Lenars/Corbis; **192** Biblioteca Nazionale Marciana, Venice/Dagli Orti/AA; **193** Louvre, Paris/BAL; **194** Museo Correr, Venice/Dagli Orti/AA; **195** BM/BAL; **196** Archivio Iconografico, S.A./Corbis; **196–197** Yann Arthus-Bertrand/Corbis; **197** Robert Francis/RHPL; **199** Museum der Stadt, Vienna/Dagli Orti/AA; **200–201** New Walk Museum, Leicester City Museum Service/BAL; **202** Rheinisches Landesmuseum, Bonn/Dagli Orti/AA; **203** Eileen Tweedy/AA; **205** Château de Versailles/BAL; **207** Musée des Beaux-Arts, Mulhouse/BAL; **208** Michael Nicholson/Corbis; **209a** and **209b** Magan Stamps, Co. Durham; **210** Nigel Chandler/Corbis Sygma; **211** SANA/Associated Press Ltd, London.